MAC OS® X LEOPARD™
QuickSteps

GUY HART-DAVIS

New York Chicago San Francisco
Lisbon London Madrid Mexico City
Milan New Delhi San Juan
Seoul Singapore Sydney Toronto

The *McGraw-Hill* Companies

Cataloging-in-Publication Data is on file with the Library of Congress

McGraw-Hill books are available at special quantity discounts to use as premiums and sales promotions, or for use in corporate training programs. To contact a special sales representative, please visit the Contact Us page at www.mhprofessional.com.

Mac OS®, Apple®, and the Apple logo are either registered trademarks or trademarks of Apple Inc. in the United States and other countries.

Microsoft® and Windows® are registered trademarks of Microsoft Corporation in the United States and other countries.

UNIX® is a registered trademark of The Open Group in the United States and/or other countries.

Information has been obtained by McGraw-Hill from sources believed to be reliable. However, because of the possibility of human or mechanical error by our sources, McGraw-Hill, or others, McGraw-Hill does not guarantee the accuracy, adequacy, or completeness of any information and is not responsible for any errors or omissions or the results obtained from the use of such information.

MAC OS® X LEOPARD™ QUICKSTEPS

1234567890 CCI CCI 0198

ISBN: 978-0-07-154978-3
MHID: 0-07-154978-1

SPONSORING EDITOR / Roger Stewart

EDITORIAL SUPERVISOR / Janet Walden

PROJECT MANAGER / Vasundhara Sawhney (International Typesetting and Composition)

ACQUISITIONS COORDINATOR / Carly Stapleton

TECHNICAL EDITOR / Dwight Spivey

COPY EDITOR / Bill McManus

PROOFREADER / Madhu Prasher

INDEXER / Claire Splan

PRODUCTION SUPERVISOR / George Anderson

COMPOSITION / International Typesetting and Composition

ILLUSTRATION / International Typesetting and Composition

ART DIRECTOR, COVER / Jeff Weeks

COVER DESIGN / Pattie Lee

To Rhonda and Teddy

About the Author

Guy Hart-Davis is the author of *How to Do Everything: iPod & iTunes, Fourth Edition, How to Do Everything with Microsoft Office Word 2007*, and *How to Do Everything with Microsoft Office Excel 2007*, all from McGraw-Hill.

About the Technical Editor

Dwight Spivey is the author of *How to Do Everything: Mac* (McGraw-Hill, 2008), and is a software and support engineer for Konica Minolta, where he specializes in working with Mac operating systems, applications, and hardware.

Acknowledgments

My thanks go to the following people, who put in a huge amount of work on this book:

- Marty Matthews, series editor, developed the first edition and made countless suggestions for improving it.

- Dwight Spivey, technical editor, reviewed this second edition for technical accuracy and made many helpful suggestions.

- Bill McManus, copy editor, edited the book deftly and with good humor.

- Vasundhara Sawhney, project manager, kept the book moving and the author under control.

- Madhu Prasher, proofreader, caught widely varied inconsistencies.

- Roger Stewart, editorial director at McGraw-Hill Professional, helped create the series and pulled strings in the background throughout the process.

- David Zielonka, EDP director/Technical at McGraw-Hill Professional, provided production guidance and support throughout the project.

Contents at a Glance

Contents

5

6

10

Introduction

QuickSteps books are recipe books for computer users. They answer the question "how do I...?" by providing a quick set of steps to accomplish the most common tasks in a particular operating system or application.

The sets of steps are the central focus of the book. QuickSteps sidebars show how to quickly perform many small functions or tasks that support the primary functions. Notes, Tips, and Cautions augment the steps, presented in a separate column so as not to interrupt the flow of the steps. The introductions are minimal rather than narrative, and numerous illustrations and figures, many with callouts, support the steps.

QuickSteps books are organized by function and the tasks needed to perform that function. Each function is a chapter. Each task, or "How To," contains the steps needed to accomplish the function, along with the relevant Notes, Tips, Cautions, and screenshots. You can easily find the tasks you need through:

- The Table of Contents, which lists the functional areas (chapters) and tasks in the order they are presented

- A How-To list of tasks on the opening page of each chapter

- The index, which provides an alphabetical list of the terms that are used to describe the functions and tasks

- Color-coded tabs for each chapter or functional area, with an index to the tabs in the Contents at a Glance (just before the Table of Contents)

Conventions Used in This Book

Mac OS X Leopard QuickSteps uses several conventions designed to make the book easier for you to follow. Among these are

- A 🔘 symbol in the Table of Contents or the How To list in each chapter references a QuickSteps sidebar in a chapter.

- A 🪐 in the Table of Contents or the How To list in each chapter references a QuickFacts sidebar in a chapter.

- **Bold type** is used for words on the screen that you are to do something with, such as "click **Save As**" or "open the **File** menu."

- *Italic type* is used for a word or phrase that is being defined or otherwise deserves special emphasis.

- <u>Underlined type</u> is used for text that you are to type from the keyboard.

- SMALL CAPITAL LETTERS IN BOLD are used for keys on the keyboard such as ENTER and RETURN.

- The ⌘ symbol represents the Mac COMMAND key, the key with the Apple symbol and ⌘ sign. The symbol represents the menu at the left end of the Mac OS X menu bar.

- When you need to enter a command, this book tells you to "press" the key(s). When you need to enter text or numbers, this book tells you to "type" them.

How to...

Chapter 1
Stepping into Mac OS X

Mac OS X is an *operating system*. Operating systems perform *the* central role in managing what a computer does and how it is done. An operating system provides the interface between you and the computer hardware: it lets you store a file, print a document, connect to the Internet, or transfer information over a local area network without knowing anything about how the hardware works.

This chapter explains how to start Mac OS X and how to log on; how to use its screens, windows, menus, and dialog boxes; how to shut it down, and how to get help.

1

2

3

4

5

6

7

8

9

10

NOTE

The desktop on your Mac may look different from the one shown in Figure 1-1. As you'll see later in this book, you can configure many aspects of the desktop to give it the look and the functionality you need.

Start Mac OS X

To start Mac OS X, turn on your Mac by pressing the **Power** button (if in doubt which button this is, consult your Mac's documentation). Sometimes that is all you need to do. If, when you turn on your Mac, you get a screen similar to Figure 1-1, then you have started Mac OS X. You may also need to log on, as explained later in this chapter.

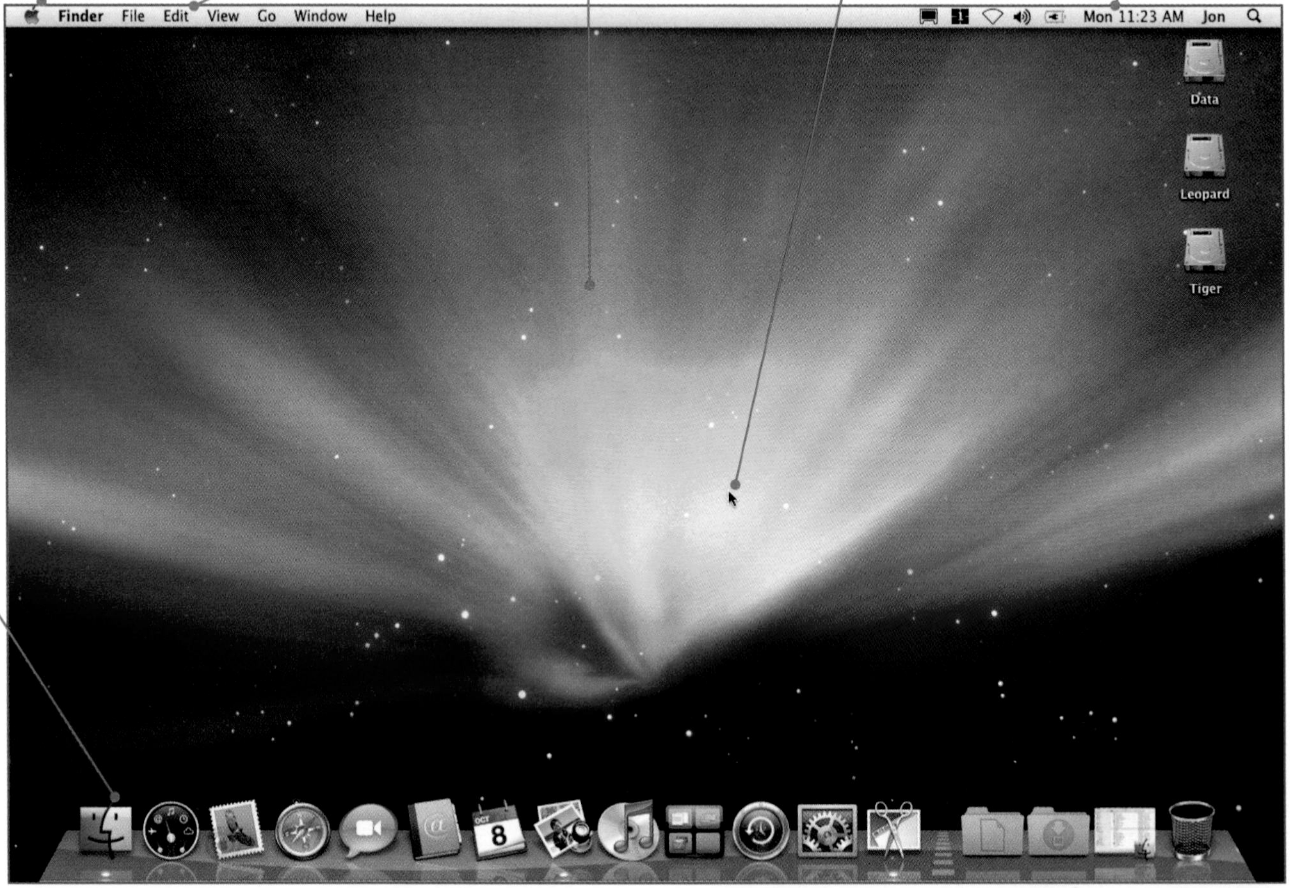
Apple menu, provides access to system-wide commands
Menu bar, provides access to commands for the active application
Desktop, used for windows, dialog boxes, and icons
Mouse pointer, identifies the focus of the mouse
Menu bar icons, provide information and give quick access to key functions
Dock, provides icons for frequently used applications and folders
Finder File Edit View Go Window Help
Mon 11:23 AM Jon
Data
Leopard
Tiger

Figure 1-1: ***When you have started Mac OS X, your screen should look something like this.***

TIP

You can skip the registration process by pressing ⌘+Q.

QUICKSTEPS

INSTALLING MAC OS X FROM SCRATCH

Another possibility is to install Mac OS X from scratch. Normally, you need to do this only if you have an old Mac (rather than having bought a new one).

1. Insert the Mac OS X DVD in your Mac.

2. If Mac OS X is running, a window opens that provides a Restart button you can click to restart the Mac from the DVD. If so, click this button. If not, restart the Mac, and when the Mac plays its startup sound, hold down **C** to start the Mac from the DVD drive.

3. On the first screen, select the language that you want Mac OS X to use—for example, English.

4. On the Welcome screen, click **Continue**, and then read and agree to the software license agreement.

5. On the Select A Destination screen, choose the disk on which you want to install Mac OS X.

6. On the Install Summary screen, you can reduce the amount of space that Mac OS X takes up. Click the **Customize** button to reach the Customize screen, and then clear the check box for any items you do not want. Mac OS X includes several gigabytes of Printer Drivers and Language Translations that you can omit if your Mac is short of disk space. Click **Done** when you've made your choices.

7. When you return to the Install Summary screen, click **Install**. The installation process then runs.

8. When the Install Succeeded screen appears, either click **Restart** or simply wait for the countdown timer to restart the Mac automatically.

Register Mac OS X and Perform Initial Setup

If you buy a new Mac with Mac OS X already installed, or if you upgrade from an older version of Mac OS, you need to set up and register your copy of Mac OS X:

1. On the Welcome screen, choose your country (for example, United States), and then click **Continue**. If your country doesn't appear in the short list, select **Show All**.

2. On the Do You Already Own A Mac? screen, you can choose to transfer information from another Mac, from another disk volume on this Mac, or from a Time Machine backup. See "Transfer User Accounts from Another Mac" in Chapter 8 for coverage of this topic. If you do not want to transfer information now, choose **Do Not Transfer My Information Now**, and then click **Continue**.

3. On the Select Your Keyboard screen, click the keyboard layout you want (for example, U.S.), and then click **Continue**. If the layout doesn't appear in the short list, select **Show All**.

4. On the Enter Your Apple ID screen, enter your .Mac member name or Apple ID from the iTunes Store or the Apple Store, and then click **Continue**. If you don't have an Apple ID, you can set one up later.

5. On the Registration Information screen, supply your name, address, and phone number. You can also enter an e-mail address if you already have one. Click **Continue**.

6. On the A Few More Questions screen, provide your occupation, and a description of where you will primarily use this Mac (for example, at home). Choose whether to receive news, software updates, special offers, and information from Apple. Click **Continue**.

SET UP YOUR USER ACCOUNT

If you've bought a new Mac or installed a fresh copy of Mac OS X (rather than migrating an existing installation to Mac OS X), you must also create your user account on the Create Your Account screen:

1. Type your name in the Name box in your preferred format—for example, Chris Smith.

2. Mac OS X enters a default version of what you typed in the Short Name box. This "short name" uses only lowercase letters and no spaces or punctuation except hyphens: for example, chrissmith. Change the name to a lowercase short name you want to use: for example, chris.

CAUTION

If you don't want to use a password for your user account, you can leave the Password box and the Verify box blank—but this is highly dangerous. Anybody who can access your Mac will then be able to log on using your user account without entering a password.

NOTE

At this point, Mac OS X attempts to find an Internet connection that it can use to communicate your registration information to Apple. If Mac OS X finds an Internet connection, it uses that connection without further ado. If Mac OS X does not find an Internet connection, it prompts you to set up a connection.

TIP

For security, create a separate user account for each person who will use a particular Mac and assign a password to each user account. That way, each user can have his or her preferred settings. Also, when you use separate accounts for users, Mac OS X's security features help you to keep each user's files secure from all other users, allowing for privacy and preventing damage to other users' files (accidentally or otherwise). If you want to share files with other users, Mac OS X enables you to do that easily too. See Chapter 8 for instructions on creating and configuring user accounts.

3. Type a password in the Password box and the Verify box. For security, Mac OS X displays dots rather than the characters you type.

4. If you want, type a reminder for the password in the Password Hint box. The hint will help any attacker break into your Mac, so it's best not to create a hint.

5. Click **Continue**. Mac OS X creates your account.

6. On the Get The Full Mac Experience screen, choose whether to use your existing .Mac membership on this Mac, sign up for a new .Mac membership, enter the activation key for a .Mac membership you've bought (but not yet used), or refrain from buying a membership right now. Click **Continue**.

7. When installation is complete, Mac OS X displays the Thank You screen to tell you that your Mac is set up and ready. Click **Go**, and your desktop appears (see Figure 1-1, earlier).

Log On to Mac OS X

If, when you start Mac OS X, you see a login screen like the one displayed in Figure 1-2, click your name, enter your password if prompted for it (as shown here), and click **Log In**.

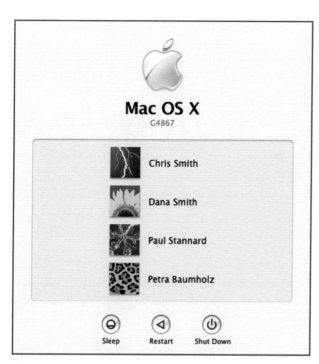

Figure 1-2: **If Mac OS X displays this login screen, click your user name. If Mac OS X prompts you for your password, type it, and then click Log In.**

 **NOTE**

There are two reasons for configuring Mac OS X to display the login screen that doesn't list user names: security and convenience. First, while the login screen that lists user names lets an unauthorized person try to guess the password for a user name that's displayed, the login screen that doesn't list user names requires an unauthorized person to guess both a user name and its corresponding password. Second, having to navigate a long list of users on the login screen can be even less convenient than typing your user name.

Figure 1-3: **If Mac OS X is configured not to display user names, type your name and password, and then click Log In.**

If you see the screen displayed in Figure 1-3, which doesn't list user names, type your user name and password, and click **Log In**. Mac OS X will open. If a systems administrator installed your Mac, he or she should have given you your user name and password. If you installed your Mac, you will have created the user name and set the password (if there is one). See "Control Who Is a User" in Chapter 8 for instructions on setting up users.

Use the Mouse in Mac OS X

A *mouse* is any pointing device—including trackballs, pointing sticks, and graphic tablets—with one or more buttons. Moving the mouse moves the pointer on the screen. You *select* an object on the screen by moving the pointer so that it is on top of the object and then pressing the button on the mouse.

If your mouse has two buttons, press the left button to click. Press the right button to right-click. You can use either your left or right hand to control

NOTE

Apple uses both "control" and "ctrl" on desktop keyboards and uses "ctrl" on PowerBook and iBook keyboards, all for the **CONTROL** key. This book uses **CONTROL** to represent that key.

the mouse. (To control a trackpad, you can use either hand or even both hands together.)

If your mouse has only one button, you produce a right-click by holding down **CONTROL** while you click.

Use the Screen

The Mac OS X screen can hold windows and other objects. In its simplest form, shown in Figure 1-1, you see a desktop picture (a background scene), a menu bar at the top, a bar containing icons at the bottom, and an icon for the hard disk from which your Mac starts. You may also see icons for your Mac's optical drive and any network drives that your Mac is connected to.

The parts of the screen are: the *desktop*, which takes most of the screen; the *menu* bar across the top; the *Dock* across the bottom; *desktop icons*, which can be anywhere on the desktop; and the *mouse pointer*, which can be anywhere on the screen.

USE THE DESKTOP

The *desktop* is the entire screen except for the Dock and the menu bar. Windows, dialog boxes, and icons (such as the icon for your Mac's hard disk) are displayed on the desktop. You can store *aliases*, which are icons for your favorite applications and documents, on the desktop (see Chapter 2). You can drag windows, dialog boxes, and icons around the desktop. Double-click an icon on the desktop to open the file, folder, or application associated with the icon.

USE THE MENU BAR

The menu bar (shown below with iTunes active) gives you access to the commands in the active application. Only one application can be active at a time; the active application is said to have the *focus*.

QUICKSTEPS

USING THE MOUSE

SELECT AN OBJECT ON THE SCREEN

Select an object on the screen by moving the mouse pointer to it and clicking it. *Click* means to point at an object you want to select and quickly press and release the mouse button.

Macintosh HD

OPEN OR START AN OBJECT

Open an object or start an application by double-clicking it. *Double-click* means to point at an object you want to select, and then press and release the mouse button twice in rapid succession.

OPEN A CONTEXT MENU FOR AN OBJECT

Open a context menu, which allows you to perform actions on an object, by **CONTROL**+clicking it or right-clicking it.

MOVE AN OBJECT ON THE SCREEN

Move an object on the screen by dragging it. *Drag* means to point at an object you want to move, and then press and hold the mouse button while moving the mouse. You drag the object as you move the mouse. When the object is where you want it, release the mouse button.

Macintosh HD

Open
Get Info
Duplicate
Make Alias
Copy "Macintosh HD"
Clean Up Selection
Label:
× ▪ ▪ ▪ ▪ ▪ ▪ ▪
More ▸

menu

Menus for the active application (iTunes)

Information icons and menulets

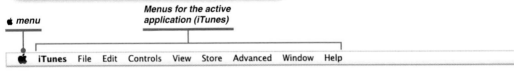

 menu

🍎 **iTunes** File Edit Controls View Store Advanced Window Help   📶 ◀ DV 🔊 Mon 10:33 PM Chris Smith 🔍

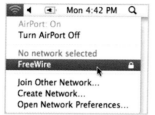

At the left end of the menu bar is the menu. This menu is referred to as the "Apple menu" and provides access to system-wide commands, such as configuring your Mac, logging out, or shutting down your Mac.

At the right end of the menu bar are information icons and small menus called *menulets*, as shown here.

USE THE DOCK

The Dock, which appears at the bottom of the screen by default, contains icons for frequently used applications, documents, and folders. "Understand the Dock," below, shows you how to understand the icons on the Dock and work with them.

USE A DESKTOP ICON

A *desktop icon* represents an application, file, or folder that can be started or opened. Double-click a desktop icon to open or activate it.

USE THE MOUSE POINTER

The *mouse pointer*, or simply the *pointer*, shows where the mouse is pointing. Move the mouse to move the pointer.

Understand the Dock

The Dock is divided into two parts by a divider bar that looks like the white stripe down the middle of a road. Shortcuts to applications appear to the left of the divider bar. Shortcuts to folders and documents appear to the right of the divider bar, together with an icon for each open window you've minimized (reduced to an icon). The Trash appears at the right end of the Dock.

NOTE

Throughout this book you'll see phrases such as "open the **File** menu." These tell you to click a menu in the menu bar (the File menu) in order to open it.

NOTE

When you position the Dock vertically on the left or right of the screen, application shortcuts appear above the divider bar, folder and document shortcuts appear below the divider bar, and the Trash appears at the bottom.

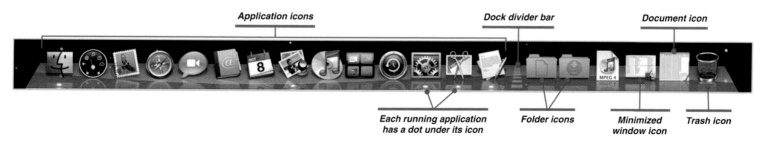

Application icons   *Dock divider bar*   *Document icon*

Each running application has a dot under its icon   *Folder icons*   *Minimized window icon*   *Trash icon*

QUICKSTEPS

STARTING AN APPLICATION

The method for starting an application depends on where the application icon is located. The alternatives are:

ON THE DESKTOP

Double-click the application icon, or "alias," on the desktop. Alternatively, double-click the icon for a document to open it in the application associated with it.

ON THE DOCK

Click the application icon on the Dock. Alternatively, click the icon for a document on the Dock to open it in the associated application.

ON THE RECENT ITEMS SUBMENU

1. Open the menu.

2. Highlight (move the mouse pointer over) **Recent Items** to display the submenu.

3. Click the item for the application or document you want to open (see Figure 1-4).

If you choose a document on the menu, Mac OS X opens the document in the application associated with it.

IN YOUR APPLICATIONS FOLDER

1. Click the desktop to activate the Finder.

2. Open the **Go** menu in the menu bar.

3. Click **Applications**. A Finder window opens showing your Applications folder.

4. Double-click the application's icon.

To identify an icon, hover the mouse pointer over it for a moment, and Mac OS X will display its name.

Click an icon to open an application, folder, or document, or to restore a minimized window to its previous size.

Use the Apple Menu

The menu provides instant access to system-wide commands for Mac OS X. These are the key items on the menu:

- **Software Update** runs the Software Update application, which checks automatically for updates to Mac OS X and major applications.

- **System Preferences** displays the System Preferences window, which contains icons for configuring most aspects of Mac OS X.

- The **Dock** submenu contains commands for quickly configuring the Dock's position and behavior.

- The **Location** submenu lets you switch quickly between sets of settings for different network locations. For example, you might switch between settings for your office and settings for home. This submenu appears only when you've created different network locations.

- The **Recent Items** submenu (see Figure 1-4) contains entries for the last ten applications and the last ten documents you've used.

- **Force Quit** displays the Force Quit Applications window, which you can use to close an application that has stopped responding. See "Quit an Application When It Goes Wrong" in Chapter 5 for instructions on using Force Quit.

- **Sleep, Restart, Shut Down, and Log Out** provide you with ways to leave your Mac. See "Leave Mac OS X," later in this chapter, for details.

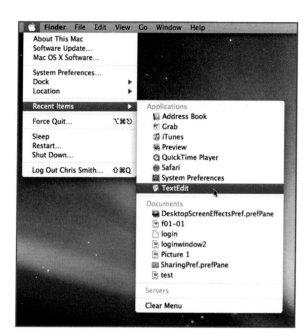

Figure 1-4: *The Recent Items submenu on the ⬢ menu lets you quickly open any of the last applications, documents, or servers you've used.*

Use a Window

When you start an application or open a folder, the application or folder appears in a "window" on your screen, as does the Applications window in Figure 1-5.

Each window has a number of features that are identified in Figure 1-5 and referred to in the rest of this book:

- The **title bar** contains the name of the application or folder in the window and is used to drag the window around the screen.

- The **toolbar** contains tools related to the contents of the window. Click a tool to use it. You can toggle the toolbar on and off by clicking the gray button at the right end of the toolbar.

- The **detail pane** displays the principal object of the window, such as files, folders, applications, documents, or images.

- The **status bar** provides messages and information about what is displayed or selected in the window. Many applications let you display and hide the status bar by using commands on the **View** menu.

- The **sizing handle** allows the window to be sized diagonally, increasing or decreasing its height and width as you drag.

- The **vertical scroll bar** lets you move the contents of the pane vertically within the window so that you can see information, further up or further down the window, that wasn't displayed within the detail pane.

- The **horizontal scroll bar** lets you move the contents of the pane horizontally within the window so that you can see information, further across to the left or the right, that wasn't displayed within the detail pane.

- The **scroll bar** moves the contents in large increments vertically or horizontally by clicking within it.

- The **scroll button** on a scroll bar can be dragged in either direction to move the contents in that direction.

- The **scroll arrows** let you move the scroll button in small increments in the direction of the arrow.

- The **Close button** closes the window but usually leaves the application running.

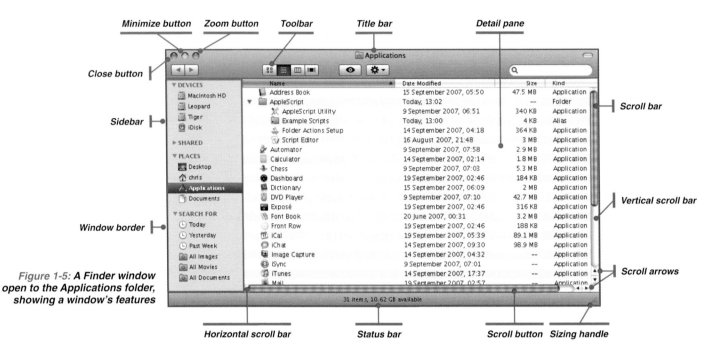

Figure 1-5: *A Finder window open to the Applications folder, showing a window's features*

Double-clicking a window's title bar minimizes the window to an icon on the Dock. This is much easier and faster than clicking the Minimize button. Hold down **SHIFT** as you double-click to minimize the window in slow motion. If double-clicking the title bar doesn't minimize a window, turn this option on by opening the menu, choosing **System Preferences**, clicking **Appearance**, and selecting the **Minimize When Double-Clicking A Windows Title Bar** check box. Open the **System Preferences** menu and click **Quit System Preferences** to close System Preferences.

- The **Minimize button** collapses the window down to an icon on the Dock. Click the window's icon on the Dock to restore the window to its previous size.

- The **Zoom button** toggles the window between its current size and the largest size at which it will fit on the screen and usefully display its contents. Zooming some windows makes them take up the whole screen, whereas zooming other windows makes them take up only the full height or width of the screen. Click the Zoom button again to restore the window to its former size.

- The **Sidebar** (in the Finder window and some other windows) provides quick access to different devices (such as hard drives), important folders, shared drives, and predefined searches.

- The **window border** separates the window from other windows or from the desktop.

Use a Menu

A menu is a panel that provides a list of actions that you can take for a particular object, such as a file or a folder. For example, the Edit menu for the Finder (and for many applications) includes commands such as Undo, Cut, Copy, and Paste.

To use a menu:

1. Click an application window to make it active. Mac OS X displays the menu bar for the application.
2. Click the menu name in the menu bar.
3. Move the pointer to the desired item.
4. Click the desired item.

Use a Dialog Box, Sheet, or Window

Dialog boxes present choices that enable you to take actions. A *dialog box* uses a common set of features called *controls* to accomplish its purpose. For example, the View Options dialog box shown in Figure 1-6 lets you choose which columns of information to display for your music library in iTunes. To display a column, you select its check box; to hide a column, you clear the check box. When you've finished making your choices, you click the OK button to close the dialog box.

Unlike some other operating systems, Mac OS X doesn't draw a very distinct line between dialog boxes and small windows. As you work with Mac OS X, you'll find that many features use windows not only to present information but also to allow you to make configuration choices. There are two main differences between a dialog box and a window in this type of usage:

- You can leave the window displayed and return to the application to continue work. (By contrast, you usually must close a dialog box before you can return to the application that displayed it.)
- Most small windows are for setting preferences or choosing configurations rather than executing a command. You close a window by clicking its Close button (the red button in its title bar) rather than by clicking a command button.

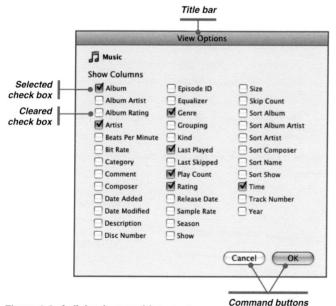

Figure 1-6: **A dialog box enables you to make choices, take actions, or both.**

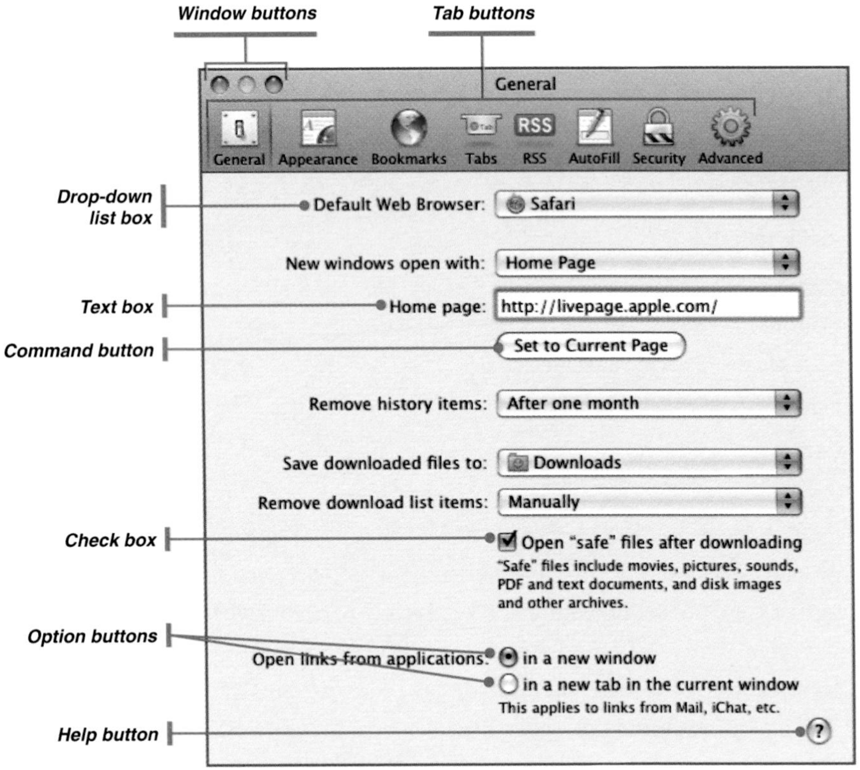

Window buttons   **Tab buttons**

Drop-down list box

Text box

Command button

Check box

Option buttons

Help button

General

General Appearance Bookmarks Tabs RSS AutoFill Security Advanced

Default Web Browser: Safari

New windows open with: Home Page

Home page: http://livepage.apple.com/

Set to Current Page

Remove history items: After one month

Save downloaded files to: Downloads

Remove download list items: Manually

☑ Open "safe" files after downloading
"Safe" files include movies, pictures, sounds,
PDF and text documents, and disk images
and other archives.

Open links from applications: ⦿ in a new window
○ in a new tab in the current window
This applies to links from Mail, iChat, etc.

*Figure 1-7: Mac OS X uses smaller windows in a similar
way to dialog boxes, particularly for setting preferences.*

Figure 1-7 shows the General pane of the Preferences
window for Safari, Mac OS X's default web browser.

A *sheet* is a special type of dialog box that's attached to
a particular document rather than floating free on the
screen. A sheet prevents you from working further in that
document until you close it, but you can work in other
documents in the same application. Most sheets don't
have a title bar and remain attached to their documents,
but otherwise they behave like dialog boxes.

Figure 1-8 shows an example of a Save As sheet for a
workbook file in Numbers.

The common controls in dialog boxes, windows, and
sheets are used in these ways:

- The **title bar** usually contains the name of the dialog box or
  window and is used to drag the dialog box or window around
  the desktop. On Mac OS X, some dialog boxes and windows
  do not have names—instead, they simply have a title bar.
  Most sheets don't have a title bar.

- **Tab buttons**, often referred to simply as "buttons," let you
  select from among several panes or tabs in a dialog box.

- A **drop-down menu** opens a list from which you can choose one item that will be
  displayed when the list is closed.

- A **list box** lets you select one or more items from a list; it may include a scroll bar if the
  list contains many items.

- **Option buttons**, also called *radio buttons*, let you select one among mutually exclusive
  options.

- A **text box** lets you enter and edit text.

- **Command buttons** perform functions such as closing the dialog box and accepting
  the changes (the OK button) or closing the dialog box and ignoring the changes (the
  Cancel button).

Sheet   **Document window**

Figure 1-8: **A sheet is a type of dialog box attached to a particular document. This is the Save As sheet for a Numbers workbook file.**

TIP

Instead of using the mouse to click a command button in a dialog box or sheet, you can sometimes "click" the button from the keyboard. Press **RETURN** to click the default button, the button that has the blue highlight. Press **ESC** to click the Cancel button. In a dialog box that provides only Yes, No, and Cancel buttons, press **Y** to click Yes, **N** to click No, or **C** to click Cancel. If the buttons have other names, you can often click them by pressing ⌘ and the first letter of the button's name. For example, press **⌘+D** to click the Don't Save button in a confirmation dialog box.

- A **spinner** lets you select from a sequential series of numbers. For example, when you're printing a document, many applications let you use a spinner to set the number of copies to print.

- A **slider** lets you select from several values.

- **Check boxes** let you turn features on or off.

- The **Help button** displays the Help Viewer and makes it show a topic appropriate to the dialog box.

You will have many opportunities to use dialog boxes, windows, and sheets. For the most part, you can try the controls in these interface elements and see what happens. If you don't like the outcome, you can return and change the setting back to what it was before you changed it.

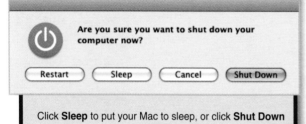
Leave Mac OS X

You can leave Mac OS X in five ways depending on what you want to do:

SLEEP

Putting your Mac to sleep suspends Mac OS X and all applications you had open. Putting your Mac to sleep is much faster than shutting it down, and waking the Mac is much faster than starting it again.

To put your Mac to sleep, open the menu and click **Sleep**. Your Mac's display will go dark and the hard drive will stop running. (You can put a laptop Mac to sleep by closing its lid.)

To reawaken your Mac, press any key or click the mouse.

LOG OUT

Log out means to close the active applications and network connections and to close your user account but leave your Mac running. To log out:

1. Open the menu and click **Log Out** *Your Name*, where *Your Name* is your user name (for example, **Log Out Lisa**). Mac OS X will display this confirmation message box:

2. Click **Log Out**. Your Mac will display the Login screen, from which you or another user can log in.

SWITCH USERS

Switch users means to leave the active applications and network connections active and keep your user account active while you let another user use the Mac. To switch users:

1. Click your user name at the right end of the menu bar.

2. Click the name of the desired user.

3. If Mac OS X prompts you for the user's password, enter it and click **Log In**.

Mac OS X will hide your desktop and will display the desktop for the user you selected. Your user session and applications continue to run, but they are hidden until you switch users back to your account.

RESTART

The Restart command is another way of leaving Mac OS X—and coming back immediately. Restart closes any running applications, prompting you to save any unsaved files that you have been using, and then shuts down and restarts Mac OS X. Restarting is usually done when there is a problem that restarting Mac OS X will fix. You may also need to restart Mac OS X after installing or updating system software or applications. To restart:

1. Open the menu and click **Restart**. Mac OS X will display the confirmation dialog box shown here.

2. Click **Restart**. Mac OS X will close all running applications, restart itself, and then display the login screen.

SHUT DOWN

Shutting down means to log off all users and shut down your Mac. To shut down:

1. Open the menu and click **Shut Down**. Mac OS X will display the confirmation dialog box shown here:

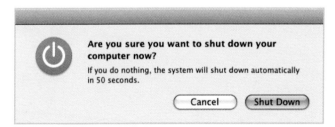

2. Click **Shut Down**. Mac OS X will close all running applications, close itself, and then turn off your Mac.

Figure 1-9: *The Mac Help home page includes links to get you started with Leopard.*

Get Help

Mac OS X Help provides both built-in documentation and online assistance that you can use to learn how to work with Mac OS X. To use Help to get started with Mac OS X:

1. If the menu bar is displaying the menus for any application except the Finder, click the desktop to activate the Finder menus.

2. Open the **Help** menu and click **Mac Help**. The Mac Help window will open, like the one in Figure 1-9, displaying its home page.

3. Click the **Exploring Mac OS X** link. A list of topics for new Mac OS X users will be displayed.

4. Click the **Back** button on the toolbar to return to the previous screen.

5. Click the **What's New In Leopard?** link to see details of Leopard's new features.

6. Click the **Back** button on the toolbar to return to the previous screen.

7. Click in the Search box, type a query, and then press RETURN to display matching results. Click a link to open it.

8. Click the **Close** button to close the window.

How to...

Chapter 2
Customizing Mac OS X

Mac OS X has many features that you can customize. You can keep the default Mac OS X setup; or you can change the display, Dock, sounds, rearrange the desktop, and enable accessibility options.

Change the Look of Mac OS X

Mac OS X has a subtle and attractive user interface that you can change to suit your preferences. Here you'll see how to change the screen's look, including the desktop background and the Dock.

Open System Preferences

Much of what you see on the Mac OS X screen is controlled by the settings in System Preferences. You'll need to open System Preferences to make many of the changes in this chapter.

1. Open the menu (at the left end of the menu bar).

2. Click **System Preferences**. The System Preferences window will open, as shown in Figure 2-1.

```
 Finder   File   Edit   \
About This Mac
Software Update...
Mac OS X Software...

System Preferences...
Dock                    ▶

Recent Items            ▶

Force Quit...        ⌥⌘⎋

Sleep
Restart...
Shut Down...

Log Out Jon...       ⇧⌘Q
```

NOTE

The selection of icons available in the System Preferences window depends on the configuration of your Mac. If you have installed third-party configuration tools on your Mac that are designed to be accessed through System Preferences, Mac OS X displays these icons in an Other category below the System category.

QUICKSTEPS

USING SYSTEM PREFERENCES

You'll probably need to open System Preferences frequently to configure Mac OS X as you find out which settings work best for you. Mac OS X provides several ways to open System Preferences. You can also change the way that System Preferences appears, as discussed in this QuickSteps section.

USE THE DOCK ICON

If you have a System Preferences icon on the Dock, you can open System Preferences by clicking it. Mac OS X places a System Preferences icon on the Dock by default, but you may choose to remove it to make space for other icons.

USE THE ⬤ MENU

Open the ⬤ menu and click **System Preferences**.

USE THE APPLICATIONS FOLDER

1. Open the **Go** menu and click **Applications** to display the Applications folder.

2. Double-click the **System Preferences** icon.

Continued . . .

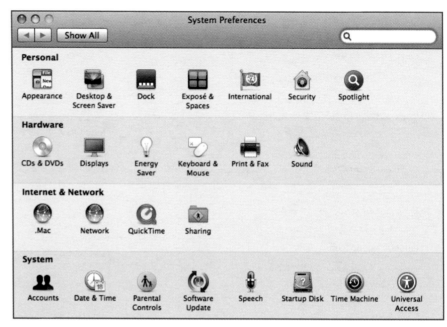

Figure 2-1: *The System Preferences window contains most of the graphical configuration tools for Mac OS X, including those for configuring the display and appearance.*

Change the Desktop Background

Because the desktop background covers almost the entire desktop (until you cover it with windows), it contributes greatly to the appearance of Mac OS X. By changing the desktop background, you can make Mac OS X look substantially different from its default settings. Mac OS X lets you put either a single picture or a changing sequence of pictures on your desktop.

CHANGE THE DESKTOP FROM SYSTEM PREFERENCES

1. **CONTROL**+click or right-click the desktop. The context menu appears.

2. Choose **Change Desktop Background**. The Desktop & Screen Saver pane of System Preferences is displayed.

UICKSTEPS

USING SYSTEM PREFERENCES

(Continued)

NAVIGATE SYSTEM PREFERENCES

The three buttons on the toolbar in the System Preferences window let you navigate quickly among preference panes:

- Click the **Back** button to return to the last preference pane.
- Click the **Next** button to return to the preference pane from which you went back to a different pane.
- Click the **Show All** button to display all the categories and icons.

To search for a particular item, click in the Search box and type the first few letters of the item's name. System Preferences displays a list of matches and highlights the icons for matching items to help you find them.

ORGANIZE SYSTEM PREFERENCES DIFFERENTLY

By default, System Preferences displays items sorted by category: Personal, Hardware, Internet & Network, System, and Other. The Other category appears only if you have third-party configuration applications installed. If you prefer to see an alphabetical list, open the **View** menu and choose **Organize Alphabetically**. To return to category view, open the **View** menu and choose **Organize By Categories**.

NOTE

When you open the Desktop & Screen Saver pane of System Preferences, Mac OS X displays the tab you used last—the Desktop tab or the Screen Saver tab.

3. If the Screen Saver tab is displayed, click the **Desktop** tab (see Figure 2-2). The preview at the top displays your current background and its name. If you've selected the Change Picture check box, the preview shows a graphic indicating a succession of pictures.

4. In the list box, select the category or folder. Its contents are displayed in the box on the right.

- Mac OS X includes several folders of backgrounds, including Apple Images, Nature, Plants, Black & White, Abstract, and Solid Colors.
- You can access pictures stored in your Pictures folder by clicking **Pictures Folder**.

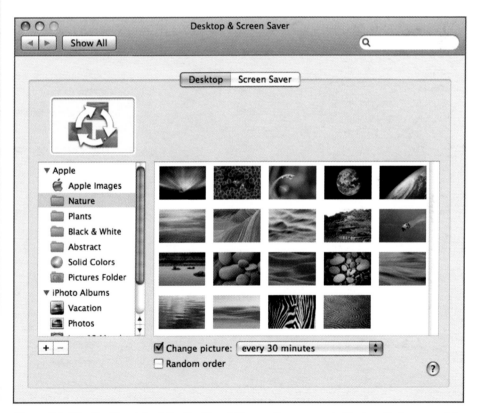

Figure 2-2: **The Desktop tab of the Desktop & Screen Saver pane in System Preferences lets you change your desktop background.**

- To add any folder to the list, click the + button, use the resulting sheet to browse the Mac and select the folder, and then click the **Choose** button. To remove a folder, select it, and then click the – button.

- To use a picture from iPhoto, select the album from the iPhoto Albums list.

5. To use a single picture, select it in the box on the right. To use all the pictures in the folder or category, don't make a selection in the box on the right.

6. If you're using multiple pictures:

- Select the **Change Picture** check box.

- Specify the frequency of change in the drop-down list box: When Logging In, When Waking From Sleep, Every 5 Seconds, Every Minute, Every 5 Minutes, Every 15 Minutes, Every 30 Minutes, Every Hour, or Every Day.

- You can also select the **Random Order** check box to display the pictures in random order.

7. If a picture doesn't fit the screen, use the drop-down list box in the preview area to specify how to treat it: Fit To Screen, Fill Screen, Stretch To Fill Screen, Center, or Tile.

8. Open the **System Preferences** menu and click **Quit System Preferences** to close System Preferences.

CHANGE THE DESKTOP FROM iPHOTO

You can also change the desktop background quickly from iPhoto, the photo-organizing application that Apple includes on most Macs and sells as part of the iLife suite. (See "View Pictures with iPhoto" in Chapter 6 for more information on iPhoto.)

To use a single picture as a desktop background:

1. Click the **iPhoto** icon in the Dock.

2. In iPhoto, crop the picture to the aspect ratio of the screen if necessary. (See the QuickSteps "Cropping Pictures to Fit Your Desktop" in Chapter 6.)

3. Select the picture.

4. Open the **Share** menu and click **Set Desktop**.

To put an album or a group of pictures on your desktop:

1. In iPhoto, crop the pictures to the aspect ratio of your screen if necessary. (See the QuickSteps "Cropping Pictures to Fit Your Desktop" in Chapter 6.)

NOTE

If you choose the Fit To Screen option, Mac OS X displays a color panel that you can use to select the background color for the parts of the screen the picture leaves uncovered.

UNDERSTANDING WHY SCREEN SAVERS ARE NOT NECESSARY

In the last millennium, if you left your computer on but didn't use it, the unchanging image on the screen could become burned into the face of the cathode-ray tube (CRT) monitor, where it would remain displayed as a ghostly image superimposed on what the screen was supposed to be displaying. To prevent burn-in from occurring, software engineers developed *screen savers*, applications that constantly change the image onscreen when the computer is left unused.

Burn-in seldom occurs on graphical operating systems (such as Mac OS X), and modern CRT monitors and liquid crystal display (LCD) monitors are largely immune to burn-in. Nevertheless, screen savers have become popular for both entertainment and security (hiding your work while you're away from your computer).

2. Select the album or the pictures:
   - To use an entire album, select it in the Source list and make sure no pictures are selected in the viewing area.
   - To use just some pictures from an album, select the album in the Source list, then select the pictures in the viewing area. To select multiple contiguous pictures, click the first, and then **SHIFT**+click the last. To select noncontiguous pictures, select the first, and then ⌘+click the other pictures.

3. Open the **Share** menu and click **Set Desktop**. iPhoto applies the first picture to your desktop. iPhoto then displays the Desktop tab of the Desktop & Screen Saver pane in System Preferences.

4. Toward the bottom of the left list box, click the sideways gray triangle next to Folders if the folders are not displayed.

5. Under Folders, click **iPhoto Selection**.

6. Select the **Change Picture** check box if it is not already selected.

7. Choose the frequency in the **Change Picture** drop-down list box, and select or clear the **Random Order** check box as appropriate.

8. Open the **System Preferences** menu and click **Quit System Preferences** to close System Preferences. Mac OS X returns the focus to iPhoto.

Pick a New Screen Saver

Mac OS X provides several screen savers you can use:

1. **CONTROL**+click or right-click the desktop to display the context menu.

2. Click **Change Desktop Background**. The Desktop & Screen Saver pane of System Preferences will appear.

3. If the Desktop tab is selected, click the **Screen Saver** tab to display the Screen Saver tab (see Figure 2-3).

4. Select a screen saver in the Screen Savers list to see it previewed in the Preview box. Click **Test** to see it previewed full screen. Move the mouse to cancel the test.

5. Click **Options** to display the Display Options sheet, on which you can choose options for the screen saver. (Which options are available depends on the type of screen

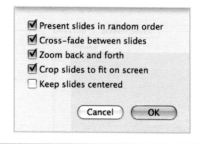

saver you chose. See the two examples here.) When you've made your choices, click **OK** to close the Display Options sheet.

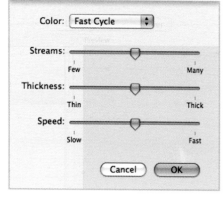

Figure 2-3: *Mac OS X lets you choose from various prebuilt screen savers or create a screen saver from your own pictures. You can also use the artwork from your songs in iTunes.*

CAUTION

You can find many screen savers on the Internet, some free and others for sale. While many free screen savers are fully functional and entertaining (or educational), others have been created or adapted deliberately to spread malicious code. Others yet are so poorly programmed as to cause Mac OS X problems. So, before installing a free screen saver on your Mac, it's a good idea to check for feedback from other users.

6. Drag the **Start Screen Saver** slider to specify how long your Mac remains inactive before the screen saver starts.

7. Select the **Use Random Screen Saver** check box if you want Mac OS X to pick a screen saver for you at random.

8. Select the **Show With Clock** check box if you want Mac OS X to superimpose a clock on the screen saver.

9. For a pictures-based screen saver, click the **Display Style** button for the effect you want: Slideshow, Collage, or Mosaic. Preview each of these to decide which you want.

10. If you want to be able to start your screen saver by moving your mouse to a particular corner of the screen, click **Hot Corners**. The Hot Corners sheet will appear. Select

Start Screen Saver in the drop-down list box that corresponds to the corner you want to use, and then click **OK** to close the sheet.

TIP

You can also set another hot corner to prevent the screen saver from activating by selecting Disable Screen Saver in that corner's drop-down list box. Being able to disable the screen saver is useful when you leave your Mac while performing a demanding operation, such as burning a DVD, that you don't want the screen saver to interrupt.

11. Open the **System Preferences** menu and click **Quit System Preferences** to close System Preferences.

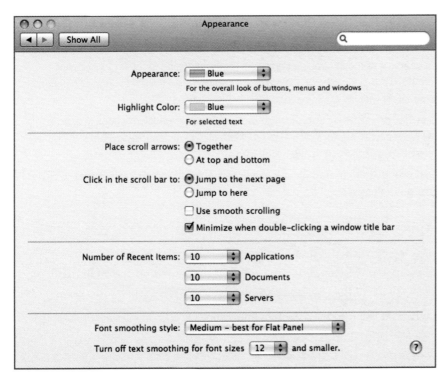

Figure 2-4: Use the controls on the Appearance pane in System Preferences to subtly change the appearance of text and windows.

Alter the Appearance of Objects

You can alter some aspects of the appearance of windows and text by working on the Appearance pane in System Preferences.

1. Open the menu and click **System Preferences** to open the System Preferences window.

2. Click **Appearance**. The Appearance pane will be displayed (see Figure 2-4).

3. In the **Appearance** drop-down list box, select **Blue** (the default) or **Graphite** to change the overall look of windows, menus, and buttons. This change has a surprisingly large effect: applying Graphite makes your Mac look subdued and sober.

4. In the **Highlight Color** drop-down list box, select the color you want to use for selected text and lists. Again, the default is Blue.

5. In the Place Scroll Arrows area, specify how to place the scroll arrows on the scroll bars by selecting the **Together** option button or the **At Top And Bottom** option button. Together (the default setting) places the scroll arrows together at the bottom of a vertical scroll bar and the right end of a horizontal scroll bar. If you've switched from Windows to a Mac, you may find the At Top And Bottom setting easier to use.

6. In the Click In The Scroll Bar To area, select the **Jump To The Next Page** option button or the **Scroll To Here** option button to specify what you want to happen when you click in an empty space in the scroll bar: move to the previous or next page of information, or move to the location in the document that corresponds to the place you click in the scroll bar.

7. Select the **Use Smooth Scrolling** check box if you want Mac OS X to make scrolling as smooth as possible. This may slow down scrolling.

8. Clear the **Minimize When Double-Clicking A Window Title Bar** check box if you don't want to be able to minimize a window by double-clicking its title bar. Normally, this behavior is helpful unless you find yourself double-clicking unintentionally.

9. In the Number Of Recent Items area, use the **Applications** drop-down list box, the **Documents** drop-down list box, and the **Servers** drop-down list box to specify how many applications, documents, and servers Mac OS X displays on the | Recent Items submenu.

10. Check that the setting in the **Font Smoothing Style** drop-down list box is suitable for your monitor. Apple recommends the **Medium** setting for LCD monitors and the **Standard** setting for CRT monitors. If you don't like the effect on your monitor, experiment with the other settings.

11. Use the **Turn Off Text Smoothing For Font Sizes** drop-down list box to specify the largest type size for which Mac OS X shouldn't use smoothing. (Smoothing on minuscule type tends to make it look fuzzy.)

12. Open the **System Preferences** menu and click **Quit System Preferences** to close System Preferences.

Change the Resolution and Color Depth

Depending on your Mac and monitor, you can display Mac OS X with varying resolutions and color quality. You can select the resolution and color depth on the Display tab of the Displays pane in System Preferences.

1. Open the menu and click **System Preferences** to open the System Preferences window.

2. Click **Displays**. The Displays pane will appear. Its title bar shows the type of display—for example, Color LCD.

3. If the Color tab is displayed, click the **Display** tab (see Figure 2-5).

TIP

You can use the | Recent Items submenu to quickly open an application, document, or server you've used recently. If having these items listed is a security concern, reduce the settings to **0** in the Number Of Recent Items area on the Appearance pane of System Preferences.

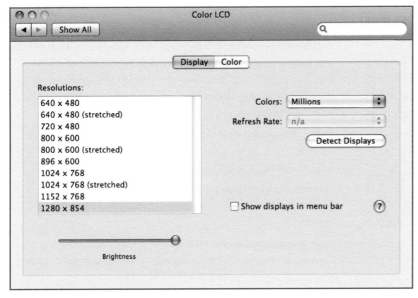

Figure 2-5: *Increasing the resolution lets you see more on the screen at once, but each item appears at a smaller size.*

4. Select the resolution in the **Resolutions** list box.

5. Select **Millions** in the **Colors** drop-down list box unless you know that you need to use fewer colors—for example, because a particular application requires thousands of colors, or because you want Screen Sharing to be faster.

6. For a CRT, choose a refresh rate in the **Refresh Rate** drop-down list box. Refresh rates of 75 hertz (Hz) or higher reduce visible flicker on CRTs. The Refresh Rate drop-down list box is not available for LCDs, which don't suffer from flicker.

7. If you need to switch display resolution or color depth frequently, select the **Show Displays In Menu Bar** check box to add the Displays menu to the menu bar. In the **Number Of Recent Modes** drop-down list box, specify how many modes (resolutions and color depths) the menu should include.

8. Drag the **Brightness** slider to change the brightness of the screen.

9. Open the **System Preferences** menu and click **Quit System Preferences** to close System Preferences.

NOTE

After changing your display, adding a display, or removing a display, you may need to click the **Detect Displays** button on the Display tab of the Displays pane.

Add a Monitor

Often the best upgrade you can make to your Mac is adding a monitor so that you can see more onscreen. To add a monitor, follow these general steps (the specifics vary depending on the type of Mac and the type of monitor):

1. Check that your Mac has a spare display connector.

2. Note the type of display connector: VGA, DVI, or Mini-DVI. (The Mac's specifications—either in the box or on Apple's web site—will tell you this.)

3. Check the type of connector on the monitor.

4. If necessary, get a connector cable. For example:
   - To connect a VGA monitor to a DVI connector, get a VGA-to-DVI connector cable.
   - To connect a DVI monitor to a mini-DVI connector, get a mini-DVI–to-DVI connector cable.

5. Connect the monitor to your Mac.

6. Connect the monitor's power supply, and power the monitor on.

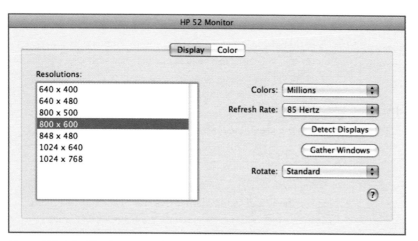

Figure 2-6: *The Displays pane for an external monitor may include the Rotate drop-down list, which lets you turn the image upside down or (more usefully) sideways so that you can use the monitor positioned vertically rather than horizontally.*

7. Normally, Mac OS X detects the monitor automatically and shows the Displays pane of the Preferences dialog box so that you can configure the monitor. The Displays pane appears on each monitor with settings appropriate to that monitor. Figure 2-6 shows the Displays pane for an HP 52 monitor. If Mac OS X doesn't open the Displays pane, open the menu, click **System Preferences**, and then click **Displays**.

8. In the new monitor's Displays pane, choose settings for the monitor.

9. In the other Displays pane, click the Arrangement tab to display its controls (see Figure 2-7), and then drag the icon for the new monitor to show its physical placement relative to the other monitor.

10. Ensure the **Mirror Displays** check box is cleared unless you want each monitor to show the same picture (for example, when you're giving a presentation via a digital projector).

11. Open the **System Preferences** menu and click **Quit System Preferences** to close System Preferences.

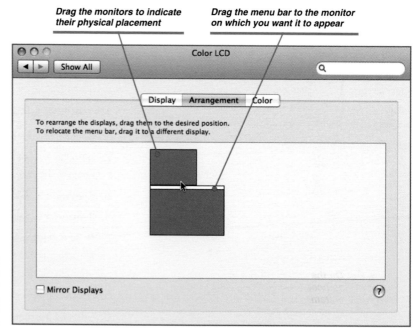

Figure 2-7: *On the Arrangement tab of the Displays pane, make sure Mac OS X knows where your monitors are physically placed, so that the mouse pointer travels correctly from one to the other.*

NOTE

Before performing an action with the Finder, you must activate the Finder so that its menus are displayed in the menu bar. If no other application is active, the Finder will already be active, and you won't need to activate it. If another application is active (either with one or more windows displayed or all its windows minimized), that application's menus will be displayed in the menu bar. When another application is active, you can activate the Finder by clicking open space or any object on the desktop. (This is because the desktop is considered to be part of the Finder.) You can also activate the Finder by clicking the Finder icon on the Dock. If no Finder window is open, Mac OS X will open a Finder window showing your default folder (typically, your Home folder) when you click the Finder icon on the Dock.

Figure 2-8: On the General pane of the Finder Preferences window, choose which categories of items appear on the desktop.

Add Icons to Your Desktop

Because your desktop is always displayed, it can be a convenient place to keep icons for applications, folders, and documents you use frequently. You can customize the icons on your desktop to suit your needs.

CONTROL ICONS FOR DISKS AND DRIVES

By default, Mac OS X displays an icon on the desktop for:

- Your Mac's main hard disk (which is always present)
- Any other hard disk in or connected to the Mac
- Any CD or DVD drive in which you have inserted a disc
- Any servers or network drives to which your Mac has established a connection

You can change these default settings:

1. Activate the **Finder**.
2. Open the **Finder** menu and click **Preferences** to display the Preferences window for the Finder.
3. If the General pane (see Figure 2-8) isn't displayed, click the **General** button.
4. Select or clear the **Hard Disks** check box, the **External Disks** check box, the **CDs, DVDs, and iPods** check box, and the **Connected Servers** check box, as appropriate.
5. Click the **Close** button (the red button) to close the Preferences window.

ADD OR REMOVE OTHER ICONS

As you'll see in Chapter 3, you can store folders and files directly on the desktop if you choose. You can also place other items on the desktop, such as aliases (shortcuts) to applications, documents, and folders:

1. Activate the **Finder** and click a file or folder that you want on the desktop.
2. Open the **File** menu and click **Make Alias**. Mac OS X creates an alias and assigns it the name of the file or folder and the word "alias." For example, an alias to the folder named My Songs receives the name "My Songs alias."
3. Mac OS X places an edit box around the default name. If you want, type a new name and press **RETURN**.
4. Drag the alias to your desktop.

Figure 2-9: *Use the options in the Desktop window to arrange and align icons on the desktop.*

NOTE

The Show Icon Preview check box controls whether the Finder displays previews for graphics files or just generic icons. Previews help you identify files but may make the desktop redraw more slowly. This isn't normally a concern, but if you notice your desktop appearing to congeal, try clearing the Show Icon Preview check box.

Rearrange Desktop Icons

When you have the icons you want on the desktop, they may be a mess. You can drag the icons to where you want them or let Mac OS X arrange them for you.

LET MAC OS X ALIGN OR ARRANGE ICONS

When you drag the icons where you want them, it may be hard to align them precisely, so let Mac OS X do that:

1. Activate the **Finder**.

2. Open the **View** menu and click **Show View Options**. The Desktop window will be displayed (see Figure 2-9).

3. In the **Arrange By** drop-down list, choose **Snap To Grid** to make Mac OS X align the icons according to an underlying, invisible grid. (The Snap To Grid item and the None item are opposites. You can choose only one at once. The current setting bears a check mark.)

4. To arrange the icons automatically, open the **Arrange By** drop-down list again, and then click the item by which you want to arrange them: Name, Date Modified, Date Created, Size, Kind (file type), or Label.

5. Leave the Desktop window open for the moment in case you want to change the icon size, spacing, or labels.

CHOOSE ICON SIZE, TEXT SIZE, AND LABELS

1. Drag the **Icon Size** slider in the Desktop window to change icon size. Watch your existing desktop icons change size.

2. In the **Text Size** drop-down list box, choose a font size that you find easy to read.

3. To change the label position, select the **Bottom** option button or the **Right** option button.

4. Click the **Close** button (the red button) to close the Desktop window.

CHANGE LABEL COLOR

To make your icons easier to sort, you can assign them different label colors. You can then sort the icons by label (as described a moment ago) to put icons with the same color next to each other.

To change label color:

1. **CONTROL**+click or right-click the icon. The context menu appears.

2. Select the color in the Label area. (To remove the color, click the **X** button.)

Rename Desktop Icons

To rename a desktop icon:

1. Click the label once, and then click it again. Mac OS X displays an edit box around it.

2. Type the new name and press **RETURN**.

Change the Dock

The Dock has several aspects you can customize, including its size, the number and selection of icons it contains, and its behavior.

You can perform major customization either from the Dock pane of System Preferences (see Figure 2-10) or by using shortcuts. To display the Dock pane, open the menu, highlight **Dock**, and click **Dock Preferences**, or open System Preferences and click **Dock**.

QUICKSTEPS

POSITIONING AND HIDING THE DOCK

CHANGE THE POSITION OF THE DOCK

You can change where the Dock is positioned, or hide the Dock when you don't need to see it:

- Press and hold **SHIFT** while dragging (**SHIFT**+drag) the **Dock divider line** to the desired side.

  –Or–

- Select the **Left** option button, the **Bottom** option button, or the **Right** option button opposite Position On Screen on the Dock pane in System Preferences.

  –Or–

- **CONTROL**+click or right-click the **Dock divider line**, highlight **Position On Screen**, and select the **Left** option button, the **Bottom** option button, or the **Right** option button on the Dock context menu.

  –Or–

Continued . . .

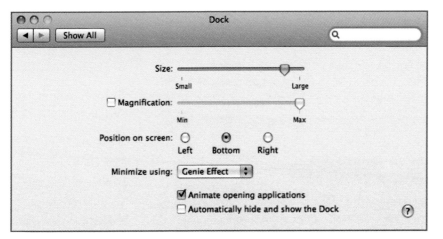

Figure 2-10: *The Dock pane of System Preferences is the central location for configuring the Dock, but you can also use shortcuts.*

QUICKSTEPS

POSITIONING AND HIDING THE DOCK *(Continued)*

- Open the menu, highlight **Dock**, and click **Position On Left, Position On Bottom**, or **Position On Right**.

HIDE AND DISPLAY THE DOCK

By default, Mac OS X keeps the Dock displayed so that you can access it at any time. But you can configure the Dock to hide automatically so you have more space onscreen:

- Select the **Automatically Hide And Show The Dock** check box on the Dock pane in System Preferences.

   –Or–

- Open the menu, highlight **Dock**, and choose **Turn Hiding On**.

   –Or–

- Press ⌘+OPTION+D.

The Dock then hides itself automatically. To display the Dock, move the mouse pointer to the side of the screen on which you've positioned the Dock.

To turn hiding off, clear the **Automatically Hide And Show The Dock** check box, choose **Turn Hiding Off**, or press ⌘+OPTION+D again.

TIP

You can toggle magnification on and off by opening the menu, highlighting **Dock**, and clicking **Turn Magnification On** or **Turn Magnification Off**.

CHANGE THE SIZE OF THE DOCK AND ITS ICONS

To change the size of the Dock:

- Drag the **Dock divider line** upward (to enlarge the Dock) or downward (to reduce it).

–Or–

- Drag the **Size** slider on the Dock pane.

The Dock resizes proportionally. Its maximum length is controlled by the length of the side of the screen on which it's positioned. As you add more icons to the Dock, Mac OS X automatically shrinks the Dock as necessary to fit it on the screen with all its icons displayed.

TURN MAGNIFICATION ON OR OFF

The Dock's magnification feature lets you see the Dock icons easily even if you've reduced the Dock to a tiny size to accommodate many icons. When you pass the mouse pointer over a Dock icon, Mac OS X magnifies it:

To apply magnification, select the **Magnification** check box on the Dock pane in System Preferences, and drag the slider to specify the degree of magnification.

CHOOSE AN EFFECT FOR MINIMIZING AND RESTORING WINDOWS

Mac OS X offers a choice of two animations for minimizing and restoring windows. Choose **Genie Effect** (the default) or **Scale Effect** in the **Minimize Using** drop-down list box on the Dock pane in System Preferences. The effects are hard to describe, but you'll see the difference easily when you try them.

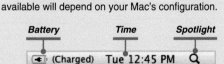
ADD AN APPLICATION TO THE DOCK

To add an application to the dock, drag its icon to the left portion of the Dock. For example:

1. Activate the **Finder**.
2. Open the **Go** menu and click **Applications**. A Finder window opens showing your Applications folder.
3. Drag an icon from the Applications folder to the left portion of the Dock.

ADD A DOCUMENT OR FOLDER TO THE DOCK

To add a document or folder to the Dock, drag its icon to the right portion of the Dock.

REARRANGE THE ICONS ON THE DOCK

To rearrange the icons on the Dock into your preferred order, drag an icon to its new position. Mac OS X makes space for the icon as you drag it.

REMOVE AN ICON FROM THE DOCK

To remove an icon from the Dock, quit the application if it's running, and then drag the icon off the Dock. When you release the mouse button, the icon vanishes in a puff of logic.

Change How Mac OS X Operates

You can customize how Mac OS X operates to suit your preferences.

Use Spaces to Extend Your Desktop Area

One of the most exciting new features in Leopard is Spaces, which enables you to extend your desktop area pretty much as far as you want. Each Space beyond the first is an extra desktop, and you can display whichever Space you want on your monitor.

CUSTOMIZING THE MENU BAR

(Continued)

VOLUME ICON

Select or clear the **Show Volume In Menu Bar** check box on any tab of the Sound pane.

BLUETOOTH ICON

Select or clear the **Show Bluetooth Status In The Menu Bar** check box on the Settings tab of the Bluetooth pane. Alternatively, select or clear the **Show Bluetooth Status In Menu Bar** check box on the Bluetooth tab of the Keyboard & Mouse pane. (The Bluetooth pane and the Bluetooth tab are available only if your Mac has Bluetooth, a wireless networking technology, installed.)

DISPLAYS ICON

Select or clear the **Show Displays In Menu Bar** check box on the Display tab of the Displays pane.

SPACES ICON

Select or clear the **Show Spaces In Menu Bar** check box on the Spaces tab of the Exposé & Spaces pane.

BATTERY STATUS ICON

Select or clear the **Show Battery Status In The Menu Bar** check box on the Options tab of the Energy Saver pane. This check box is available only for Mac laptops.

INPUT MENU ICON

Select or clear the **Show Input Menu In Menu Bar** check box on the Input Menu tab of the International pane.

AIRPORT ICON

Select or clear the **Show AirPort Status In Menu Bar** check box on the AirPort section of the Network pane, with **AirPort** selected in the Show drop-down list. (The AirPort section is available only if your Mac has an AirPort card.)

Continued . . .

For example, you can put your web browser and e-mail program on one Space, your Word document and Excel spreadsheet on another, iTunes on a third, and your Finder windows on a fourth. Rather than trying to marshal all the windows on a single desktop, you can devote a Space to each set of windows, and switch from Space to Space as needed.

Before you can use Spaces, you must configure it. Don't worry—the process is easy.

SET UP SPACES

To set up Spaces for the first time, follow these steps:

1. Click the **Spaces** button on the Dock.

2. Mac OS X displays a dialog box telling you that Spaces has not yet been set up and inviting you to set it up.

3. Click the **Set Up Spaces** button. Mac OS X opens System Preferences, loads the Exposé & Spaces pane, and displays the Spaces tab. Figure 2-11 shows the Spaces tab with some choices made, so that you can see the controls enabled.

4. Select the **Enable Spaces** check box to start Spaces running and make the other options available.

5. Select the **Show Spaces In Menu Bar** check box if you want Mac OS X to display the Spaces icon in the menu bar so that you can switch Spaces from the menu bar and also configure Spaces easily. This is usually helpful.

6. In the central area of the window, set up the configuration of Spaces you want:
   - Mac OS X starts you off with four Spaces, arranged in two columns of two rows. You may want to use this default configuration to get used to Spaces.

QUICKSTEPS

CUSTOMIZING THE MENU BAR

(Continued)

TIME DISPLAY

Select or clear the **Show The Date And Time** check box on the Clock tab of the Date & Time pane.

PPPoE ICON

Select or clear the **Show PPPoE Status In Menu Bar** check box on the PPPoE tab of the Network pane, with the appropriate network interface (for example, Built-in Ethernet) selected in the **Show** drop-down list box. (*PPPoE* stands for Point-to-Point Protocol over Ethernet, a networking standard for fast Internet connections.) The PPPoE tab appears only if you've created a PPPoE connection manually.

MODEM ICON

Select or clear the **Show Modem Status In Menu Bar** check box in the Modem section of the Network pane, with the appropriate modem entry selected in the **Show** drop-down list box.

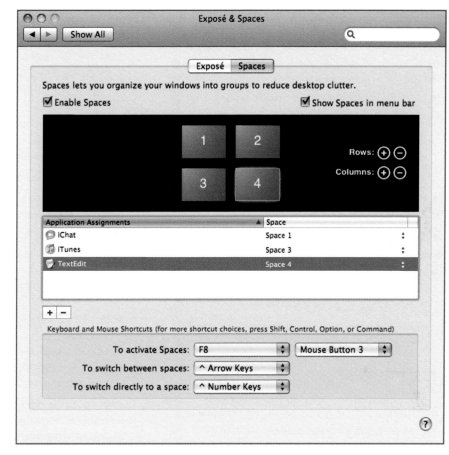

Figure 2-11: **On the Spaces tab of the Exposé & Spaces pane in System Preferences, choose how many Spaces to use, how to arrange them, and how to switch among them.**

NOTE

When you remove a column or row, Mac OS X warns you if doing so will remove an application binding (an application assignment). Click **Cancel** if you don't want to have Mac OS X remap the assignment to the nearest adjacent Space. Otherwise, click **OK**, and then change any remapped application assignment afterward.

Removing Spaces will modify your bindings

Removing this column of Spaces will modify application bindings to those Spaces. Application bindings will be redirected to the nearest adjacent Space to the one deleted.

Cancel   OK

- Click the + button next to Rows to add another row. Click the – button next to Rows to remove one existing row.

- Click the + button next to Columns to add another column. Click the – button next to Columns to remove one existing column.

NOTE

You can have up to four rows and four columns, giving a total of 16 Spaces. If this isn't enough for you, consider getting a virtual-desktop program such as CodeTek's Virtual Desktop Pro, www.codetek.com, which provides up to 100 virtual desktops.

NOTE

For any of the keyboard and mouse shortcuts for Spaces, you can add a modifier key—⌘, **OPTION**, **CONTROL**, or **SHIFT**—or a combination of modifier keys. Open the drop-down list, hold down the key or keys to make the list change, and then choose the item you want.

TIP

If you use Spaces (and you should), you'll probably want to be able to trigger it from the mouse. If your mouse has a third, fourth, or fifth button that Mac OS X recognizes, you can simply choose that button in the right-hand **To Activate Spaces** drop-down list. If your mouse has only two buttons, add a modifier key. For example, you can set ⌘ and the secondary mouse button (the right-click button) to activate Spaces. Open the right-hand **To Activate Spaces** drop-down list, and then hold down ⌘ while you choose **Secondary Mouse Button**.

7. In the Application Assignments area, tell Mac OS X which applications you want to keep in particular Spaces:

- At first, the Application Assignments list will probably be blank. Click the + button below the list to add a new assignment. Mac OS X opens a dialog box showing the applications in your Applications folder. Click the application, and then click **Add**. Mac OS X adds the application to the list.

- In the Space column, click the drop-down list opposite the application you added, and then choose which Space to assign it to. Choose **Every Space** if you want the application to be able to appear in whichever Space you park it.

- To remove an application assignment, click it, and then click the – button.

8. If you want to be able to control Spaces using the keyboard and mouse, customize the Keyboard And Mouse Shortcuts area:

- In the left-hand **To Activate Spaces** drop-down list, choose the key you want to press to activate Spaces—or choose the – item (the "nothing" item) if you don't want to use keys for activating Spaces. In the right-hand drop-down list, choose the mouse button (see the nearby Tip). You can also click the **Spaces** button on the Dock to activate Spaces.

- In the **To Switch Between Spaces** drop-down list, choose the arrow-key combination you want to use to move between spaces. The default setting is to use **CONTROL** with an arrow key—for example, **CONTROL+UP ARROW** to move to the Space above the current Space. This works well unless you use an application that also uses **CONTROL** and the arrow keys in combination.

- In the **To Switch Directly To A Space** drop-down list, choose the number-key combination you want to use to jump directly to a space. The default setting is to use **CONTROL** and the appropriate number—for example, **CONTROL-1** to display Space 1. This too works well unless you need the **CONTROL**-key combinations for other purposes.

9. Open the **System Preferences** menu and click **Quit System Preferences** to close System Preferences.

SWITCH AMONG SPACES

Once you've set up Spaces, you'll find them easy and intuitive to use:

- To see your Spaces, click the **Spaces** button on the Dock, press the keyboard shortcut you defined for Spaces (for example, **F8**), or invoke Spaces using another means (for example, a hot corner).

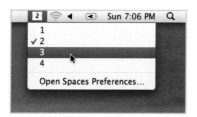

- To move a window to a different Space, drag it from its current Space to the Space on which you want it to appear.

- When you start an application that you've assigned to a Space, Mac OS X automatically positions that application's window on that Space.

- If you selected the Show Spaces In Menu Bar check box, the Spaces icon shows the number for the current space. To switch to another Space, open the Spaces menulet and choose the Space you want.

REARRANGE SPACES

You can rearrange Spaces on the Spaces tab of the Exposé & Spaces pane in System Preferences, but there's an easier way. Click the **Spaces** icon on the Dock, or trigger Spaces using a hot corner or shortcut. Then simply click a Space (not a window in a Space) and drag it to where you want it to appear.

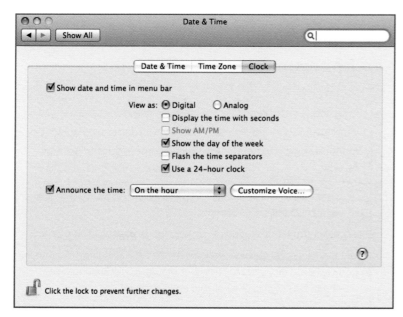

*Figure 2-12: **The Clock tab of the Date & Time pane in System Preferences offers various options, including displaying the seconds, flashing the time separators, and announcing the time aloud.***

Set and Use the Date and Time

The time display at the right end of the menu bar may seem simple enough, but you can customize it out of all recognition—or dispense with it:

1. Click the **time readout** in the menu bar. The time menu is displayed, including the full date.

2. To switch the clock quickly between digital and analog, select **View As Analog** or **View As Digital**, as appropriate. The analog clock icon in the menu bar is hard to read, so you'll probably want to use the digital readout.

3. Click **Open Date & Time** to display the Date & Time pane in System Preferences.

4. Click the **Clock** tab to display its contents (see Figure 2-12).

5. Choose options for the clock:

   - The **Show The Date And Time In Menu Bar** check box controls whether the clock appears at all.

- Select the **Digital** option button or the **Analog** option button to control the format.
- Choose other options, which include showing seconds, showing A.M./P.M., showing the day of the week, flashing time separators, using a 24-hour clock, and announcing the time out loud.

6. To change the time or date, click the **Date & Time** tab:
   - To set the date and time automatically using a time reference on the Internet, select the **Set Date & Time Automatically** check box, and choose the appropriate server in the drop-down list box.
   - To set the date and time manually, clear the **Set Date & Time Automatically** check box. Use the controls to set the date and time.

7. To specify the time zone, click the **Time Zone** tab. Choose your location on the map or use the **Closest City** drop-down list box to specify your closest city (and thus your time zone).

8. Open the **System Preferences** menu and click **Quit System Preferences** to close System Preferences.

Improve Accessibility with Universal Access

Mac OS X's Universal Access feature provides alternatives to the normal way the mouse and keyboard are used as well as some settings that make the screen more readable (or make it audible).

1. Open the menu and click **System Preferences** to open the System Preferences window.

2. Click **Universal Access** to display the Universal Access pane.

3. Select the options you want to use on the Seeing tab, Hearing tab, Keyboard tab, and Mouse tab or Mouse & Trackpad tab (see Table 2-1). Figure 2-13 shows the Seeing tab.

4. Open the **System Preferences** menu and click **Quit System Preferences** to close System Preferences.

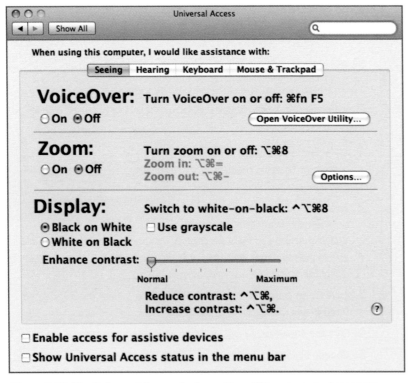

Figure 2-13: The Universal Access feature offers different ways of accessing Mac OS X and the applications that run on it. The Seeing features can be useful not only when you have vision problems but also when you're using a portable Mac in sunlight.

TAB	OPTION	DESCRIPTION	TURN ON OR OFF
Seeing	VoiceOver	Makes Mac OS X announce the names of onscreen items such as dialog boxes, sheets, and controls.	Select the **On** option button or the **Off** option button on the Seeing tab, or press **⌘+FUNCTION+F5**.
Seeing	Zoom	Enables you to zoom the screen to a large size to see small items more easily.	Select the **On** option button or the **Off** option button in the Zoom area on the Seeing tab, or press **⌘+OPTION+8** to toggle Zoom on and off.
Seeing	Zoom In	Zooms the display in.	Press **⌘+OPTION+=**.
Seeing	Zoom Out	Zooms the display out.	Press **⌘+OPTION+−** (hyphen).
Seeing	White On Black	Reverses the video to improve readability in some lighting conditions.	Select the **Black On White** option button or the **White On Black** option button on the Seeing tab, or press **⌘+OPTION+CONTROL+8**.
Seeing	Grayscale	Changes the display from color to grayscale to improve visibility of colors.	Select the **Use Grayscale** check box on the Seeing tab.
Seeing	Enhance Contrast	Increases the contrast to make elements on the screen more visible.	Drag the **Enhance Contrast** slider on the Seeing tab or press **⌘+OPTION+CONTROL+.** (period). Press **⌘+OPTION+CONTROL+,** (comma) to reduce contrast again.
Hearing	Flash The Screen	Makes the screen flash once when Mac OS X plays an alert sound.	Select the **Flash The Screen When An Alert Sound Occurs** check box on the Hearing tab.
Keyboard	Sticky Keys	Simulates pressing a pair of keys, such as ⌘+A, by pressing one key at a time. The modifier keys ⌘, **OPTION**, **CONTROL**, and **SHIFT** "stick" down until the final key of the command sequence is pressed. This is interpreted as the key sequence pressed together. Select the **Beep When A Modifier Key Is Set** check box to make Mac OS X beep when you press a modifier key. Select the **Display Pressed Keys On Screen** check box to receive a visual readout of modifier key presses.	Select the **On** option button or the **Off** option button in the Sticky Keys area of the Keyboard tab. Alternatively, press **SHIFT** five times in succession when the Press The Shift Key Five Times To Turn Sticky Keys On Or Off check box is selected.
Keyboard	Slow Keys	Makes Mac OS X wait for the specified delay before it registers a keystroke. Drag the **Acceptance Delay** slider to set the delay. Select the **Use Click Key Sounds** check box to make Mac OS X play a click when it registers the keystroke.	Select the **On** option button or the **Off** option button in the Slow Keys area of the Keyboard tab.

*Table 2-1: **Universal Access Features***

TAB	OPTION	DESCRIPTION	TURN ON OR OFF
Mouse	Mouse Keys	Enables you to use the numeric keypad instead of the mouse to move the pointer on the screen. Drag the **Initial Delay** slider to configure the delay before starting to move the mouse, and the **Maximum Speed** slider to set the maximum speed at which the mouse pointer moves. On a Mac with a trackpad, you can select the **Ignore Trackpad When Mouse Keys Is On** check box to disable the trackpad when you're using Mouse Keys.	Select the **On** option button or the **Off** option button in the Mouse Keys area of the Mouse tab. Alternatively, press **OPTION** five times in succession when the Press The Option Key Five Times To Turn Mouse Keys On Or Off check box is selected.
Mouse	Cursor Size	Enables you to enlarge the mouse pointer by dragging the **Cursor Size** pointer.	This option is always on, but the cursor size is set to **Normal** by default.
All tabs	Assistive Devices	Enables you to use extra assistive devices to control your Mac.	Select or clear the **Enable Access For Assistive Devices** check box at the bottom of the Universal Access pane.
All tabs	Universal Access Icon	Displays a Universal Access icon in the menu bar, giving you quick access to Universal Access options.	Select or clear the **Show Universal Access Status In The Menu Bar** check box at the bottom of the Universal Access pane.

*Table 2-1: **Universal Access Features (Continued)***

Customize the Keyboard

Mac OS X requires a keyboard for textual communications and typing. You can change the length of the delay before a key that is held down is repeated and the rate at which the key is repeated. On a portable Mac, you can also choose whether to use the function keys primarily for default actions or for custom actions.

NOTE

If you have a Mac laptop, the Keyboard tab of the Keyboard & Mouse pane also lets you choose between using the function keys as normal function keys or for custom actions (such as changing the screen brightness or the audio volume). Select the **Use All F1, F2, Etc. Keys As Standard Function keys** check box to use the standard actions (which will depend on the application that's active); you'll then need to press **FN** and the function key to use the custom actions. Clear the check box (which is cleared by default) to use the custom actions. You'll then need to press **FN** and the function key to perform a standard action.

1. Open the menu and click **System Preferences** to open the System Preferences window.

2. Click **Keyboard & Mouse** to display the Keyboard & Mouse pane.

3. If the Keyboard tab isn't displayed, click the **Keyboard** tab to display it (see Figure 2-14).

4. Drag the **Key Repeat Rate** slider to change the rate at which a key repeats when you hold it down.

5. Drag the **Delay Until Repeat** slider to change the delay until a key starts repeating.

6. When you have set up the keyboard the way you want, open the **System Preferences** menu and click **Quit System Preferences** to close System Preferences. Alternatively, if you want to customize other aspects of your system, click **Show All** to display all the categories.

QUICKSTEPS

PERFORMING ADVANCED KEYBOARD CUSTOMIZATION

If you use the keyboard extensively, you may want to customize it in two advanced ways: by applying a different layout, or by customizing the modifier keys.

APPLY A DIFFERENT KEYBOARD LAYOUT

Mac OS X also lets you apply a different logical layout, such as the Dvorak layout, to the keyboard. The keys themselves don't change, but they deliver different letters from what's indicated on the keys. You will want to apply a different layout only if you've learned (or are learning) to type using a particular layout.

To apply a different layout:

1. Open the menu and click **System Preferences** to open the System Preferences window.

2. Click **International**, and then click the **Input Menu** tab.

3. Select the check box for each layout you want to use.

4. Open the **System Preferences** menu and click **Quit System Preferences** to close System Preferences.

If you select two or more layouts, you can switch among them by using the Input menu on the menu bar. Alternatively, press ⌘+SPACEBAR to switch between the last two layouts you've used, or press ⌘+OPTION+SPACEBAR to step through all the layouts in the Input menu.

CUSTOMIZE THE MODIFIER KEYS

The modifier keys—⌘, OPTION, CONTROL, and SHIFT— are vital to using Mac OS X effectively from the keyboard. If you attach a nonstandard keyboard to your Mac, you may need to customize the modifier keys. For example,

Continued . . .

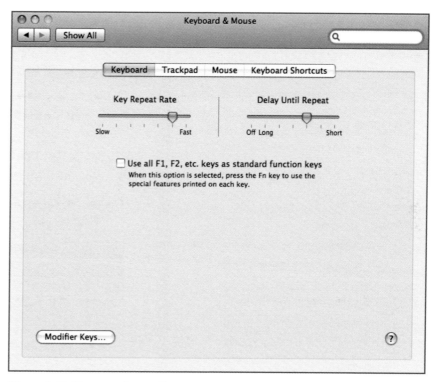

Figure 2-14: *You can change the repeat rate and the repeat delay for your keyboard to suit your typing style.*

Customize the Mouse and Trackpad

In a graphical user interface such as that of Mac OS X, you can perform many actions using the mouse rather than the keyboard. This makes it vital to configure your mouse so that it works as comfortably as possible.

If your Mac has a built-in trackpad, you can configure the trackpad for speed and comfort. This configuration is independent of the mouse configuration.

CUSTOMIZE THE MOUSE

1. Open the menu and click **System Preferences** to open the System Preferences window.

2. Click **Keyboard & Mouse**. The Keyboard & Mouse pane will be displayed.

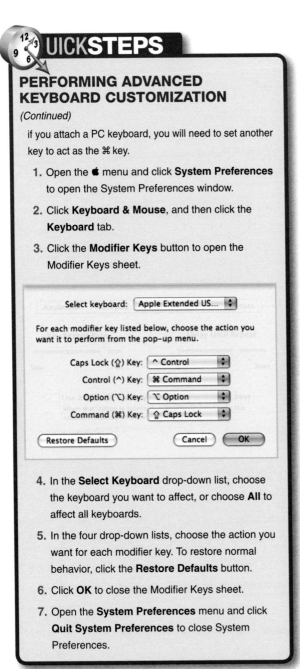

if you attach a PC keyboard, you will need to set another key to act as the ⌘ key.

1. Open the **⌘** menu and click **System Preferences** to open the System Preferences window.

2. Click **Keyboard & Mouse**, and then click the **Keyboard** tab.

3. Click the **Modifier Keys** button to open the Modifier Keys sheet.

> Select keyboard: Apple Extended US... ⬦
>
> For each modifier key listed below, choose the action you want it to perform from the pop-up menu.
>
> Caps Lock (⇪) Key: ⌃ Control ⬦
> Control (⌃) Key: ⌘ Command ⬦
> Option (⌥) Key: ⌥ Option ⬦
> Command (⌘) Key: ⇪ Caps Lock ⬦
>
> (Restore Defaults)   (Cancel) (OK)

4. In the **Select Keyboard** drop-down list, choose the keyboard you want to affect, or choose **All** to affect all keyboards.

5. In the four drop-down lists, choose the action you want for each modifier key. To restore normal behavior, click the **Restore Defaults** button.

6. Click **OK** to close the Modifier Keys sheet.

7. Open the **System Preferences** menu and click **Quit System Preferences** to close System Preferences.

3. Click the **Mouse** tab. The Mouse tab contains the same controls as the upper part of the Trackpad tab, shown in Figure 2-15.

4. Drag the **Tracking Speed** slider to control the speed at which the mouse pointer moves as you move the mouse.

5. Drag the **Double-Click Speed** slider if you want to change the double-click speed.

6. Open the **System Preferences** menu and click **Quit System Preferences** to close System Preferences.

CUSTOMIZE THE TRACKPAD

To configure the trackpad on a Mac that includes one:

1. Open the **⌘** menu and click **System Preferences** to open the System Preferences window.

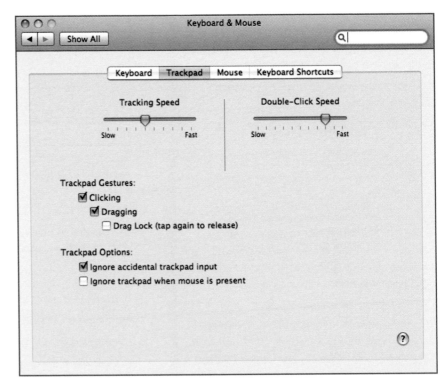

Figure 2-15: If your Mac has a trackpad, configure it on the Trackpad tab of the Keyboard & Mouse pane in System Preferences.

2. Click **Keyboard & Mouse** to display the Keyboard & Mouse pane.

3. Click the **Trackpad** tab (see Figure 2-15).

4. Drag the **Tracking Speed** slider to control the speed at which the mouse pointer moves as you move your finger on the trackpad.

5. Drag the **Double-Click Speed** slider as necessary to change the double-click speed.

6. Choose whether to use the trackpad for clicking, dragging, and drag lock by selecting the **Clicking** check box, the **Dragging** check box, and the **Drag Lock** check box in the Trackpad Gestures area.

   - You must select the **Clicking** check box to enable the Dragging check box, and you must select the **Dragging** check box to enable the Drag Lock check box.

   - If you turn on dragging, tap twice with your finger on the trackpad and then move your finger to drag the object.

   - If you turn on drag lock, tap twice with your finger on the trackpad to lock dragging on. Move your finger to drag the object, and then tap again to release the lock.

7. Select the **Ignore Accidental Trackpad Input** check box if you want Mac OS X to ignore trackpad movements it thinks are accidental. For example, you may brush the trackpad with the base of your thumbs while typing. This option is usually helpful.

8. Select the **Ignore Trackpad When Mouse Is Present** check box if you want Mac OS X to deactivate the trackpad when you plug a mouse into your Mac. This option is helpful if you do not use the trackpad when you have plugged in a mouse.

9. Open the **System Preferences** menu and click **Quit System Preferences** to close System Preferences.

Change Sounds

Mac OS X plays an alert sound when you try to do something that doesn't work or when something happens that needs your attention. Mac OS X plays other sounds to give feedback for interface actions, such as moving files to the Trash or pressing the volume keys. You can change the alert sound or prevent Mac OS X from playing feedback sounds by using the Sound pane in System Preferences.

1. Open the menu and click **System Preferences** to open the System Preferences window.

2. Click **Sound** to display the Sound pane.

CHANGING LANGUAGE AND REGIONAL SETTINGS *(Continued)*

CHANGE REGIONAL SETTINGS

To change the regional settings Mac OS X uses:

1. Open the menu and click **System Preferences** to open the System Preferences window.

2. Click **International** to display the International pane.

3. If the Formats tab isn't displayed, click the **Formats** tab to display it.

4. In the **Region** drop-down list box, select the region whose formats you want to use—for example, United States or Canada. Mac OS X initially displays only the most widely used regions in the Region drop-down list box. To display all regions, select the Show All Regions check box. The Dates readout, Times readout, and Numbers readout will display samples of those formats.

5. To change one of the formats, click the appropriate **Customize** button and work on the option sheet that Mac OS X displays. When you've finished choosing options, click **OK** to close the option sheet.

6. In the **Measurement Units** drop-down list box, select **US** or **Metric** if you want to change the default setting for the region you chose.

7. Open the **System Preferences** menu and click **Quit System Preferences** to close System Preferences.

3. If the Sound Effects tab isn't displayed, click the **Sound Effects** tab to display it.

4. Click the sound in the **Choose An Alert Sound** list. Mac OS X will play the sound to help you choose a suitable one. If you don't want to hear an alert sound, drag the Alert Volume slider all the way to the left.

5. If the **Play Alerts And Sound Effects Through** drop-down list is available, select the speakers or other device you want to use. If the only choice is Internal Speakers, Mac OS X makes this drop-down list unavailable.

6. Drag the **Alert Volume** slider to set the volume for the alert sound relative to the other audio output (for example, music) on your Mac.

7. If you don't want Mac OS X to play feedback sounds for actions, clear the **Play User Interface Sound Effects** check box.

8. If you don't want Mac OS X to play feedback sounds when you press the volume keys, clear the **Play Feedback When Volume Is Changed** check box.

9. If you want to change the overall sound volume, drag the **Output Volume** slider to the left or right.

10. If you want Mac OS X to display a volume control in the menu bar, select the **Show Volume In Menu Bar** check box. Being able to control the volume from the menu bar is helpful if you don't have another volume control within reach.

11. Open the **System Preferences** menu and click **Quit System Preferences** to close System Preferences.

How to...

- *Identify Disk Storage Devices*
- *Changing Views in the Finder*
- *Select and Open Folders*
- *Create New Folders*
- *Renaming and Deleting Files and Folders*
- *Customize the Finder*
- *Customize Finder Preferences*
- *Select Multiple Files or Folders*
- *Use the Trash*
- *Copying and Moving Files and Folders*
- *Create Aliases*
- *Search for Files and Folders*
- *Creating Smart Folders to Repeat Searches*
- *Look Quickly Inside Files*
- *Get Info About a File or Folder*
- *Work with Ownership and Permissions*
- *Write Files and Folders to a CD or DVD*
- *Creating Compressed Files from Files and Folders*

Chapter 3
Storing Information

The information on your Mac—documents, e-mail, photographs, music, and applications—is stored in *files*. So that your files are organized and can be found more easily, they are kept in *folders*, and folders can be placed in other folders for further segmentation. For example, a folder labeled "Music" contains folders for GarageBand and iTunes. The GarageBand folder contains a song file named Trialling Error, as shown in Figure 3-1.

In this chapter, you'll see how to create, use, and manage files and folders like these. (In this chapter the term "objects" refers to any mix of files, folders, and disk drives.)

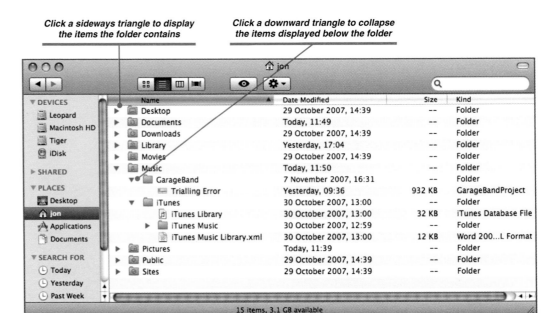

Click a sideways triangle to display the items the folder contains

Click a downward triangle to collapse the items displayed below the folder

Figure 3-1: The Finder in List view can show files in folders within other folders.

Display Files and Folders

The tool that Mac OS X provides to display and work with files and folders is called the *Finder*. The Finder is always running; its icon (shown at right) appears by default at the left end of the Dock. The Finder has four views:

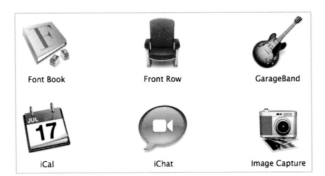

Font Book   Front Row   GarageBand

iCal   iChat   Image Capture

- **Icons view** displays a medium-size icon for each object, as shown. Icons view is good for viewing folders that contain icons—for example, the Applications folder or the Utilities folder.

- **List view** displays a list of objects with brief details (as shown in Figure 3-1).

- **Columns view** (see Figure 3-2) shows a columnar display of the folder path (the route) to the selected object, together with a preview of the object and brief details.

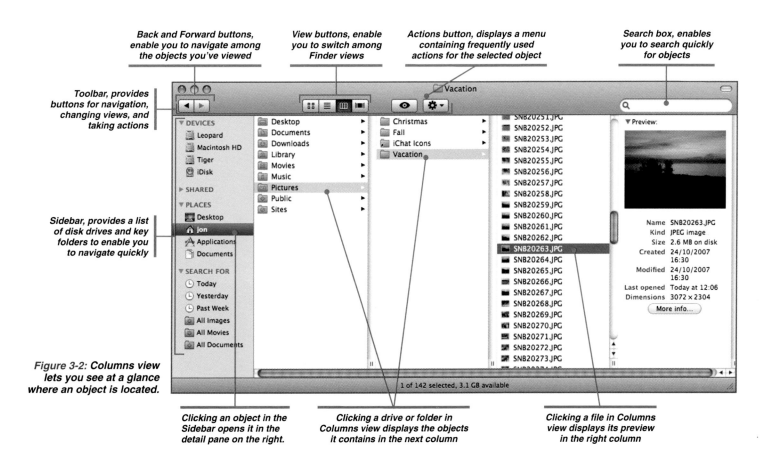

Back and Forward buttons, enable you to navigate among the objects you've viewed

View buttons, enable you to switch among Finder views

Actions button, displays a menu containing frequently used actions for the selected object

Search box, enables you to search quickly for objects

Toolbar, provides buttons for navigation, changing views, and taking actions

Sidebar, provides a list of disk drives and key folders to enable you to navigate quickly

Figure 3-2: Columns view lets you see at a glance where an object is located.

Clicking an object in the Sidebar opens it in the detail pane on the right.

Clicking a drive or folder in Columns view displays the objects it contains in the next column

Clicking a file in Columns view displays its preview in the right column

- **Cover Flow view** (see Figure 3-3) shows a scrolling graphical display of the folders or files contained in the folder you're viewing. You can click an object to bring it to the center position, where it is displayed larger, or scroll through the objects by clicking the scroll bar.

In each view, the Finder displays the Sidebar on its left side. The Sidebar is a navigation tool that contains a list of disk drives and key folders on your computer and other connected computers, broken up into the following categories:

- **Devices**   Your Mac's hard disks, and your iDisk
- **Shared**   Computers and drives shared on the network

*Click another picture or item to
bring it to the center of the display*

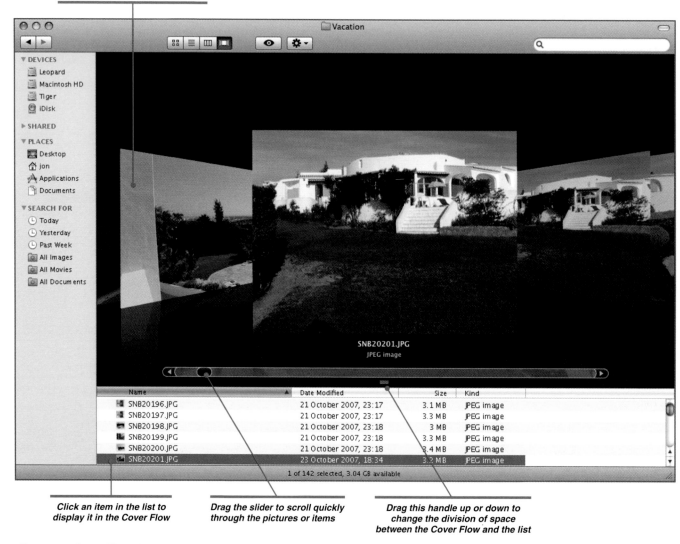

*Click an item in the list to
display it in the Cover Flow*

*Drag the slider to scroll quickly
through the pictures or items*

*Drag this handle up or down to
change the division of space
between the Cover Flow and the list*

Figure 3-3: *Cover Flow view shows you a graphical representation of the contents of the folder. This works better for some types of files than for others.*

- **Places**   Key folders on your Mac (see the following discussion)
- **Search For**   Predefined searches that let you see files and folders you've changed today, yesterday, and in the past week; all images; all movies; and all documents

To expand one of the categories in the Sidebar, click the sideways-pointing gray triangle next to it. You can then click a drive, folder, computer, or search in the Sidebar to display its contents in the detail pane. Click the downward-pointing triangle next to an expanded item to collapse its contents.

The Places category in the Sidebar includes the following folders, which Mac OS X creates automatically for each user:

- Your **Home** folder, identified by your short user name, contains all your personal folders, including the Documents, Movies, Music, and Pictures folders.
- The **Desktop** folder contains items stored on your desktop.
- The **Applications** folder contains applications you can run.
- The **Documents** folder is the main folder for storing documents that aren't music, movies, or pictures. For example, if you create a document using Microsoft Word, Word uses the Documents folder by default.

Identify Disk Storage Devices

Files and folders are held on various physical storage devices called *disk drives*. Your Mac almost certainly has a primary hard disk and a primary optical drive. It may also have further hard disks or optical drives, and it may be connected to one or more network drives, either via a wired network or via a wireless network. Mac OS X also treats iPods as drives if they are configured for disk use, so if you connect an iPod to your Mac and configure it for disk use, the iPod will appear as a drive.

Mac OS X automatically mounts all disk drives that it detects (but see the nearby Note). By default, Mac OS X displays an icon for each mounted disk drive on your desktop, giving you instant access to them. You can also access the disk drives through the Finder or via common dialog boxes and sheets (such as the Open dialog box and the Save As sheet).

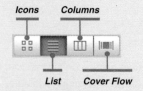
Select and Open Folders

When you open a Finder window, you see the disk drives and key folders on your computer in the Sidebar. You can:

- See the contents of a disk drive, computer, key folder, or search by clicking it in the Sidebar.

- In Icons view, List view, or Cover Flow view, open a folder and display its contents by double-clicking it.

- In Columns view, display a folder's contents in the next column by clicking it.

Create New Folders

While you could store all your files within the ready-made folders that Mac OS X provides for you—your Home, Documents, Movies, Music, and Pictures folders—you will probably want to make your files easier to find by creating some subsidiary folders.

For example, to create the Family folder in your Movies folder:

1. Click the **Finder** button on the Dock to open a Finder window to your default folder for new windows. (Your default folder is normally your Home folder unless you change it in the New Finder Windows Open pop-up menu on the General tab in Finder Preferences.)

2. If the Finder is using any other view than Columns view, click the **Columns** button to switch to Columns view. (You can create a folder in any view, but this example uses Columns view.)

3. In the first column, click the **Movies** folder to display its contents.

4. Open the **File** menu and click **New Folder**. Mac OS X will create a new folder, assign it the default name "untitled folder," and display an edit box around it so that you can change the name immediately.

5. Type the new name for the folder and either press **RETURN** or click elsewhere to apply the name.

6. Click the new folder to open it.

QUICKSTEPS

RENAMING AND DELETING FILES AND FOLDERS

RENAME A FILE OR FOLDER

1. Click the file or folder once to select it.
2. Click again. An edit box will be displayed around the name.
3. Type the new name or edit the existing name.
4. Press **RETURN** or click elsewhere to apply the new name.

MOVE A FILE OR FOLDER TO THE TRASH

To move a file or folder to the Trash, use any of these techniques:

- Drag the file or folder to the **Trash** icon on the Dock.

  –Or–

- Select the object and press ⌘+**DELETE**.

  –Or–

- Select the object. Open the **File** menu and click **Move To Trash**.

  –Or–

- **CONTROL**+click or right-click the object. Click **Move To Trash** on the context menu.

RECOVER A FILE OR FOLDER FROM THE TRASH

To recover a file or folder that has been moved to the Trash:

- Immediately after moving the file or folder to Trash, open the **Edit** menu and choose **Undo Move Of** *filename*.

  –Or–

- Click the **Trash** icon on the Dock to display a Finder window showing the contents of the Trash. Drag the file or folder from the Trash to the desired location.

Customize the Finder

To make the Finder even quicker and easier to use, you can customize various aspects of its behavior, including Icons view, List view, Columns view, Cover Flow view, and the Sidebar.

Start by activating the **Finder** (for example, click the Finder icon on the Dock, or click the desktop), opening the Go menu, and choosing **Home** to open a Finder window showing your Home folder.

CUSTOMIZE ICONS VIEW

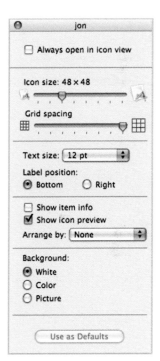

1. If the Finder window isn't using Icons view, click the **Icons** button, or open the **View** menu and click **As Icons**, to switch to Icons view.
2. Open the **View** menu and click **Show View Options**. The options window will open, showing the short name of your user account (in the example, "jon") in its title bar (because your Home folder is selected).
3. Select the **Always Open In Icon View** check box if you want the Finder always to use Icon view when you open a window showing this folder.
4. Drag the **Icon Size** slider to make the icons your preferred size.
5. Drag the **Grid Spacing** slider to adjust the size of the grid on which the icons are aligned. For example, drag the slider toward the left end to position the icons closer together.
6. Use the **Text Size** drop-down list box to choose a text size that you find easy to read.
7. Specify the label position relative to the icon by selecting the **Bottom** option button or the **Right** option button.
8. Select the **Show Item Info** check box if you want to display brief information about the contents of a folder with its icon.
9. Select the **Show Icon Preview** check box if you want graphics to be displayed as miniature versions of their contents rather than as generic icons. This option is useful for folders that contain pictures.

10. If you want Mac OS X to arrange the icons automatically, choose an item other than None in the **Arrange By** drop-down list: Name, Date Modified, Date Created, Size, Kind (file type), or Label. You can also select **Snap To Grid** in the **Arrange By** drop-down list to make Mac OS X align the icons to the underlying grid.

11. In the Background area, specify the background for the folder by selecting the **White** option button, the **Color** option button, or the **Picture** option button.

   ● If you select Color, click the **Color** button that appears, use the resulting Colors window to pick the color, and click **OK**.

   ● If you select Picture, click the **Select** button, choose the picture in the Select A Picture dialog box, and click **OK**.

12. If you want to use the settings you've chosen here for all windows, click the **Use As Defaults** button. Any customization you've applied to other windows remains in place.

13. Leave the options window open so that you can perform further customization.

CUSTOMIZE LIST VIEW OR COVER FLOW VIEW

1. With the options window still open, click the **List** button or **Cover Flow** button (as appropriate) on the toolbar, or open the **View** menu and click **As List** or **As Cover Flow** (as appropriate) in the Finder window. The Finder window will switch to List view or Cover Flow view, and the options window will switch to displaying the options for List view or Cover Flow view. All the options are the same except for the first option (see step 2).

2. In List view, select the **Always Open In List View** check box if you want the Finder always to use List view when you open a window showing this folder. In Cover Flow view, select the **Always Open In Cover Flow View** check box if you want the Finder always to use Cover Flow view for this folder.

3. In the Icon Size area, click the option button for the size you prefer, small or large.

4. Use the **Text Size** drop-down list box to choose a text size that you find easy to read.

5. In the **Show Columns** area, select the check boxes for the columns you want to have displayed in List view. The Name column is always displayed; you can't switch it off.

6. Select the **Use Relative Dates** check box if you want any date columns you display to use relative date descriptions, such as Today or Yesterday, instead of standard date formats (for example, 1 September 2008).

7. Select the **Calculate All Sizes** check box if you want Mac OS X to display the sizes of folders as well as files. Calculating the size of folders (especially those that contain many files) takes more processor cycles and may take a while when you open a Finder window.

TIP

Applying a background color or picture to a Finder window can help you pick that window out more easily from other Finder windows.

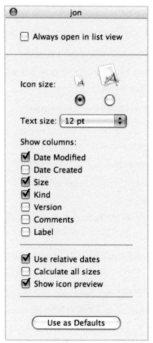

8. Select the **Show Icon Preview** check box if you want the Finder to display a preview on each icon, where possible, rather than a generic icon.

9. If you want to use the settings you've chosen here for all windows, click the **Use As Defaults** button. Any customization you've applied to other windows remains in place.

10. Leave the options window open so that you can perform further customization.

CUSTOMIZE COLUMNS VIEW

1. With the options window still open, click the **Columns** button on the toolbar, or open the **View** menu and click **As Columns** in the Finder window. The Finder window will switch to Columns view, and the options window will switch to displaying the options for Columns view.

2. Select the **Always Open In Column View** check box if you want the Finder always to use Columns view when you open a window showing this folder.

3. Use the **Text Size** drop-down list box to choose a text size that you find easy to read.

4. Select the **Show Icon Preview** check box if you want to include icons in the listings. For a more compact display, clear this check box.

5. Select the **Show Preview Column** check box if you want to display the preview in the rightmost column. The preview is helpful for identifying files visually.

6. In the **Arrange By** drop-down list, choose how you want the Finder to arrange the icons: Name, Date Modified, Date Created, Size, Kind (the file type), or Label.

7. Click the **Close** button (the red button on the left).

Customize Finder Preferences

You can also customize various aspects of the Finder's look and behavior by using the Finder Preferences window:

1. Open the **Finder** menu and click **Preferences** to open the Finder Preferences window.

2. If the General pane (see Figure 3-4) isn't displayed, click the **General** button to display it.

3. In the Show These Items On The Desktop area, choose which drives to show on the desktop by selecting or clearing the **Hard Disks** check box, the **External Disks** check box, the **CDs, DVDs, And iPods** check box, and the **Connected Servers** check box.

Figure 3-4: The General pane of Finder Preferences lets you specify which disk drives, external disks, and servers to show on the desktop, where and how new Finder windows open, and how to treat spring-loaded folders.

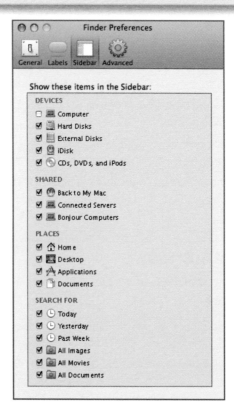

NOTE

Spring-loaded folders and windows are a Mac OS X feature that make moving and copying objects easier. Instead of having to open the destination before dragging an object, you can drag the object over the destination folder, wait a moment (still holding down the mouse button), and have Mac OS X open the folder automatically. Still dragging or holding down the mouse button, you can open further folders inside that folder if necessary.

Figure 3-5: On the Sidebar pane of Finder Preferences, choose which drives and folders to display in the Sidebar. For example, if you do not use an iDisk, you will probably want to remove the iDisk item.

4. In the **New Finder Windows Open** drop-down list box, choose the location you want each new Finder window to display: Computer, Macintosh HD, iDisk, Home, Documents, or another folder. The default is Home.

5. If you want each folder you open from a Finder window to be displayed in a new window instead of the same window, select the **Always Open Folders In A New Window** check box. If you prefer to use the Forward button and Back button to navigate among folders, clear this check box.

6. Select the **Spring-Loaded Folders And Windows** check box if you want to use the spring-loaded folders feature. (See the Note.) Drag the **Delay** slider to specify how quickly the spring-loading works.

7. Click the **Labels** button to display the Labels pane, on which you can change the names used for the colored labels. (For example, you might change the name "Red" to "Urgent.")

8. Click the **Sidebar** button to display the Sidebar pane (see Figure 3-5).

9. Select the check boxes for the drives and folders you want the Sidebar to contain. Clear the check boxes for other items.

10. Click the **Advanced** button to display the Advanced pane (see Figure 3-6).

11. Select the **Show All File Extensions** check box if you want Mac OS X to display all file extensions (instead of hiding most of them).

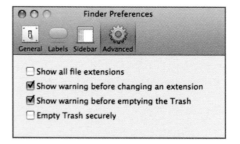

Figure 3-6: The Advanced pane of Finder Preferences lets you choose whether to display file extensions and Trash warnings. Most people find the warning before emptying the Trash helpful. If you prefer to empty the Trash securely so that nobody can salvage its contents, select the Empty Trash Securely check box.

A *file extension* is the "second part" of a filename that serves to tell some operating systems which type of data a file contains. For example, if you save a Rich-Text Format document in TextEdit under the name Cats, TextEdit adds the file extension .rtf to indicate that the file is a Rich-Text Format document. The full file name is Cats.rtf, but Mac OS X by default hides the file extension from you, because you do not normally need to see it.

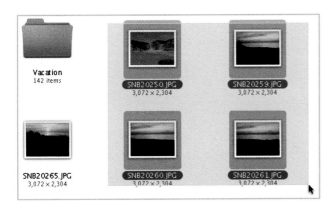

Vacation
142 items

SNB20250.JPG
3,072 × 2,304

SNB20259.JPG
3,072 × 2,304

SNB20265.JPG
3,072 × 2,304

SNB20260.JPG
3,072 × 2,304

SNB20261.JPG
3,072 × 2,304

12. Clear the **Show Warning Before Emptying The Trash** check box if you don't want Mac OS X to display a confirmation message box when you empty the Trash. (See "Empty the Trash," later in this chapter.)

13. Click the **Close** button (the red button) to close the Finder Preferences window.

Select Multiple Files or Folders

Often, you will want to perform one or more operations—such as copy, move, or delete—on several files and/or folders at the same time. You can select objects using any of several techniques:

- In Icon view, move the mouse pointer to just beyond the corner of the block of icons you want to select. Drag the mouse across the icons, creating a selection box around the icons and making Mac OS X select them. You can drag in whichever direction you find easiest.

  –Or–

- In List view, Columns view, or Cover Flow view, drag up or down through the objects you want to select.

  –Or–

- Click the first object, hold down **SHIFT**, and click the last object. Mac OS X selects both of those objects and the objects between them. This method works best for selecting contiguous objects in List view, Columns view, or Cover Flow view.

  –Or–

- Click the first object, hold down ⌘, and click each of the other objects. You can use this technique in any view. ⌘+click a selected object to deselect it.

Use the Trash

The Mac operating system has long used the metaphor of trash for deleting items. Instead of deleting an object immediately (and removing it from your Mac's hard disk so that you can never retrieve it again), you move the object to the Trash. An object remains in the Trash until you empty the Trash, at which point you can't retrieve it any more. This two-stage process is not only clear and familiar but helps you avoid deleting objects permanently by making hasty choices in the Finder.

QUICKSTEPS

COPYING AND MOVING FILES AND FOLDERS

You can copy files and folders using the mouse, the menu, or the keyboard. You can move files and folders using the mouse.

COPY WITH THE MOUSE

To copy with the mouse, press and hold **OPTION** while dragging any file or folder from one folder to another on the same disk drive. To copy from a folder on one disk drive to a folder on another disk drive, drag without holding down **OPTION**.

MOVE WITH THE MOUSE

To move with the mouse, drag any file or folder from one folder to another on the same disk drive. To move from a folder on one disk drive to a folder on another disk drive, press and hold down ⌘ while dragging the object.

COPY USING THE MENU

1. Select the object to copy.
2. Open the **Edit** menu and click **Copy** *object*, where *object* is the object's name.
3. Navigate to the destination.
4. Open the **Edit** menu and click **Paste Item**.

COPY USING THE KEYBOARD

1. Select the object to copy.
2. Press ⌘+C to copy the object.
3. Navigate to the destination.
4. Press ⌘+V to paste the object.

The Trash is a special system folder that can contain both files and folders. You can open the Trash in a Finder window by clicking the **Trash** button on the Dock. Figure 3-7 shows the Trash open in Cover Flow view. You can sort the Trash and search through it as you would any other folder.

EMPTY THE TRASH

Before emptying the Trash, you may want to double-check that you haven't moved any valuable files to it by mistake. Then:

1. Activate the **Finder**.

Figure 3-7: The Trash is a special folder that holds files and folders you've deleted until you empty it, at which point the deleted items vanish forever.

TIP

One action you can't take in the Trash folder is double-click a file to open it; when you do this, Mac OS X displays a message box telling you that the document could not be opened because it is in the Trash. You're supposed to move the file out of the Trash before you open it—presumably so that you don't forget to move it out of the Trash afterward if you want to keep the file. However, you can open a file in the Trash by dragging it to a suitable application's icon on the Dock. This trick is useful for checking what a file in the Trash contains before removing the file from the Trash or emptying the Trash.

NOTE

You can turn off the confirmation message box by clearing the **Show Warning Before Emptying The Trash** check box in the Advanced pane of Finder Preferences (open the **Finder** menu and choose **Preferences**).

TIP

You can also empty the Trash by **CONTROL**+clicking or right-clicking the **Trash** icon on the Dock and choosing **Empty Trash** from the shortcut menu.

2. Open the **Finder** menu and click **Empty Trash**. Mac OS X displays a confirmation message box.

3. Click **OK**. Mac OS X empties the Trash, permanently deleting all the objects it contains.

USE THE SECURE EMPTY TRASH FEATURE

Emptying the Trash by using the technique described in the previous section gets rid of the files and folders well enough for conventional purposes, but the files leave fragments that computer recovery experts might be able to reassemble. If you need to ensure that your deleted material cannot be recovered like this, use the Secure Empty Trash feature instead of emptying the Trash.

1. Activate the **Finder** if it isn't already.

2. Open the **Finder** menu and click **Secure Empty Trash**. Mac OS X displays a confirmation message box.

3. Click **OK**. Mac OS X empties the Trash, permanently deleting all the objects it contains and overwriting the disk sectors that contained them.

Secure Empty Trash takes longer than emptying the Trash in the conventional way, but usually not long enough to be inconvenient.

Create Aliases

Aliases allow you to quickly access files from places other than where the files are stored. For example, you can start an application from the Dock even though the actual application file is stored in another folder. Similarly, you can store aliases for the documents you need most frequently in a convenient location, such as on your desktop (or on the Dock).

To create an alias:

1. Select the file or folder.
2. Open the **File** menu and click **Make Alias**. Mac OS X will create an alias to the object and assign it the object's name and the word "alias." For example, an alias to the file named "Work Plans" receives the name "Work Plans alias."
3. Mac OS X places an edit box around the default name. If you want, type a new name and press **RETURN**.
4. Drag the alias to where you want to keep it.

Search for Files and Folders

It's often difficult to remember where particular files and folders are on a computer, especially if it has a large hard disk (or several of them) and one or more network drives. To help you locate the files you need, Mac OS X provides a search feature called Spotlight. You can search directly from the desktop across your entire computer or open a Finder window and perform either a predefined search or a more specific custom search.

SEARCH QUICKLY FROM THE DESKTOP

The quickest way to find files and folders is to use Spotlight from the desktop:

1. Click the **Spotlight** icon at the right end of the menu bar. Mac OS X opens a Spotlight panel.

2. Type the first few letters of the item you want to find. Spotlight searches as you type, and displays matching results, as shown in the following illustration.

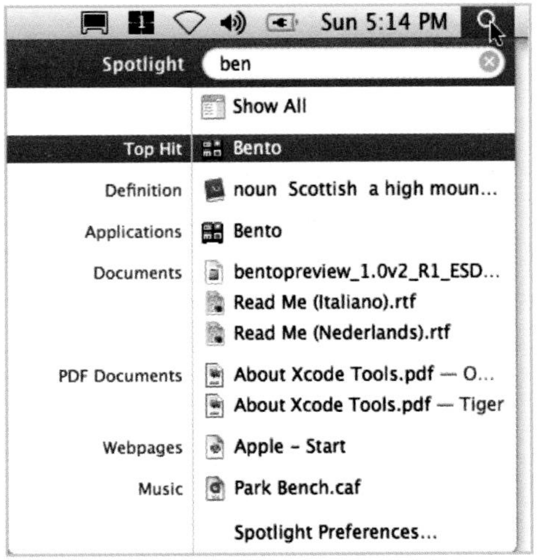

3. If Spotlight finds many results, you may need to narrow down the list by typing further search terms. Alternatively, click the × button in the Spotlight panel to clear the current search, and then type a new search term.

4. If you see the file or folder you want, click it. To see all results, click the **Show All** item at the top of the list. Mac OS X opens a Finder window showing the search results (see Figure 3-8).

5. From the Finder window, you can then refine the search as needed by using the techniques described in the upcoming section "Perform a Detailed Search from the Finder."

USE AN EXISTING SEARCH

To use one of Mac OS X's built-in searches:

1. Activate the **Finder**.

2. Open a Finder window. For example, press ⌘-**N** to open a new Finder window.

3. If the Search For area of the Sidebar is collapsed, click the gray triangle to expand it.

4. Click the search you want. For example, click the **Today** search to see all the files you have created or opened today.

PERFORM A DETAILED SEARCH FROM THE FINDER

To perform a detailed search from the Finder, or to refine the search results you've reached by using the technique described in the previous section:

1. Activate the **Finder**.

2. Open a Finder window showing the drive or folder from which to start the search. For example, open the **Go** menu and choose **Computer** to display your Mac's contents, or open the **Go** menu and choose **Home** to display your Home folder. Alternatively, click a drive or folder in the Sidebar.

3. Open the **File** menu and click **Find**. The Searching window is displayed, showing basic search settings (see Figure 3-9). If you've run a Spotlight search as described in the previous section, you'll already have results displayed.

Figure 3-8: By opening a Finder window, you can see more detail on the Spotlight results. You can also refine the search as needed.

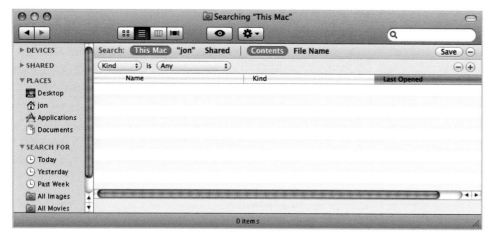

Figure 3-9: Mac OS X's Searching window quickly locates files matching the criteria you specify.

TIP

Searching filenames is much faster than searching contents, so if you can remember enough of the name of the file you want, try searching by filename first.

TIP

For further search options, hold down OPTION as you click the + button. You can then choose between matching **Any**, **All, or None** of the following criteria.

4. On the left side of the Search bar, tell Mac OS X where to search:

   - **This Mac** searches everywhere on your Mac to which you have access. (Mac OS X doesn't allow you to search other users' folders.) This search is thorough but may be slow. Use it if you don't know where the target file or folder is on your Mac.

   - **(Current Object)**, the second item on the Search bar, shows the name of the current drive or folder—for example, your user name if you've chosen your Home folder.

   - **Shared** searches all shared folders to which your Mac is connected.

5. On the right side of the Search bar, make sure **Contents** is selected if you want to search within files as well as search their names. Click **File Name** if you want to search only filenames.

6. On the line below the Search bar, use the first line of controls to specify the first search criterion (see Table 3-1).

7. To add another search criterion, click the + button. The Find window adds a second line of controls. Specify the next criterion using the same technique. This is an AND search: the search result must meet all the criteria you specify. Therefore, each criterion you add restricts the search further.

8. Mac OS X continues to search as you add criteria, so you can see the results. Figure 3-10 shows an example.

9. Click an object to display the *Path bar*, a partial tree diagram showing the object's location in the lower part of the window.

10. Double-click an object to open it. Double-click a folder in the tree diagram to open that folder.

11. Click the **Close** button (the red button) on the Searching window to close it.

QUICKSTEPS

CREATING SMART FOLDERS TO REPEAT SEARCHES

If you will need to perform a particular search more than once, you can save it for reuse. Mac OS X calls these saved searches Smart Folders. Smart Folders are great for keeping related items organized.

The easiest way to create a Smart Folder is by saving a search:

1. Perform your search as described in the section "Perform a Detailed Search from the Finder."

Continued . . .

ITEM	COMPARISON	COMMENTS
Kind	Is	Specify the type: Any, Applications, Documents, Folders, Images, Movies, Music, PDF, Presentations, Text, or Other.
Last Opened Date	Within Last	Choose the date you want—for example, choose Last Opened Date.
Last Modified Date	Exactly	Choose the comparison.
Created Date	Before After Today Yesterday This Week This Month This Year	If necessary, specify the date or number of time periods. For example, choose Within Last 10 Days or Before 4/1/2008.
Name	Matches Contains Begins With Ends With Is	Specify the comparison and the appropriate text string. For example, you might specify Contains Jane to find files and folders whose names contain "Jane."
Contents	Contains	Specify the text to find in the file's contents.
Other	[Various]	Opens the Select A Search Attribute panel, which lets you choose another attribute to search by. For example, select Size if you want to search for files bigger than, smaller than, or of a certain size. Select the In Menu check box if you want to add that attribute to the menu in the Searching window.

Table 3-1: Search Criteria for Finding Objects with the Searching Window

Look Quickly Inside Files

When you have many files, finding exactly the file you need can be hard, even if you've used descriptive filenames. Often, you'll need to look inside a file to see whether it's the one you want. Or you may want to scan through several files easily—without opening them.

CREATING SMART FOLDERS TO REPEAT SEARCHES *(Continued)*

2. Click the **Save** button at the right end of the Search bar. Mac OS X displays a Save sheet.

3. Type a name for the saved search, and choose where to save it. (The default location is the Saved Searches folder, which is a good place to start.)

4. Select the **Add To Sidebar** check box if you want to add the search to the Search For category in the Sidebar. This gives you instant access to the search.

5. Click **Save**.

If you selected the **Add To Sidebar** check box, Mac OS X puts the search at the bottom of the Search For category. You can drag it to a different position. To remove a search from the Sidebar, drag it out of the Sidebar (the document area is usually easiest).

You can also create a Smart Folder from scratch:

1. Activate the **Finder**.

2. Open the **File** menu and choose **New Smart Folder** (or press ⌘+SHIFT+N).

3. In the New Smart Folder window, search as usual.

4. Click the **Save** button at the right end of the Search bar, and then save the Smart Folder.

Creating a Smart Folder from scratch has one advantage: when you close the Finder window, Mac OS X prompts you to save the Smart Folder if you haven't already done so.

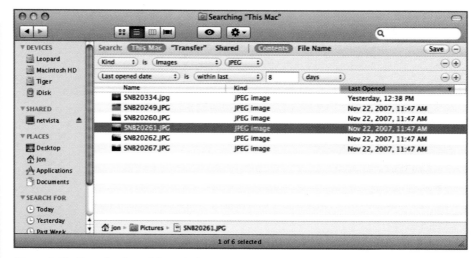

Figure 3-10: From the Searching window, you can check the location of an object or double-click the object to open it.

LOOK QUICKLY INSIDE A FILE

To look quickly inside a file without opening it, use the Quick Look feature:

1. In a Finder window, select the file.

2. Click the **Quick Look** button on the toolbar, or CONTROL+click (or right-click) the file and choose Quick Look. The Finder opens a Quick Look window showing the contents of the file (see Figure 3-11).

3. To view the file full screen, click the **Full Screen** button. Click the **Exit Full Screen** button to return to the window.

4. To look inside another file, click it in the Finder window.

5. To open the current file, double-click it in the Quick Look window.

6. Click the **Close** button (the × button) to close the Quick Look window.

SCAN QUICKLY THROUGH MULTIPLE FILES

You can also use Quick Look to scan quickly through multiple files:

1. In a Finder window, select the files you want to scan through. For example, click the first file, and then hold down ⌘ as you click each of the other files in turn.

Full Screen button, click to switch to full-screen view

Figure 3-11: Quick Look lets you quickly view the contents of a file without actually opening it in an application. You can resize the window, and scroll up and down, but you can't edit the file.

TIP

You can also launch Quick Look for the selected file or files by pressing **SPACEBAR**.

2. Click the **Quick Look** button on the toolbar, or **CONTROL**+click (or right-click) the file and choose **Quick Look**. The Finder opens a Quick Look window showing the contents of the first file (see Figure 3-12).

3. Use the **Previous** and **Next** buttons to navigate among the files. Click the **Play** button to play a slide show of the files.

4. To get an overview of the files, click the **Index Sheet** button. Click the miniature for the file you want to view.

5. To open the current file, double-click it in the Quick Look window.

6. Click the **Close** button (the × button) to close the Quick Look window.

Get Info About a File or Folder

List view displays some information about the selected object (such as its kind, its size, and the date it was last modified), and the Preview pane in Columns

Figure 3-12: Quick Look lets you scan quickly through multiple files—even if they're of different types.

Previous   Play   Next   Index Sheet   Full Screen

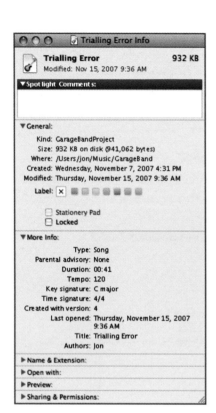

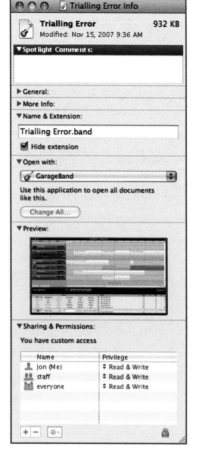

Figure 3-13: The Info window provides full information about an object.

view displays substantially more information. But to get a full set of information about an object, you need to display its Info window:

1. Select the object in a Finder window or on the desktop.

2. Open the **File** menu and click **Get Info**. The Info window will be displayed (see Figure 3-13).

3. Verify the information you want to know. You can expand and collapse the different sections of the window by clicking the gray triangles.

4. Click the **Close** button (the red button) to close the Info window.

Work with Ownership and Permissions

For security, Mac OS X assigns different levels of permissions to different objects. These permissions control what each user can do with an object: whether the user can see it but not change it (Read Only permission), see it and change it (Read & Write permission), not see it but add files to it (Write Only permission, which is used for public folders in which users can deposit files), or not access it at all (No Access permission). Each object also has an *owner*, a user or system process that has ultimate control over the object. For a file or folder that you create, you are the owner. For a system folder, the system is the owner.

Mac OS X's permissions are set up to give you free rein over your Home folder and its contents, keep you out of other users' folders (and keep them out of yours), and prevent you from damaging system folders. Administrator users have wider-reaching privileges than Standard users, who in turn have more privileges than Managed With Parental Controls users and Sharing Only users. (See Chapter 8 for a discussion of the different types of users.)

CHECK AN OBJECT'S OWNERSHIP AND PERMISSIONS

To check an object's ownership and permissions, display the Info window for the object (open the **File** menu and click **Get Info**) and expand the Ownership

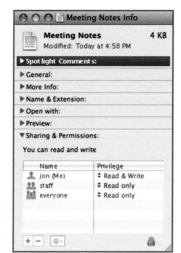

Figure 3-14: Use the Sharing & Permissions section of the Info dialog box to check and change permissions for an object.

& Permissions section (if necessary) by clicking the **Sharing & Permissions** gray triangle. Figure 3-14 shows an example.

CHANGE AN OBJECT'S PERMISSIONS AND OWNERSHIP

Sometimes, you may need to change the permissions on an object—for example, to upgrade a user from Read Only access to Read & Write access so that the user can change a file. You'll need to be an administrator to do this.

1. If the Lock icon shows a closed lock, click it to open it. Type your login password in the authentication dialog box, and then click **OK**. Mac OS X enables the controls.

2. In the Name list, select the user or the group whose permission you want to change.

3. In the Privilege list, select the necessary level of permission—for example, Read Only or Read & Write.

4. If Mac OS X displays the Authenticate dialog box, type your administrator password and click **OK**.

5. If you want to apply the new permissions to the objects contained in the object you're changing (for example, the files in a folder), click the **Action** button and choose **Apply To Enclosed Items**. Mac OS X will display a confirmation dialog box, as shown at left.

6. Click **OK**.

7. Click the **Lock** icon to change it from an open lock to a closed lock.

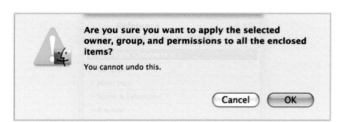

Write Files and Folders to a CD or DVD

Mac OS X allows you to copy ("burn," or record) files to a writable or rewritable CD or DVD. You must have a CD-R (writable) or CD-RW (rewritable) drive and suitable blank media to burn CDs. To burn DVDs, you need an Apple SuperDrive or a compatible DVD burner and writable or rewritable blank media.

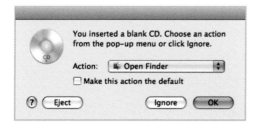

1. Insert a blank CD or DVD (as appropriate) into your CD burner or DVD burner. Mac OS X will display a dialog box asking what you want to do with the disc.

QUICKSTEPS

CREATING COMPRESSED FILES FROM FILES AND FOLDERS

Mac OS X enables you to create compressed files in the zip format. Zip files are useful for reducing the space that files take on your Mac or for sending files via e-mail or file transfer.

1. In the Finder, select the files or folders you want to put in the archive.

2. Open the **File** menu and click **Compress**. (The name of the command varies depending on the objects selected.) Mac OS X will create a zip file.

   - If the archive contains two or more objects, Mac OS X will name it Archive.zip.

   - If the archive contains only one object, Mac OS X gives the archive the same name as the object but adds the .zip extension.

3. If necessary, click the object's name once (in Icons view) or twice with a pause (in any other view), type the new name, and press **RETURN**.

To open a zip file, double-click it. If the zip file contains a single file, Mac OS X displays that file. If the zip file contains multiple files, Mac OS X automatically creates a folder that has the same name as the zip file (but without the .zip extension) in the same folder as the zip file, and then uncompresses the zip file's contents to this folder. Double-click the new folder to view its contents.

TIP

When buying writable or recordable media, put quality above price. If your data is valuable, there's no point in using low-quality discs that won't preserve it perfectly, no matter how much of a bargain those discs may appear to be.

2. Select **Open Finder** in the **Action** drop-down list box. (It may be selected already.)

3. Click **OK**. Mac OS X will mount the disc as a drive on the desktop with a name such as *untitled CD*.

4. Click the disc's name to select it, type the name you want to assign, and press **RETURN**.

5. Double-click the disc's icon to open a Finder window showing its contents (nothing yet).

6. Drag files and folders to the disk from another Finder window or from your desktop. Rearrange the files and folders in the Finder window for the disc as desired.

7. When you're ready to burn the disk, click the **Burn** button below the Search box, or open the **File** menu and click **Burn Disc**. Mac OS X will display a confirmation dialog box, as shown here:

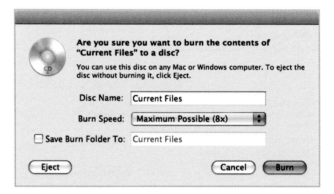

8. If you want to change the disc name, type the new name in the Disc Name text box.

9. If you want to save the burn folder so that you can use it again, select the **Save Burn Folder To** check box. If necessary, change the name that appears in the text box.

10. Click **Burn**. Mac OS X will burn the disc and then mount it on the desktop.

11. Drag the disk to the **Trash** to eject it, and then label it. Dragging the disk to the Trash is the Mac convention for ejecting a removable disc or drive—it doesn't delete the files you've burned to the disk.

Chapter 4

Using the Internet

The Internet provides a major means for worldwide communications between both individuals and organizations, and for locating and sharing information. To use the Internet, you must have a connection to it, either a dial-up connection or a broadband connection. You can then send and receive e-mail, access the World Wide Web, and use instant messaging.

Connect to the Internet

You can connect to the Internet using a telephone line, a cable TV connection, or a satellite link. With a telephone line, you can connect with either a dial-up connection or a DSL (digital subscriber line) connection (see comparison in Table 4-1). DSL, cable TV, and satellite connections are called broadband connections because of their higher (than dial-up) speed and common setup (see comparison in Table 4-2). You must have access to at least one of these forms of communication in order to connect to the Internet. You must also set up the Internet connection itself.

NOTE

To connect to the Internet via dial-up, you must have an existing account with an Internet service provider (ISP), and you must know your ISP's phone number for your modem to dial. You also need to know the user name and password for your account. This information is provided by your ISP when you establish your account.

FEATURE	DIAL-UP	DSL
Cost	From around $10/month	From around $15/month
Speed	Up to 48 Kbps* download** 33 Kbps upload	Speeds vary: download 512 Kbps upward; upload 128 Kbps upward
Connection	Dial up each time	Always connected
Use of line	Ties up line, may want a second line	Line can be used for voice and fax while connected to the Internet

* Kbps is kilobits (thousands of bits, 1 or 0) per second.
**Download is receiving information from the Internet on your computer.

Table 4-1: Comparison of Dial-Up and DSL Connections

SERVICE	DOWNLOAD SPEED	UPLOAD SPEED	MONTHLY COST	RELIABILITY
Dial-up	48 Kbps	33.6 Kbps	$10	Fair
DSL	768 Kbps to 6 Mbps or more	128 Kbps to 1 Mbps	$15	Good
Cable Internet	1–6 Mbps or more	500 Kbps	$35	Good
Satellite Internet	1 Mbps	150–512 Kbps	$50	Fair

Table 4-2: Representative Speeds, Costs, and Reliability for Internet Connections

Set Up Communications

Communications is the physical link between your Mac and the Internet. To set up connections, you must first choose between a dial-up and a broadband connection.

SET UP A BROADBAND CONNECTION

A broadband connection—which typically uses a DSL phone line, a TV cable, or a satellite connection—is normally made with a device that connects to your wired or wireless local area network (LAN) and allows several computers on the network to use the connection. (See Chapter 9 for instructions on setting up a network.) With a network set up, your computer connected to the network via either a network cable or a wireless link, and a broadband service connected to the network, your computer is connected to the broadband service. There is nothing else you need to do to set up a broadband connection.

SET UP A DIAL-UP CONNECTION

To set up a *dial-up connection* that uses the modem to dial and connect to your ISP via the phone line:

NOTE

All Macs include a built-in Ethernet network interface, so you do not need to add one to connect your Mac to the Internet. However, while older Macs include modems, newer models do not, so you may need to add a modem. The easiest way to add a modem is to get a Mac-compatible USB modem from a source such as the Apple Store (http://store.apple.com). You then simply plug the modem into a USB connector, and your Mac can start using it.

NOTE

Sometimes a DSL or TV cable connecting device is called a "modem," but it is not an analog-to-digital converter, which is the major point of a **mo**dulator-**dem**odulator; instead, the data remains in digital form throughout. For this reason, this book doesn't describe DSL and cable connecting devices as modems.

1. Open the menu and click **System Preferences** to open the System Preferences window.

2. Click **Network**. The Network pane will be displayed.

3. In the left list box, select the modem entry. For example, if your Mac has an internal modem, select **Internal Modem**. The modem controls will be displayed (see Figure 4-1).

4. Leave **Default** selected in the Configuration drop-down list. (You use this drop-down list to create different dial-up configurations for different locations—for example, one for home, one for the road.)

5. Type the ISP's telephone number in the Telephone Number text box.

6. Type your account name in the Account Name text box and your password in the Password text box.

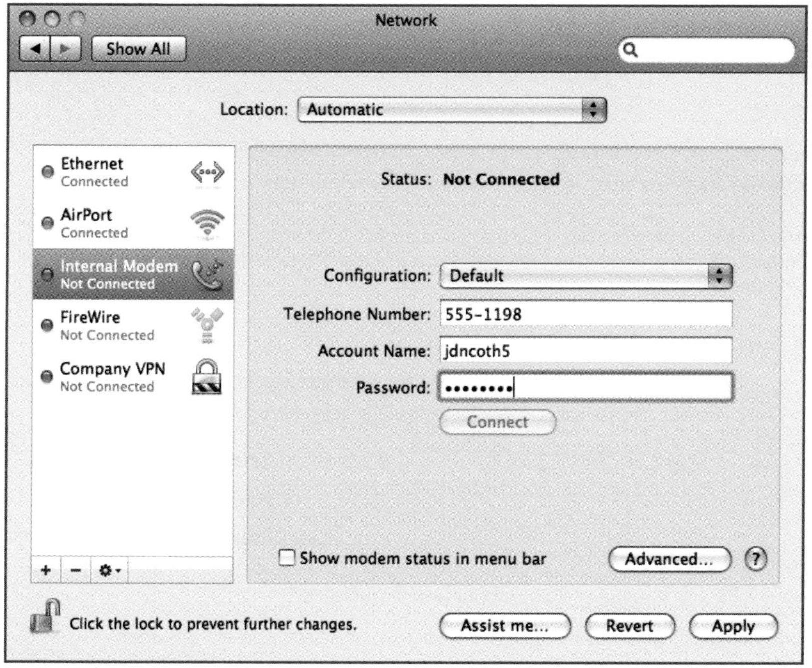

7. Select the **Show Modem Status In Menu Bar** check box to make modem details appear in the menu bar. (This enables you to quickly check the status of your connection.)

8. Click the **Advanced** button to display the Advanced pane for the dial-up connection.

9. Choose essential settings on the **Modem** tab (see Figure 4-2). The settings required vary by ISP, but the following settings are fairly typical:

   ● Select the **Enable Error Correction And Compression In Modem** check box.

   ● In the **Dial Mode** drop-down list, select **Wait For Dial Tone Before Dialing**. This setting helps avoid your Mac dialing when you're making a phone call.

   ● In the Dialing area, select the **Tone** option button unless you have pulse dialing (in which case, select the **Pulse** option button). If in doubt, pick up your phone and press any of the higher numeric keys (7, 8, or 9). If you hear a single beep, select the **Tone** option button. If you hear rapid clicks, select the **Pulse** option button.

   ● In the Sound area, select the **On** option button so that you can hear your modem dialing. Hearing the modem is helpful when setting up your connection. When the connection is working reliably, you may prefer to turn the sound off by selecting the **Off** option button.

Figure 4-1: A dial-up connection requires an account name, password, and phone number.

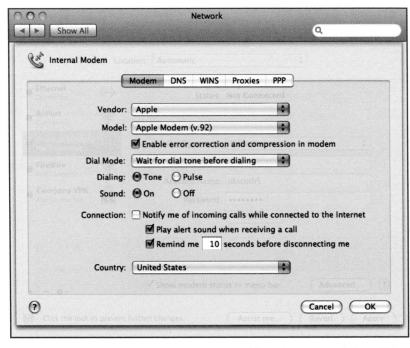

Figure 4-2: On the Modem tab, you can tell Mac OS X whether to wait for a dial tone before dialing and whether to notify you of incoming calls when you've made a dial-up connection to the Internet.

NOTE

PPP is the abbreviation for Point-to-Point Protocol, the network protocol used for connecting to the Internet via dial-up.

- In the Connection area, select the **Notify Me Of Incoming Calls While Connected To The Internet** check box if you want Mac OS X to alert you to incoming calls. Choose whether to receive an alert sound.

- Select the **Remind Me *NN* Seconds Before Disconnecting Me** check box if you want Mac OS X to warn you before disconnecting the connection. Set the number of seconds you want.

10. Click the **PPP** tab to display its contents (see Figure 4-3).

11. In the **Settings** drop-down list, choose **Session**, and then choose options:

   - Whether Mac OS X connects automatically when needed (for example, when you open an application that requires an Internet connection)

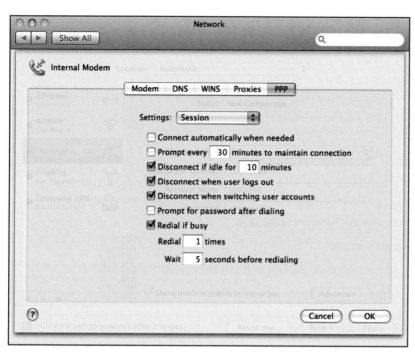

Figure 4-3: The most important Session settings on the PPP tab control whether Mac OS X automatically connects to the Internet and whether it disconnects you automatically when you log out, switch users, or leave the connection idle for too long.

- Whether to disconnect after a specified interval of inactivity or when you log out or switch users

- Whether (and if so, how many times) to redial the connection if it's busy

12. Click **OK** to close the Advanced pane.

13. Click **Apply** to apply your settings. Mac OS X creates the connection.

14. Press ⌘+Q or open the **System Preferences** menu and choose **Quit System Preferences** to close System Preferences.

CONNECT TO THE INTERNET

You're now ready to connect to the Internet:

1. Click the **Modem** icon in the menu bar and choose the **Connect** command for the modem (for example, **Connect Internal Modem** if you're using an internal modem).

2. Mac OS X dials your ISP, establishes the connection, and registers your Mac on the Internet. The Modem icon displays information about the progress of the connection. You will hear the modem dialing and going through the *handshaking* (beeps and pinging sounds) with the ISP's modem.

3. To disconnect, click the **Modem** icon in the menu bar and choose **Disconnect**.

NOTE

Instead of closing System Preferences, you can connect by clicking the **Connect** button on the Modem pane. Normally, however, connecting using the modem icon in the menu bar is easier than opening System Preferences.

Test Your Internet Connection

By now, you should have configured your Internet connection. The easiest way to test that it's working is to try to connect to the Internet by clicking the **Safari** icon on the Dock.

If an Internet web page is displayed, then you are connected and you need do no more. If you are unable to establish an Internet connection even though you have verified that your dial-up or broadband connection is working, you may need to contact your ISP for further advice.

Use the World Wide Web

The *World Wide Web* (or just the *Web*) is the sum of all the web sites in the world—examples of which are CNN's web site, the eBay web site, and the Apple web site. The Web is what you can access with a *web browser*, such as Safari, which comes with Mac OS X and is Mac OS X's default web browser.

Search the Internet

You can search the Internet in two ways: by using the search facility built into Safari (which is powered by Google, a major search site) and by using an independent search facility on the Web.

SEARCH FROM SAFARI

To search using Safari's built-in Google search facility:

1. Click the **Safari** icon on the Dock to start Safari.

2. Click in the **Search** text box in the upper-right corner of the Safari window.

3. Type what you want to search for.

4. Press **RETURN**. Safari displays a web page of search results. Figure 4-4 shows an example.

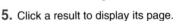

5. Click a result to display its page.

SEARCH FROM AN INTERNET SEARCH SITE

There are many independent Internet search sites. A popular one is Yahoo!

1. Click the **Safari** icon on the Dock to open Safari.

2. Click the icon at the left end of the Address text box (the blue icon in the example shown here) to select the address.

3. Type www.yahoo.com and press **RETURN** to go to the Yahoo! site. Alternatively, if a Yahoo! button appears on the Address bar, simply click that button.

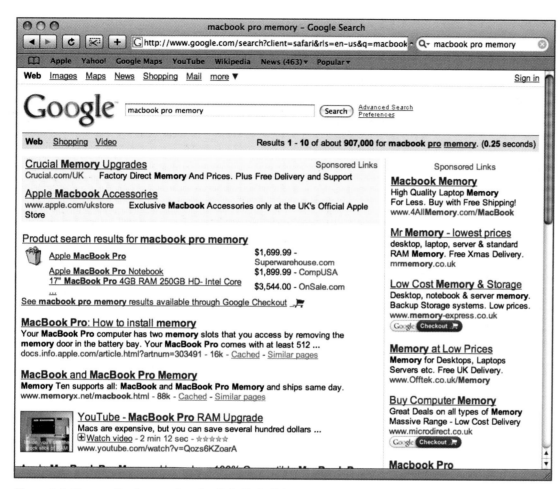

Figure 4-4: The results of a search using Safari's built-in Google search facility

4. In the **Web Search** text box on the Yahoo! site, type the text you want to search for.

5. Press **RETURN** or click the **Web Search** button on the site. Safari displays a web page of search results.

6. Click the link of your choice to go to that page.

Keep Bookmarks of Your Favorite Sites

Sometimes you visit a site that you would like to return to quickly or often. Safari provides a feature called "bookmarks" that you can use to save markers to specific pages on sites so that you can access them quickly. You can access bookmarks via the Bookmarks bar, which Safari displays below the Address bar by default, the Bookmarks menu, or the Bookmarks window.

You can add as many bookmarks as you want to the Bookmarks bar. Once the bookmarks reach the right edge of the window, Safari adds the bookmarks to an extension panel, which you can display by clicking the >> button. You can also add bookmarks to the Bookmarks menu and to the Bookmarks window.

What's usually easiest is to use the Bookmarks bar for your primary bookmarks—for example, those you access every day—and to create only

QUICKSTEPS

BROWSING THE INTERNET

Browsing the Internet requires use of a browser, such as Safari, to go from one web site to another to see the sites' contents. You can browse to a site by directly entering a site address, or *URL* (uniform resource locator), by navigating to a site from another site, or by using the browser controls. First, you must start the browser.

START THE SAFARI BROWSER

To start Safari, click the **Safari** icon on the Dock or activate the **Finder**, open the **Go** menu, click **Applications**, and double-click **Safari**.

ENTER A WEB SITE DIRECTLY

To go directly to a web site:

1. Start Safari.

2. Click the icon at the left end of the Address text box to select the entire address.

3. Type the address of the web site you want to open and press **RETURN**.

USE SITE NAVIGATION

Site navigation means using a combination of links and menus on one web page to locate and open another web page, either in the same site or in another site.

● **Links** are words, phrases, sentences, or graphics that you click to display the linked pages. When you position the mouse pointer over a link, the pointer changes to display a hand icon with the forefinger pointing upward. Links are often underlined, either all the time or when you hover the mouse pointer over them.

McGraw-Hill Professional (including McGraw-Hill Trade;

Continued . . .

---

as many bookmarks as fit on the bar without using the extension panel. You can then put your next most important bookmarks on the Bookmarks menu, limiting its length to what will fit within the Safari window without requiring you to scroll down. Finally, relegate your least important bookmarks to the Bookmarks window.

CREATE A BOOKMARK ON THE BOOKMARKS BAR

To create a bookmark on the Bookmarks bar:

1. Navigate to the web page you want to bookmark.

2. Drag the icon at the left end of the Address text box to the Bookmarks bar.

3. Safari will display a naming sheet showing the page's title. If the sheet is too small, drag the dotted handle in the lower-right corner to enlarge it. Type the name you want (keep it short so that it doesn't waste space on the Bookmarks bar), and click **OK**.

Type a name for the bookmark.

Amazon.com

Cancel OK

CREATE A BOOKMARK IN ANOTHER LOCATION

To create a bookmark either on the Bookmarks bar or in another location:

1. Navigate to the web page you want to bookmark.

2. Open the **Bookmarks** and click **Add Bookmark**. Safari will display a naming sheet showing the page's title. Again, drag the lower-right corner if the sheet is too small.

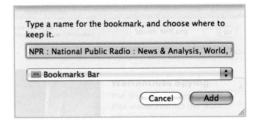

3. Edit the name or type a new name. Make the name as compact yet descriptive as possible so that you can grasp instantly what the web page contains.

QUICKSTEPS

BROWSING THE INTERNET (Continued)

- **Menus** contain one or a few words, in either a horizontal or vertical list, that you click to display the linked pages.

USE BROWSER NAVIGATION

Browser navigation means using the controls within your browser to go to another web page:

- Click the **Back** button to go to the previous page in the stack of pages you have viewed. You can also press ⌘+[.

- Click the **Forward** button to move forward again. You can also press ⌘+].

- To navigate quickly, click the **Back** button or the **Forward** button and hold down the mouse button for a second to display a menu of the recent pages available. Drag down to select the page you want.

- Press **BACKSPACE** to go back to the previous page. Press **SHIFT+BACKSPACE** to go forward to the next page.

Continued . . .

4. Use the drop-down list box to specify where to save the bookmark:

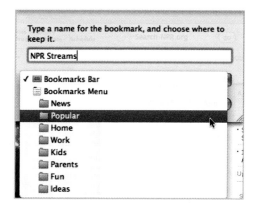

- Choose **Bookmarks Menu** to create the bookmark as an entry on the Bookmarks menu. Doing this makes the bookmark quickly accessible, but your Bookmarks menu will soon grow long.

- Choose a folder or subfolder to create the bookmark in that folder. You can then access the bookmark through the Bookmarks window.

5. Click **Add**.

REARRANGE BOOKMARKS ON THE BOOKMARKS BAR

To move a bookmark on the Bookmarks bar, drag it to the new position.

To remove a bookmark from the Bookmarks bar, drag it into the Safari window or anywhere outside the Bookmarks bar. Alternatively, **CONTROL**+click or right-click the bookmark and then click **Delete**.

OPEN A BOOKMARKED PAGE

To open a bookmarked page:

- Click the appropriate button on the Bookmarks bar.

  –Or–

- Open the **Bookmarks** menu and click the bookmark's item.

  –Or–

- Display the Bookmarks window, click the appropriate bookmarks folder or subfolder, and double-click the bookmark.

QUICKSTEPS

BROWSING THE INTERNET (Continued)

USE WINDOWS AND TABS

Safari lets you open multiple windows, so that you can view two or more web pages in different windows at the same time. With default settings, you can open a link in a new window by holding down ⌘ as you click a link.

Safari also enables you to use multiple tabs in the same window. Make sure first that Safari is set to open new tabs. Open the **Safari** menu and click **Preferences**, click the **Tabs** button, select the **⌘-Click Opens A Link In A New Tab** check box, and click the **Close** button (the red button).

You can then open a link on a new tab in the current window by holding down ⌘ as you click the link. When you open the first new tab, Safari displays the tab bar below the Address bar and the Bookmarks bar. You can navigate to another tab by clicking it. To close a tab, click the **Close** button (the × button) that appears on it.

USE THE BOOKMARKS WINDOW

To see all your bookmarks in your current Safari tab, open the **Bookmarks** menu and click **Show All Bookmarks**. Safari displays the Bookmarks window (see Figure 4-5). If you want to have the bookmarks on another tab, open a fresh tab first. The easiest way to open a new tab is to **CONTROL**+click or right-click an existing tab and then click **New Tab**.

Click a collection in the Collections pane to display its contents. Then:

- Double-click a bookmark to open it.

  –Or–

- **CONTROL**+click or right-click a bookmark and choose **Delete** to delete it.

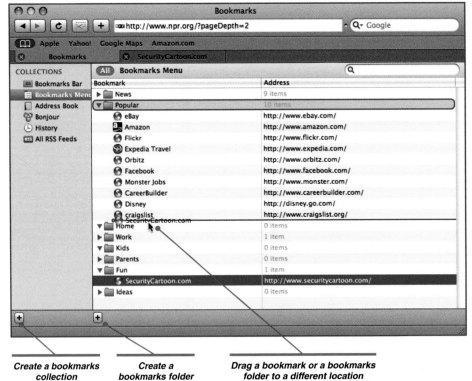

Figure 4-5: Use the Bookmarks window to navigate through and manage your full set of bookmarks.

Create a bookmarks collection

Create a bookmarks folder

Drag a bookmark or a bookmarks folder to a different location

To leave the Bookmarks window, open the **Bookmarks** menu and click **Hide All Bookmarks**. Alternatively, double-click a bookmark to open it in the current window.

Change Your Home Page

Each time you start Safari, it automatically opens a specific web page called your "home page." You can also display your home page at any time by opening the **History** menu and clicking **Home** or pressing ⌘+SHIFT+H.

To change your home page:

1. Go to the page you want to use as your home page.
2. Open the **Safari** menu and click **Preferences**. The Preferences window will open.
3. Click the **General** tab. The General pane will be displayed.

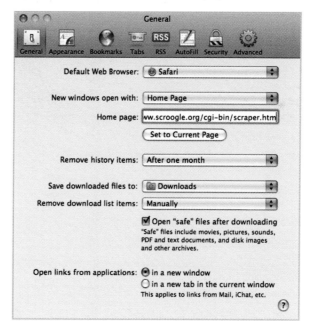

4. Click **Set To Current Page** to make the current page your home page.
5. Click the **Close** button (the red button) to close the Preferences window.

CONTROLLING INTERNET SECURITY

Safari allows you to control several aspects of Internet security to help keep your browsing sessions safe. To configure settings for these features, display the Security pane of the Preferences window:

1. Click the **Safari** button on the Dock. Safari will launch.

2. Open the **Safari** menu and click **Preferences**. The Preferences window will be displayed.

3. Click the **Security** tab. The Security pane will be displayed (see Figure 4-6).

HANDLE COOKIES

Cookies are small files containing text data that web sites store on your computer so that they can identify your Mac when you return to the web site. Cookies have a positive side: they can save you from having to enter your name and ID frequently. Many e-commerce web sites (sites where you can execute a payment transaction over the Web) require cookies for their shopping carts and payment mechanisms to work at all.

Cookies can also be dangerous, enabling web sites to identify you when you do not want them to be able to do so, and potentially letting outsiders access sensitive information on your Mac. Safari lets you choose whether to accept or reject requests to store cookies on your Mac.

To determine whether Safari accepts cookies, select the **Always** option button, the **Never** option button, or the **Only From Sites You Navigate To** option button in the Accept Cookies area of the Security pane.

The default setting is Only From Sites You Navigate To, which makes Safari accept cookies from sites you

Continued . . .

Access Your Browsing History

Safari keeps a history of the web pages you visit so that you can easily return to a site you've visited in the past. Safari normally keeps a month's worth of History items, but you can change the period if you want. You can also clear your history when you want to get rid of its contents.

USE HISTORY

To use History, open the **History** menu and choose the page from the History menu or from one of the submenus named by day and date.

To see your history as a list that's easier to navigate than the menu, open a new tab, open the **History** menu, and choose **View All History**. Close the tab when you've finished.

CLEAR HISTORY

You may want to clear your history so that nobody who can access your Mac can see which pages you've visited. To clear your history, open the **History** menu and click **Clear History**.

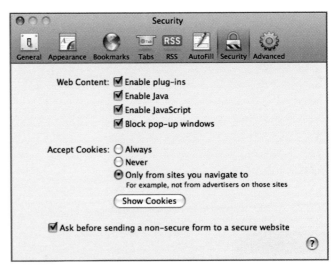

Figure 4-6: Use the options on the Security pane of Safari's Preferences window to control how Safari handles cookies, web content, and pop-up windows.

CONTROLLING INTERNET SECURITY *(Continued)*

actively navigate to (for example, by clicking a link) but reject cookies from other sites, such as advertisers on the sites you navigate to. Choosing the Never setting, which causes Safari to reject all cookies, protects your privacy but may prevent e-commerce sites from working. Choosing the Always setting is seldom a good idea.

CONTROL WEB CONTENT

You can control the content that Safari allows to run by selecting or clearing the top three check boxes in the Web Content area of the Security pane:

- **Enable Plug-Ins** Controls whether Safari runs content that requires plug-ins, such as movie files that require a QuickTime plug-in. Plug-ins can potentially be used to execute malicious content, but they're vital for watching movies and other content while browsing.

- **Enable Java** Controls whether Safari runs *applets*, or little applications, written in the Java programming language. Java operates in a security zone called a *sandbox*, so it's usually safe to run Java applets. However, Java also has the potential for malicious misuse, which is why Safari lets you prevent Java from running.

- **Enable JavaScript** Controls whether Safari runs scripts (programs) written in the JavaScript scripting language. As with Java, JavaScript is widely used for positive purposes, but it can be misused by malefactors.

BLOCK POP-UP WINDOWS

Web scripting (programming) languages enable web developers to automatically open extra windows, called

Continued . . .

Use SnapBack

In addition to History, Safari provides SnapBack, a feature that lets you quickly return to the SnapBack page for each window or tab. The SnapBack page is:

- The first page you opened in a window or tab (until you change the SnapBack page)
- The last page you opened in this window or tab by typing its address in the Address text box
- The last page you opened in this window or tab from History or using a bookmark
- The last page you marked as a SnapBack page by opening the **History** menu and choosing **Mark Page For SnapBack**

When a SnapBack page is available in a window, Safari displays an orange icon with a white arrow at the right end of the Address text box. Click this icon to return to the SnapBack page:

Copy Information from the Internet

You'll sometimes find information on the Internet that you want to copy—a picture, some text, or a web page.

CAUTION

Material you copy from the Internet is normally protected by copyright; therefore, what you can do with it legally is limited. Basically, you can store it on your hard disk and refer to it. You cannot put it on your web site, sell it, copy it for distribution, or use it for a commercial purpose without the permission of the owner. Unless a web page states specifically that its content is in the public domain (which is the body of out-of-copyright works that anyone is free to reuse), or the page grants you permission to reuse specific content for particular purposes, you should assume that the content is copyrighted.

QUICKSTEPS

CONTROLLING INTERNET SECURITY *(Continued)*

pop-up windows, when you display a page or take actions on it (such as following a link or attempting to leave the page). Pop-up windows occasionally display helpful content, but they're usually used to display ads or to show you content that you probably wouldn't have chosen to see.

Safari enables you to block pop-up windows. To do so, select the **Block Pop-Up Windows** check box on the Security pane of the Preferences window. You can also open the **Safari** menu and choose **Block Pop-Up Windows** to toggle blocking on and off. When it's on, a check mark appears next to this menu item.

In most cases, there's little downside to blocking all pop-up windows. But occasionally you'll find a web site that requires pop-up windows in order to work. If such a web site is well designed, it will display an error message telling you that you must allow pop-up windows for it to work; if not, it may simply fail to work. If you find a web page apparently not working, try temporarily enabling pop-up windows (open the **Safari** menu and click **Block Pop-Up Windows** to toggle off the blocking) and see if it suddenly starts working. After you finish using the site, open the **Safari** window and click **Block Pop-Up Windows** again to restore the blocking.

COPY A PICTURE FROM A WEB PAGE

To copy a picture from the current web page to your hard disk:

1. CONTROL+click or right-click the picture and click **Save Image As**. Safari will display a Save As sheet.
2. In the Save As text box, change the picture's default name if you want. (For example, you might assign a more descriptive name.)
3. In the Where drop-down list box or in the Sidebar and folder list, choose the folder in which you want to save the picture.
4. Click **Save**.

COPY TEXT FROM THE INTERNET

To copy some text from the current web page to a text editor or word processor:

1. Drag across the text to select it.
2. CONTROL+click or right-click the selection, and choose **Copy**.
3. Open or switch to a text editing application (for example, Text Editor) or a word processor (for example, Microsoft Word).
4. CONTROL+click or right-click where you want the text to appear, and choose **Paste**.

COPY A WEB PAGE FROM THE INTERNET

To copy the current web page and store it on your hard disk:

1. Open the **File** menu and choose **Save As**. Safari will display a Save sheet.
2. In the Save As text box, change the page's default name if you want. (For example, you might assign a more descriptive name to help you identify the page.)
3. In the **Where** drop-down list box, choose the folder in which you want to save the picture.
4. In the **Format** drop-down list, make sure that **Web Archive** is selected. (The alternative, Page Source, saves the HTML code that produces the graphical page.)
5. Click **Save**.

Play Internet Audio and Video

You can play audio and video from the Internet with Safari by clicking an audio or video link on a web page. Safari launches the appropriate plug-in or helper application for the content.

Chapter 7 discusses working with audio and video in depth.

NOTE

If your Dock doesn't include a Mail icon, click the **desktop**, open the **Go** menu and click **Applications** to open a Finder window showing your Applications folder, and then double-click the **Mail** icon. Alternatively, drag the **Mail** icon to the Dock to add it, and then click the icon you just added.

Use Internet E-Mail

Mac OS X includes a powerful e-mail application named Mail that allows you to send and receive e-mail.

Establish an E-Mail Account

To send and receive e-mail, you must establish an e-mail account with an Internet service provider (ISP) and configure that account in Mail. To set up your e-mail account, you need to know the following information, which your ISP will provide:

- Your e-mail address (for example, csmith6446@example.com)
- Your account name with the e-mail provider (for example, csmith)
- Your password

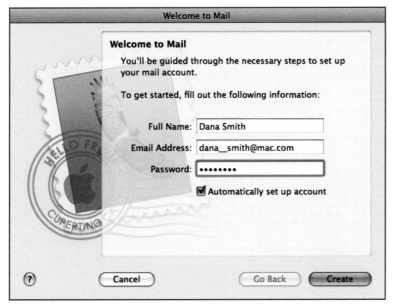

- The incoming mail server's name (for example, pop3.example.com) and its type (POP3, IMAP, or Microsoft Exchange)
- The outgoing mail server's name (for example, smtp.example.com)

With an Internet connection established and with this information, you can set up an account in Mail:

1. Click the **Mail** icon on the Dock. The first time you start Mail it will display several messages, and then it will display the Welcome To Mail dialog box (see Figure 4-7)—unless you have already set up an e-mail account, as you may have when installing Mac OS X.

2. Enter the account details in the text boxes and then click the corresponding button to proceed:

   - If you enter a .Mac or Gmail e-mail address, the Welcome To Mail screen displays the Automatically Set Up Account check box and selects it. Click the **Create** button to create the account. You need enter no more information.

   - If you enter a non-.Mac or non-Gmail e-mail address, click the **Continue** button, and then follow the remaining steps in this list.

Figure 4-7: Enter the details of your e-mail account in the Welcome To Mail dialog box. If the address is at Apple's .Mac service or Google's Gmail, the Automatically Set Up Account check box appears, as shown here.

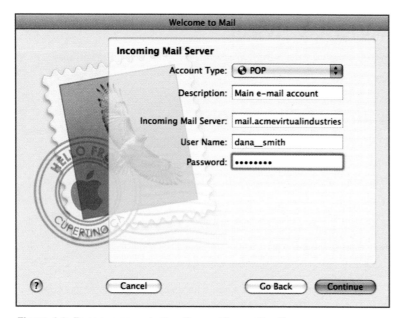

Figure 4-8: For any account other than a .Mac or Gmail account, you must choose the type of incoming mail server type and enter your user name and password.

3. On the Incoming Mail Server screen (see Figure 4-8), specify the details of the incoming mail server—the server from which you receive your messages:

- In the **Account Type** drop-down list, choose **POP**, **IMAP**, or **Exchange**, as appropriate.

- Optionally, type a description in the Description text box—for example, Main e-mail account.

- In the Incoming Mail Server text box, type the server's name—for example, pop3.example.com or imap.example.com.

- In the User Name text box, type your user name for the mail server.

- In the Password text box, type your password for the mail server.

4. Click the **Continue** button to display the Outgoing Mail Server screen (see Figure 4-9), and then specify the details of the server you use to send your messages:

- Optionally, type a description of the server in the Description text box (so that you can identify it easily; this is more useful if you use multiple accounts and servers).

Figure 4-9: For any account other than a .Mac or Gmail account, specify the address of the outgoing mail server. Select the Use Authentication check box only if your ISP has told you to use authentication for sending messages.

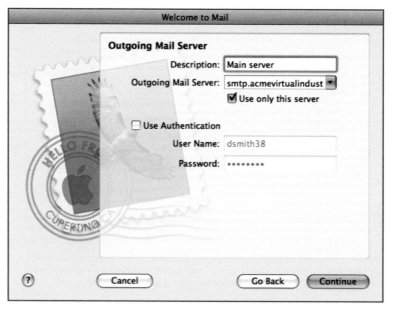

- Type the server's name in the Outgoing Mail Server text box. Select the **Use Only This Server** check box if this is the only server you will use, as is normally the case.

- Select the **Use Authentication** check box if your ISP has told you to use authentication when sending e-mail. Type your user name and password in the boxes provided.

5. Click the **Continue** button to display the Account Summary screen.

6. Verify that the details are correct; if not, click **Go Back** and fix them. When they are correct, make sure the **Take Account Online** check box is selected, and then click **Create**. Mail creates the account and displays your Inbox (see Figure 4-10).

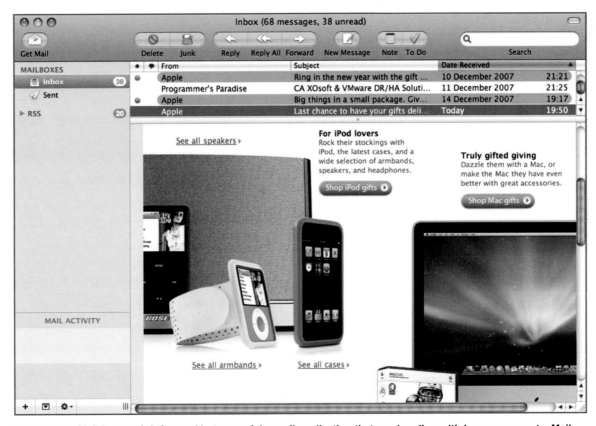

Figure 4-10: Mail is a straightforward but powerful e-mail application that can handle multiple user accounts. Mail also lets you create notes and to-do items.

Figure 4-11: Sending e-mail messages is a fast and easy way to communicate. You can include photos or other content in your messages.

Create and Send E-Mail

To create and send an e-mail message:

1. Open or activate **Mail** and click **New Message** on the toolbar. The New Message window will open (see Figure 4-11).

2. Start to type a name in the To text box. If Mail recognizes the name as one you've previously sent a message to, or as an entry in your address book (shown in Figure 4-12; also see the "Using Address Book" QuickSteps, later in this chapter), it suggests the match or matches.

   • To select the single match offered (after typing, for example, "chri" as shown on the left below), press **RETURN**. Mail creates a button for the address (as shown on the right below).

   • To select one of multiple matches, either continue typing to narrow down the list or click the correct match in the list. Mail creates a button for the address.

   • If Mail has no suggestions, finish typing the address.

3. To send the message to more than one addressee, type a comma after the first address, and then type the second address. If Mail has created an address button for the first addressee, you needn't type the comma.

TIP

Once you've entered an address in a message, Mail remembers it for you, even if you don't add it to Address Book. But sometimes you may need to remove an address from the previous-recipients list. To do so, first add the address to the To or Cc field of a message. Then **CONTROL**+click or right-click the address and choose **Remove From Previous Recipients List** from the context menu. **CONTROL**+click or right-click the address again, and then choose **Remove Address** from the context menu to remove the address from the message.

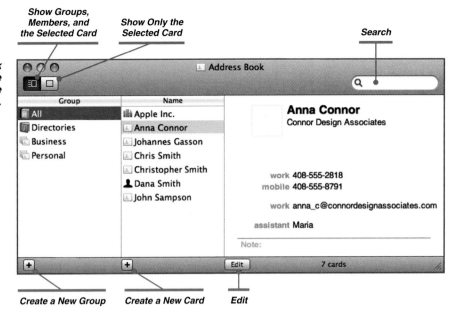

Figure 4-12: Address Book provides a place to store information about the people you correspond with.

Show Groups, Members, and the Selected Card

Show Only the Selected Card

Search

Create a New Group   Create a New Card   Edit

CAUTION

E-mail often appears to be an informal means of communication, an impression enhanced by the speed with which you can dash off a message and send it in moments to one or more people. But it's worth remembering that e-mail, like other written forms of communication, can easily be kept and stored by the recipient, and can come back to haunt the sender many years later. Worse, unlike other written forms of communications, an e-mail can also be forwarded instantly to people you never intended should read it. So before you send a "quick" e-mail message, read it through again to check that you won't regret sending it.

NOTE

When Mail is running, its Dock icon displays a red circle showing the number of messages you've received but haven't read. (If you've read all the messages you've received, the red circle doesn't appear.)

4. If you want to differentiate the addressees to whom the message is principally being sent from those for whom it is being copied for information, press **TAB** (or click in the Cc text box) and enter the other addressees' addresses there.

5. Press **TAB** (or click in the Subject text box) and type the subject of the message. Make it descriptive (so that the recipient can tell what the message is about) and brief (so that the recipient can see the full subject line).

6. Press **TAB** again (or click in the large text box) and type your message.

7. When you have completed your message, click **Send** in the upper-left corner. Mail will contact your outgoing mail server and send the message, complete with sound effects.

8. If you're ready to close Mail, open the **Mail** menu and choose **Quit Mail**.

Receive E-Mail

Depending on how Mail is configured, it may automatically receive any e-mail destined for you when your Mac is connected to your ISP. If not, or if you need

SENDING BLIND CARBON COPIES FOR DISCRETION

When you send a message, each recipient of the message sees all the addresses in the To box and the Cc box. Normally, this is helpful—each recipient knows the other recipients, and can decide whether to include them on replies.

Like most e-mail applications, Mail also lets you send blind carbon copies, or bccs—copies of a message that go to recipients whose addresses are not visible to other recipients. A bcc recipient cannot see other bcc recipients but can see all regular recipients.

Bccs tend to feel sneaky, and you shouldn't need them often, but they can be useful in some circumstances (both business and personal). The time when bccs are most useful is when you need to send a message to a group of people without sharing any recipient's e-mail address with any other recipient—for example, when you send a message giving your new e-mail address. By sending the message to yourself, and by placing each other recipient in the Bcc field, you avoid disclosing any e-mail address unnecessarily. Most recipients will appreciate this courtesy.

To send a bcc, click the button to the left of the Subject line, and then select **Bcc Address Field** on the pop-up menu. Mail will add a Bcc box. Type the recipients' e-mail addresses in this box, and then send the message as normal.

To get rid of the Bcc field for subsequent messages, open the pop-up menu again, and then select **Bcc Address Field** on the pop-up menu once more.

to dial to connect to your ISP, click **Get Mail** on the toolbar. In either case, the mail you receive will go into your Inbox. To open and read your mail:

1. Open **Mail**. Mail displays the Inbox.
2. Click a message in the Inbox to read it in the Preview pane at the bottom of the window, or double-click a message to open the message in its own window (see Figure 4-13).
3. Choose what action (if any) to take with the message:
   - Respond to it as described in the next section.
   - Print it by clicking **Print** in a message window or by opening the **File** menu and choosing **Print** in the Inbox or a message window.

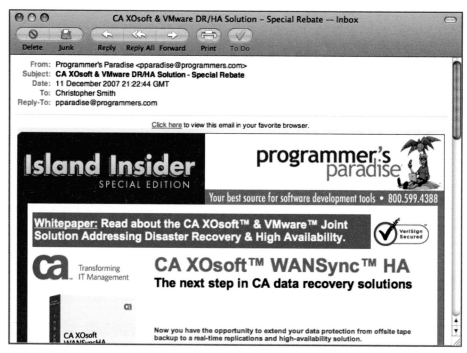

Figure 4-13: To see as much as possible of a message you've received, open it in its own window rather than reading it in the Inbox's Preview pane.

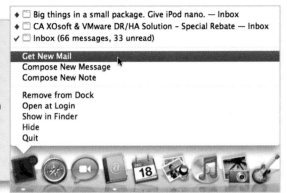

- Drag it to a mail folder.
- Delete it by clicking **Delete** in either a message window or the Inbox.

4. If you're ready to close Mail, open the **Mail** menu and choose **Quit Mail**.

Respond to E-Mail

You can respond to messages you receive in three ways. First, click the message in your Inbox (or open it in its own window), and then:

- Click **Reply** to return a message to only the person who sent the original message.

  –Or–

- Click **Reply All** to return a message to all the people who were addressees (both To and Cc) in the original message.

  –Or–

- Click **Forward** to send on a message to people not shown as addressees on the original message.

When you take any of these actions, Mail opens a window very similar to the New Message window and allows you to add or change addressees and the subject, and add a message. Click **Send** to send the message.

Apply Formatting to an E-Mail Message

The simplest e-mail messages are sent in plain text without any formatting. These messages take the least bandwidth and are the quickest and easiest to receive. If you wish, you can send messages with formatting using HTML, the Internet's Hypertext Markup Language, with which many web sites have been created. You can do this for an individual message or for all messages.

NOTE

All modern e-mail applications can properly receive formatted e-mail messages. However, complex formatted messages may not always look exactly as the sender intended.

QUICKSTEPS

USING ADDRESS BOOK

Mac OS X's Address Book, shown in Figure 4-12, enables you to collect addresses and other information about your contacts so that you can contact them quickly via e-mail or instant messaging.

OPEN ADDRESS BOOK

To open Address Book, click the **Address Book** icon on the Dock.

ADD A NEW ADDRESS

To add a new address to Address Book:

1. Click the + button beneath the Name column, or open the **File** menu and click **New Card**. Address Book adds a card with the provisional name *No Name*, opens the card for editing in the right column, and selects the First field.

2. Enter as much of the information as you have or deem desirable. Use **TAB** or the mouse to move from field to field. For e-mail, you need a name and an e-mail address. You can have multiple e-mail addresses for each contact. To add another e-mail address, click the green + button next to the existing addresses, and choose the type of address in the pop-up menu to the left of the e-mail address box.

Continued . . .

CHOOSE WHETHER TO APPLY FORMATTING TO ALL MESSAGES

1. Open the **Mail** menu and click **Preferences**. The Preferences window will open.

2. Click **Composing** to display the Composing sheet.

3. In the Message Format drop-down list box, choose **Rich Text** if you want to apply formatting. Choose **Plain Text** to send plain text messages.

4. Click the **Close** button (the red button) to close the window.

CHOOSE WHETHER TO APPLY FORMATTING TO AN INDIVIDUAL MESSAGE

You can override your default setting (specified in the previous section) for applying formatting:

1. From the main Mail window, click the **New** button on the toolbar to open a new message window.

2. Open the **Format** menu and click **Make Plain Text** or **Make Rich Text** as appropriate.

3. Address, compose, and send the message as usual.

Attach Files to E-Mail Messages

You can attach and send files, such as documents or images, with e-mail messages:

1. In Mail, click the **New** button on the toolbar. A New Message window will be displayed.

2. Click **Attach** on the toolbar. In the resulting dialog box, navigate to and select the file you want to send.

3. If you're sending the file to someone using a Windows computer, select the **Send Windows Friendly Attachments** check box.

4. Click **Choose File**. Mail will close the dialog box and add details of the file to the message.

5. Address, type, and send the message as you normally would.

USING ADDRESS BOOK *(Continued)*

3. When you've finished entering address information, click **Edit**.

ADD A GROUP OF ADDRESSES

To add a group of addresses that you want to be able to send a single message to:

1. Click the + button beneath the Group column, or open the **File** menu and click **New Group**. Address Book will add an entry to the Group column and will display an edit box around the default name, *Group Name*.

2. Type the name for the group and press **RETURN**. Address Book will apply the name and will leave the new group selected.

3. Click the **All** group entry or another group's entry that contains contacts you want to add to the new group. Drag an entry from the Name column and drop it on the new group to add that contact to the group.

After you have created a group like this, you can address a new message to the group by starting to type the group's name in the To box in the New Message window. When you complete the name, or accept Mail's suggestion for completing it automatically, Mail inserts the names of the group members in the To box.

NOTE

Mail displays some attachments, such as images and PDF files, in the message, allowing you to view them easily. You can still save these attachments to separate files if you want to keep them.

Receive Files Attached to E-Mail Messages

When someone sends you a message with a file attached, Mail displays information about the attachment in the Preview pane and in the message window:

Click the gray triangle if you want to see the details of the attachment:

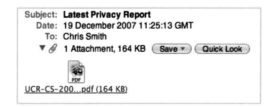

To view the attachment quickly without using an application, click **Quick Look**. In many cases, a quick look lets you determine whether to keep the attachment or delete it. Quick Look also helps protect you against opening attachments that contain viruses—but it is still a good idea to run anti-virus software.

To save the attachment or attachments, click **Save** or **Save All**, use the resulting dialog box to choose the folder in which to save the file or files, and click **Save**.

Use iChat

iChat is an application for *instant messaging*, or *IM*—instantly sending and receiving messages with others who are online at the same time as you.

NOTE

The easiest video camera to use with iChat is Apple's iSight, which comes built into consumer desktop Macs and all laptop Macs. You can also use other webcams that connect via USB or FireWire. Another option is to use a digital video camcorder that attaches to your Mac via FireWire.

NOTE

If you're using a .Mac subscription, iChat will offer to encrypt your chats with other .Mac subscribers who have also decided to use encryption. This encryption offers you some protection against snoopers and is usually a good idea. It works only with .Mac users, not users of AIM, Jabber, or Google Talk.

(Instant messaging is often referred to as "chat"—hence, iChat's name.) iChat can also handle teleconferencing, the live, remote interaction of several people complete with audio and video transmission.

To use iChat, you need to have an account with Apple's .Mac online service, an AOL Instant Messenger (AIM) screen name and password, a Jabber account (www.jabber.com), or a Google Talk account (www.google.com/talk). Whomever you want to chat with must also have an account of the same type.

To transmit audio, your Mac must have a microphone; and for you to hear audio, your Mac must have speakers or headphones. To send video, you must have a video camera either built into your Mac or connected to it via USB or FireWire.

Set Up iChat

To set up iChat:

1. If you plan to use an external video camera with iChat, attach it to your Mac. If the camera has a power control, turn it on. If you're using a built-in video camera, you needn't do anything.

2. Click the **iChat** icon in the Dock. iChat will display a Welcome To iChat dialog box.

3. Click **Continue**. iChat will display the Account Setup dialog box (see Figure 4-14).

4. Choose the account type, enter your details, and click **Continue**. Follow through the remaining setup screens, and then click **Done** when you reach the end.

Use iChat

Now that iChat is set up, you're ready to use it. First, you must enter contacts, or *buddies*, with whom you want to communicate.

ADD BUDDIES TO iCHAT

1. If iChat isn't running, click the **iChat** icon on the Dock to launch it. iChat will display the AIM Buddy List window.

CONFIGURING iCHAT

iChat contains several dozen configurable options that enable you to customize its behavior to suit your needs and preferences. To start configuration, open the **iChat** menu and click **Preferences** to open the Preferences window. Click the button for the pane you want to work with.

GENERAL PANE OPTIONS

Options on the General pane include controlling whether iChat automatically logs you in when it opens, choosing whether to show your status in the menu bar, specifying what iChat should do when you return to your Mac and your status is Away, and deciding where to save files you receive.

ACCOUNTS PANE OPTIONS

On the Accounts pane's Account Information tab, you can check the account type and details you're using for iChat. On the Security tab, you can block others from seeing that you're idle, set a privacy level (for example, allowing only specific people, or blocking specific people), and turn encryption on and off (if you're using a .Mac account). On the Server Settings tab, you can change server settings when you're not logged in—but you should not need to change them.

MESSAGES PANE OPTIONS

On the Messages pane, you can choose:

- Colors and fonts for your text balloons and senders' text balloons
- Whether to confirm the sending of files
- Whether to automatically save chat transcripts (which can be useful for work and love)
- Whether to remember your open chats, and whether to collect chats into a single window

Continued . . .

Figure 4-14: Enter your .Mac, AIM, Jabber, or Google Talk details to set up a new iChat account. If you don't have an account, click the Get An iChat Account button, and then sign up for a free trial of the .Mac service.

2. Click the + button, and then choose **Add Buddy** from the pop-up menu. iChat will display a sheet for adding a buddy via their AIM or .Mac account.

QUICKSTEPS

CONFIGURING iCHAT *(Continued)*

You can also set a keyboard shortcut that allows you to display the iChat window easily from the keyboard.

ALERTS PANE OPTIONS

On the Alerts pane, you can choose what kinds of alerts iChat uses when a particular event occurs. For example, when a buddy becomes available, you might choose to have iChat bounce its icon in the Dock and announce out loud that your buddy is now online.

AUDIO/VIDEO PANE OPTIONS

The Audio/Video pane lets you check the video camera you're using, choose which microphone to use, control the bandwidth iChat uses (for example, to prevent it from hogging your Internet connection), automatically open iChat when you turn on the camera, and play the repeated ring sound when you're invited to a conference.

After choosing suitable options in the Preferences window, click the **Close** button (the red button) to close the window.

TIP

To choose a buddy from Address Book, click the blue arrow button next to the Last Name text field to reveal a hidden section of the sheet. Select your buddy, choose the group to which you want to add him or her, and then click **Add**.

3. Choose the account type in the drop-down list, and type the account name in the Account Name box.

4. Choose which group to add the buddy to—for example, **Buddies** or **Family**—and type the first and last names. Click **Add**.

5. Your buddies will appear in the Buddy List, together with an icon indicating their status if they're online: a green dot for online and active, a yellow dot for online but inactive, a red dot for online but away, and no dot if they're offline.

START AN AUDIO CHAT

To start an audio chat:

1. **CONTROL**+click or right-click a buddy who's online and click **Invite To Audio Chat**.

2. iChat will display an Audio Chat window while it waits for your buddy to reply:

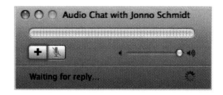

3. If your buddy accepts the invitation, iChat will establish audio contact. Speak to your buddy as you would in a telephone conversation. Drag the **Volume** slider to adjust the audio volume. Click the **Microphone** button to temporarily mute your microphone. Click the + button to add another buddy to the conversation.

4. To end the chat, click the **Close** button (the red button).

START A VIDEO CHAT

To start a video chat:

1. **CONTROL**+click or right-click a buddy who's online and click **Invite To Video Chat**. iChat will display a Video Chat window while it waits for your buddy to reply.

2. If your buddy accepts the invitation, iChat will establish audio and video contact. Chat as you would on a normal video phone. Click the **Microphone** button to temporarily mute your microphone. Click the **Full-Screen Mode** button (the button with two arrows) to zoom the Video Chat window to full screen. Double-click anywhere to exit full-screen mode.

3. To end the chat, click the **Close** button (the red button).

NOTE

If your buddy's Mac doesn't have a microphone, the Invite To Audio Chat item will be unavailable, and the Invite To One-Way Audio Chat item will be available instead. This item lets your buddy hear you and respond using text.

NOTE

If your buddy's Mac doesn't have a video camera, the Invite To Video Chat item will be unavailable, and the Invite To One-Way Video Chat item will be available instead. This item lets your buddy see you and respond verbally.

TIP

If you want to check your video camera before starting a call, click the **green-and-white camera** button at the top of the Buddy List window. iChat will display a window showing you what the camera is seeing. Click the **Close** button (the red button) when you've finished admiring that handsome devil.

START A TEXT CHAT

To start a text chat:

1. **CONTROL**+click or right-click a buddy who's online and click **Send Instant Message** or **Send Direct Message** (see the Note on the next page). iChat will display a Chat window. Type the message, and then press **RETURN**.

2. If your buddy responds, iChat shows the responses on the other side of the window from yours.

3. Type messages and press **RETURN** to send them. To send an *emoticon*, or "smiley," click the symbol at the right end of the text box and choose from the panel. The text below the panel shows the name of the emoticon and the key sequence for entering it from the keyboard.

4. When you've finished chatting, click the **Close** button (the red button).

SEND A FILE

To send a file to a buddy:

1. During a chat, open the **Buddies** menu and click **Send File**. Use the resulting dialog box to select the file, and then click **Open**. Type any necessary message and press **RETURN** to send the message and the file.

2. To send a file without starting a chat, **CONTROL**+click or right-click your buddy's entry in the Buddy List window, and then click **Send File**. Use the resulting dialog box to select the file, and then click **Open**.

In either case, your buddy can choose whether to download the file (by clicking the downward arrow that appears in its button).

NOTE

iChat provides two different ways to send a text message to a buddy, both from the menu that iChat displays when you **CONTROL**+click or right-click a buddy. Send Instant Message sends a text message to your buddy through the central messaging server. This method ensures the message will reach your buddy, but it's less secure than a direct connection. Send Direct Message sends a text message to your buddy directly (avoiding the central messaging server) if your network settings and your buddy's permit this connection. Because Send Direct Message is less sure to work, Send Instant Message is a better choice for general use.

TIP

To add several descriptors at once, click **Edit Status Menu** and work in the resulting dialog box.

RESPOND TO CHAT INVITATIONS

1. When a buddy sends you an invitation, iChat displays a pop-up window to let you know. To the right is an example of an audio invitation.

2. Click the **pop-up window** to display more detail:

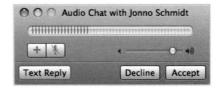

3. Click **Accept** to accept the invitation. iChat sets up the connection.

4. When you've finished chatting, click the **Close** button (the red button).

CONTROL YOUR STATUS

To control how iChat shows your status, click the **status** button in the toolbar and choose the appropriate entry from the pop-up menu. Click one of the **Custom** entries to display a text box in which you can type your preferred descriptor—for example, *Caffeinated*, *Bored*, or *Pretending to work*.

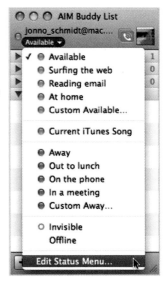

If you leave your Mac unused for a while, iChat changes your status to Idle (meaning that the Mac is idle—not necessarily that it thinks you're idle); after a long while, iChat changes your status to Away. If your Mac goes to sleep, iChat changes your status to Offline.

After you return from being away, iChat offers to change your status back to Available. Click **Available** if you want to accept this offer. Otherwise, click **No**. Select the **Don't Show Again** check box if you don't want to see this prompt again.

Chapter 5
Managing Mac OS X

To get almost anything done on Mac OS X, you'll run one or more applications (also called *programs*). Managing Mac OS X entails setting up the starting and stopping of applications in a number of different ways. Managing also includes maintaining Mac OS X, adding and removing hardware and software as needed, and backing up and restoring data.

Start and Stop Applications

In previous chapters, you have learned how to start applications from the Dock, from aliases on the desktop, and from the Applications folder. All of these methods of starting applications require a direct action from you. Mac OS X also provides several ways to start applications automatically and to monitor and manage them while they are running.

UNDERSTANDING WHY LEOPARD DOESN'T RUN SYSTEM 9 APPLICATIONS

Mac OS X is a completely different operating system from earlier versions of Mac OS, such as System 8 and System 9, and requires applications to be written especially for it. Versions of Mac OS X before Leopard included a feature called Classic that enabled you to run applications written for System 9. However, Leopard does not include Classic.

If you have a System 9 application you need to run, you have three main options:

- Look for a new version of the application that will run on Mac OS X.

- Install System 9 on a Mac (perhaps an older one), and then install the application.

- Install a previous version of Mac OS X (Tiger, Panther, or Jaguar), and then install the application on Classic.

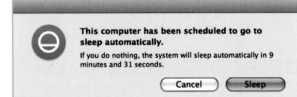

You can also add an item to the These Items Will Open Automatically When You Log In list box by dragging it from a Finder window or from your desktop.

Start and Stop Mac OS X Automatically

Mac OS X allows you to start it and stop it automatically at times you specify:

1. Open the menu and click **System Preferences** to open the System Preferences window.

2. Click **Energy Saver** to display the Energy Saver pane.

3. Click the **Schedule** button to open the Schedule sheet, shown here:

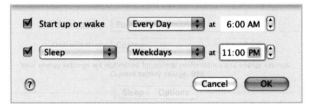

4. To start your Mac automatically, select the **Start Up Or Wake** check box and use the controls to its right to specify which days (Weekdays, Weekends, Every Day, or a specific day of the week) and the time.

5. To make your Mac shut down, sleep, or restart automatically, select the lower check box, click **Shut Down, Sleep,** or **Restart** in the drop-down list, and use the controls to its right to specify which days and the time.

6. Open the **System Preferences** menu and click **Quit System Preferences** to close System Preferences.

If you choose to shut your Mac down, put it to sleep, or restart it, Mac OS X gives you ten minutes' notice at the specified time in case you're still working. Click **Shut Down** (or **Sleep** or **Restart**) to shut down (or sleep or restart) immediately; click **Cancel** to cancel the shutdown, nap, or restart; or just leave Mac OS X to complete the countdown and shut down, sleep, or restart the Mac.

Start Applications Automatically When You Log In

Sometimes you will want to start an application automatically every time you start your Mac. For example, you might start an antivirus application automatically and have it run in the background. Or you might want, each time

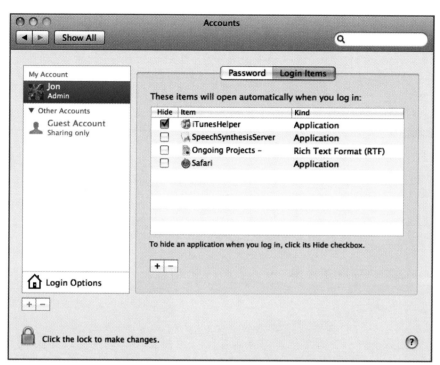

These items will open automatically when you log in:

Hide	Item	Kind
☑	iTunesHelper	Application
☐	SpeechSynthesisServer	Application
☐	Ongoing Projects –	Rich Text Format (RTF)
☐	Safari	Application

To hide an application when you log in, click its Hide checkbox.

Figure 5-1: Use the Login Items tab of the Accounts pane in System Preferences to tell Mac OS X which applications and documents to open automatically when you log in.

you log in, to open all the applications you use in a typical session. You can also open specific documents when you log in, which can save time at the start of a work session.

1. Open the menu and click **System Preferences** to open the System Preferences window.

2. Click **Accounts** to display the Accounts pane.

3. Select your account in the list box on the left.

4. Click the **Login Items** tab (see Figure 5-1).

5. To add an item to the list, click the + button beneath the These Items Will Open Automatically When You Log In list box, select the item in the resulting dialog box, and click **Add**.

6. Drag the items into the order in which you want them to be opened. (The first item in the list will be opened first.)

7. To remove an item from the list, click it, and then click the – button beneath the list box.

8. To make Mac OS X hide an item after opening it (instead of displaying the item in a window), select the **Hide** check box in the item's row. Hiding is mostly useful for system items (such as the iTunesHelper application listed in Figure 5-1), but you may want to hide regular applications on login so that your desktop remains uncluttered.

9. Open the **System Preferences** menu and click **Quit System Preferences** to close System Preferences.

Switch Applications

Like most modern operating systems, Mac OS X lets you have multiple applications open at the same time. Mac OS X makes it easy to switch from one open application to another.

SWITCH USING EXPOSÉ

The easiest way to switch to another application is to click its window. If you can see the window, this is easy. If not, you need to use Exposé.

Press **F9** to reduce all your open windows in the current Space and display them at a smaller size onscreen so you can see all of them at once. Move the mouse over a window to see its title (see Figure 5-2). Click a window to restore the screen display to normal size with the window you clicked at the front.

Figure 5-2: Pressing F9 makes Exposé shrink all open windows in the current Space so that you can see them all at once and pick the one you want.

Press **F10** to reduce all the open windows in the active application and arrange them so that you can see them (see Figure 5-3). Mac OS X grays out the other applications in the background. Click the window you want to bring to the front. Exposé then restores the rest of the screen display to normal size and displays the window you clicked at the front.

Figure 5-3: *Pressing F10 makes Exposé shrink the open windows in the active application so that you can pick the one you want to use.*

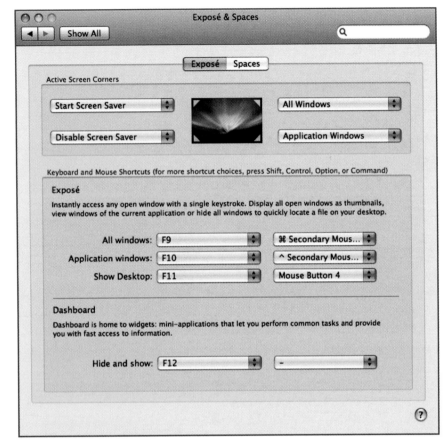

Figure 5-4: *You can configure Exposé to use different keystrokes, active screen corners, or mouse shortcuts.*

Press **F11** to move all open windows to the edges of the desktop so that you can access items on the desktop. Press **F11** again to restore the windows to their previous positions.

You can press **SHIFT** with any of these keystrokes to slow down the animation for visual entertainment.

CONFIGURE EXPOSÉ

If the Exposé keystrokes conflict with keyboard shortcuts in the applications you use, configure Exposé to use different keystrokes, active screen corners, or mouse shortcuts. Mouse shortcuts are available only for mice that have two or more buttons.

1. Open the menu and click **System Preferences** to open the System Preferences window.

2. Click **Exposé & Spaces** to display the Exposé & Spaces pane (see Figure 5-4). Click the **Exposé** tab to show the Exposé features.

3. Choose the methods of executing Exposé's All Windows, Application Windows, and Show Desktop commands. For example, open one of the menus in the Active Screen Corners box and choose the appropriate command from it.

4. Open the **System Preferences** menu and click **Quit System Preferences** to close System Preferences.

SWITCH USING THE HEADS-UP DISPLAY

You can also switch applications by pressing ⌘+**TAB** or ⌘+**SHIFT**+**TAB**. When you press one of these shortcuts, Mac OS X displays the Head-Up Display—a bar showing an icon for each running application:

NOTE

For any of the keyboard and mouse shortcuts for Exposé, you can add a modifier key—⌘, **OPTION**, **CONTROL**, or **SHIFT**—or a combination of modifier keys. Open the drop-down list, hold down the key or keys to make the list change, and then choose the item you want.

Holding down ⌘, press **TAB** to move the highlight to the next icon, or press **SHIFT+TAB** to move the highlight to the previous icon. Release the keys to display that application.

Alternatively, hold down ⌘ to keep the Heads-Up Display onscreen, and click the application you want to display.

Press ⌘+**TAB** once to switch to the last application you were using. You can then press ⌘+**TAB** again to switch back to the application you switched from, toggling between two applications.

SWITCH USING THE MOUSE

To switch applications using the mouse:

- Click the window you want to activate. If the window is in another Space, navigate to that Space first. For example, click the **Spaces** icon on the Dock, and then click the Space that contains the application.

- Double-click a title bar to minimize a window to get it out of the way.

- Click an application's icon on the Dock to switch to that application (and, if necessary, to the Space that contains it).

- Click a minimized window's icon on the Dock to switch to that window.

HIDE AND SHOW APPLICATIONS

Instead of minimizing an application window to an icon on the right side of the Dock, you can hide the application so that it's not visible, even though it's still running. To hide an application, open its application menu (for example, open the **Address Book** menu when Address Book is the active application) and click the **Hide** command. The command is named Hide *application*, where *application* is the application's name—for example, Hide Address Book.

To hide all applications *except* the active application, open the application menu and click **Hide Others**.

To show all hidden applications, open the application menu of the active application and click **Show All**. Alternatively, use the Heads-Up Display (press ⌘+**TAB**) to display one application.

TIP

You can execute whatever feature you put in an active screen corner by simply moving the mouse to that corner until the mouse pointer disappears. You don't have to click.

TIP

You can hide the active application by pressing ⌘+**H**. You can hide all other applications *except* the active application by pressing ⌘+**OPTION+H**.

QUIT AN APPLICATION WHEN IT GOES WRONG

When an application won't respond to the mouse or keyboard, you have to quit it forcibly by using the Force Quit command or the Force Quit Applications window.

Usually, it's easy to tell when an application isn't responding: Mac OS X displays a spinning, colored disc in place of the mouse pointer, and you can't perform any actions with the mouse. (Mac users know this disc semi-affectionately as the *Spinning Beachball of Death*, or SBOD.) Neither will you be able to take any actions from the keyboard in the application that's stopped responding.

Quit an Application Using the Force Quit Command

Your first tool for quitting an application forcibly is the Force Quit command. **OPTION**+click the application's icon in the Dock and click **Force Quit** on the menu.

Mac OS X will force the application to quit. If this command doesn't work, try using the Force Quit Applications window.

Quit an Application Using the Force Quit Applications Window

1. Open the ⌘ menu and click **Force Quit**. Mac OS X will display the Force Quit Applications window (see Figure 5-5).

2. Select the application that's not responding.

3. Click **Force Quit**. Mac OS X will force the application to quit.

4. Click the **Close** button (the red button) to close the Force Quit Applications window.

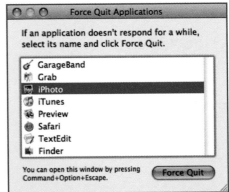

Figure 5-5: Use the Force Quit Applications window to quit an application that won't respond. The application's name may be marked "Not Responding."

QUITTING APPLICATIONS

When you've finished using an application, quit it so that it stops taking up memory and processor cycles.

USE QUIT FROM A MENU

The standard way of quitting an application is to open the application menu (the menu that bears the application's name) and click the **Quit** command (which also bears the application's name). For example, to quit Mail, open the **Mail** menu and click **Quit Mail**.

QUIT USING THE KEYBOARD

Press ⌘+Q.

QUIT FROM THE DOCK

CONTROL+click or right-click the icon for a running application in the Dock and click **Quit** on the resulting menu. You can also display this menu by clicking and holding down the mouse button for a couple of seconds.

If none of these options work, see "Quit an Application When It Goes Wrong."

Start an Application from the Terminal

Underneath its stunning interface, Mac OS X runs on UNIX, a powerful and stable operating system first developed in the 1970s and updated continuously since then. Darwin, the version of UNIX under Mac OS X, includes many applications that use a *command-line interface*—an interface with which you interact by typing commands rather than by using a mouse to manipulate graphical objects.

Should you need to, you can run UNIX commands from Mac OS X by using the Terminal application. You'll seldom need to do this unless you know UNIX and you need to perform an operation that Mac OS X and its applications can't manage—for example, adjusting Mac OS X in a way that Apple doesn't allow you to do through the user interface. But here's a quick example for you to try:

1. Click the **Finder** icon on the Dock.

2. Open the **Go** menu and click **Utilities**. The Finder window will display the contents of the Utilities folder (which is located inside the Applications folder).

3. Double-click **Terminal**. A Terminal window will be displayed (see Figure 5-6).

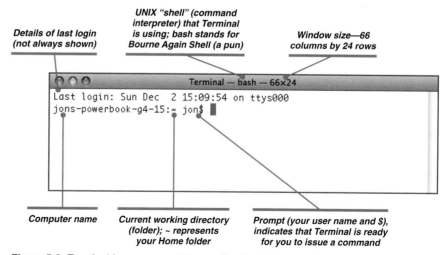

Figure 5-6: **Terminal is a command-line application for executing UNIX applications.**

```
000                Terminal — bash — 66×24
Last login: Sun Dec  2 15:09:54 on ttys000
jons-powerbook-g4-15:~ jon$ ls
Desktop        Library        Pictures
Documents      Movies         Public
Downloads      Music          Sites
jons-powerbook-g4-15:~ jon$ █
```

Figure 5-7: Using the ls command to list the contents of a folder.

```
000                Terminal — bash — 66×24
Last login: Sun Dec  2 15:09:54 on ttys000
jons-powerbook-g4-15:~ jon$ ls
Desktop        Library        Pictures
Documents      Movies         Public
Downloads      Music          Sites
jons-powerbook-g4-15:~ jon$ cd Documents
jons-powerbook-g4-15:Documents jon$ ls
Business Letters                __wireless_network_settings.txt
Ongoing Projects - Planning.rtf tm01.tiff
Personal Letters                tm02.tiff
Time Machine.rtf                tm03.tiff
To Process
jons-powerbook-g4-15:Documents jon$ █
```

4. Type ls and press **RETURN**. *ls* stands for "list" and is a command that lists the files and folders in the current directory. Terminal will display a list of the directory's contents, followed by the prompt to indicate that it is ready (see Figure 5-7).

5. Type cd Documents and press **RETURN** to change directory to your Documents folder, which is contained in your Home folder. UNIX is case sensitive, so use the capitalization specified—any other capitalization, such as **cd documents**, won't work.

6. Type ls and press **RETURN** to list the contents of your Documents folder. At left is an example of a sparsely populated Documents folder. Your Documents folder will have different contents.

7. Choose a file (not a folder) to copy as an example. Type cp (which stands for *copy*), a space, the file's name, another space, and the name you want to assign to the copy. If the file's name or the copy's name contains spaces, put the name in double quotation marks ("")—for example, cp "Time Machine.rtf" "Copy of Time Machine.rtf". Otherwise, type just its name—for example, cp testfile1 testfile2.

```
jons-powerbook-g4-15:Documents jon$ ls
Business Letters                __wireless_network_settings.txt
Ongoing Projects - Planning.rtf tm01.tiff
Personal Letters                tm02.tiff
Time Machine.rtf                tm03.tiff
To Process
jons-powerbook-g4-15:Documents jon$ cp "Time Machine.rtf" "Copy of Time Machine.
rtf"
jons-powerbook-g4-15:Documents jon$ █
```

```
jons-powerbook-g4-15:Documents jon$ cp "Time Machine.rtf" "Copy of Time Machine.
rtf"
jons-powerbook-g4-15:Documents jon$ ls
Business Letters        To Process
Copy of Time Machine.rtf        __wireless_network_settings.txt
Ongoing Projects - Planning.rtf tm01.tiff
Personal Letters                tm02.tiff
Time Machine.rtf                tm03.tiff
jons-powerbook-g4-15:Documents jon$ █
```

8. Type ls and press **RETURN** to list the contents of the Documents folder again. The copy you created will be included in the list, as shown here.

9. Delete the copy by typing rm (which stands for *remove*) and the filename, using double quotation marks again if the name contains spaces—for example, rm "Copy of Time Machine.rtf" or rm testfile2. The copy is deleted without confirmation.

10. Press ⌘+Q, or open the **Terminal** menu and click **Quit Terminal** to close Terminal.

Running Accessory Applications

Mac OS X comes with several small applications (located in your Applications folder—open a **Finder** window and click **Applications** in the Sidebar) that you can use to perform common tasks. Most of these applications are discussed elsewhere in this book, but we will look at Calculator, Stickies, and TextEdit here.

CALCULATOR

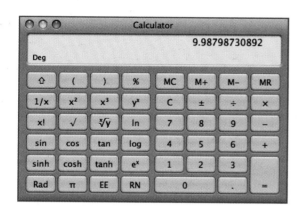

Figure 5-8: The Calculator's Advanced view provides powerful scientific functions.

The Calculator has three views: Basic view (open the **View** menu and click **Basic**) shows a standard desktop calculator, Advanced view (open the **View** menu and choose **Advanced**; see Figure 5-8) shows a powerful scientific calculator, and Programmer view (open the **View** menu and choose **Programmer**) lets you work with hexadecimal notation and bytes. To use the calculator, click the numbers onscreen or type them on the keyboard.

Calculator can also speak the buttons you've pressed or speak the result of calculations, which can be helpful for confirming what you're doing; open the **Speech** menu and click **Speak Button Pressed** or **Speak Result**, as appropriate. Calculator can also display a window showing the calculations you've performed, which helps you track your work and identify errors; open the **Window** menu and click **Show Paper Tape** to display this window.

STICKIES

Stickies is a sticky-note application that you can use to take quick notes and post reminders. Create a note by opening **File** and clicking **New Note**, then type text into it or drag in other content, such as a picture or a movie clip, from a Finder window (or your desktop) or another application. Drag the note to wherever you want to position it on your screen. Open the **File** menu and click **Save All** to save all notes. To change the color of a sticky note, click the note, open the **Color** menu, and click the color.

TEXTEDIT

TextEdit (see Figure 5-9) is a text editor that you can use to create either plain text documents or Rich Text Format (RTF) documents. (*Plain text* is text without

Figure 5-9: *TextEdit supports character and paragraph formatting, and uses Mac OS X's built-in spelling checker.*

formatting such as bold, italic, or styles. *Rich Text Format* is text with formatting.) You can even save documents in the Word 2007 format (.docx) even though TextEdit does not support all Word 2007 objects (such as charts and equations). If you double-click a text file in the Finder, TextEdit will probably open and display the file.

TextEdit's toolbar and Format menu offer straightforward formatting choices, including character formatting (such as bold, italic, and underline), paragraph alignment, and styles. TextEdit uses Mac OS X's spelling checker, which you can turn on and off by opening the **Edit** menu and choosing the **Spelling And Grammar | Check Spelling While Typing** command.

Before printing a document, open the **File** menu and click **Page Setup**, then choose the paper size, orientation, and scaling for the document.

Maintain Mac OS X

Maintaining Mac OS X includes applying updates for fixes and new features, restoring Mac OS X when hardware or other software damages it, getting information about your Mac's system status, and installing new hardware and software.

Keep Mac OS X Up to Date

Mac OS X's Software Update feature helps you to keep Mac OS X and key applications up to date. Mac OS X automatically runs Software Update periodically when your Mac is connected to the Internet, and Software Update informs you when new updates are available, as shown here.

You can also check for updates manually. To do so, open the ⌘ menu and click Software Update. You'll see the Update

window shown here while Software Update checks. If updates are available, Software Update displays the details.

If you want to install all the items, you can simply click the **Install And Restart** button. But what you'll normally want to do is choose manually which updates to install.

CHOOSE WHICH UPDATES TO INSTALL

To choose which updates to install:

1. Click the **Show Details** button. Software Update expands the window to show which updates it has found (see Figure 5-10).

2. Clear the check boxes for any updates that you don't want to install.

   - For example, if you don't have an iPod, you can probably live without updates to the iPod Software; if your Mac doesn't have an AirPort, you won't need updates for that either.

   - Sometimes, you may also not want to download a particular update right now—for example, because its file size is so large that the download will take several hours over your dial-up connection.

3. Click the **Install Items** button (its name changes to show the number of updates selected: Install 1 Item, Install 2 Items, and so on) to install the updates. Mac OS X will prompt you for your password.

4. Type your password and click **OK**. Software Update then downloads the updates and installs them.

5. After installing the updates, you may need to restart your Mac. If so, Software Update will prompt you, as shown here. Save any unsaved work in other applications, and then click **Restart** to restart your Mac. (You can also click **Not Now** if you need to finish other tasks before you restart your Mac.)

> **NOTE**
>
> Depending on the updates you're installing, you may need to agree to a license agreement.

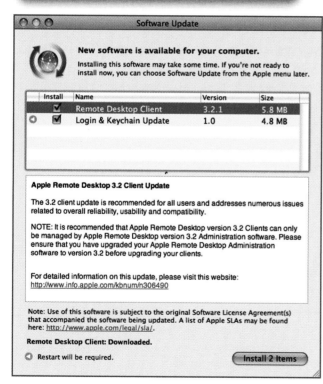

Figure 5-10: **In the New Software Is Available For Your Computer dialog box, choose which updates you want to download and install.**

If there are no updates available, Software Update displays a message box telling you so. Click **OK**, and Software Update will close itself.

IGNORE UPDATES

After you choose not to install an update, Software Update will present it to you again the next time it checks to see which updates are available. If you never want a particular update, you must tell Software Update to ignore it:

1. Select the update from the list in the New Software Is Available For Your Computer dialog box (see Figure 5-10).
2. Open the **Update** menu and click **Ignore Update**. A confirmation dialog box will be displayed.
3. Click **OK**.

RESET IGNORED UPDATES

After ignoring updates, you can reset ignored updates so that Software Update will notice them again. Open the **Software Update** menu and click **Reset Ignored Updates**. Software Update will check immediately for updates, will find those you've ignored, and will offer them in the New Software Is Available For Your Computer dialog box.

Configure Software Update

To configure how often Software Update checks for updates:

1. Open the menu and click **System Preferences** to open the System Preferences window.
2. Click **Software Update**. The Software Update pane will be displayed.
3. If the **Scheduled Check** tab isn't displayed, click it (see Figure 5-11).
4. To make Software Update check automatically for updates, select the **Check For Updates** check box and choose **Daily, Weekly**, or **Monthly** in the drop-down list box.

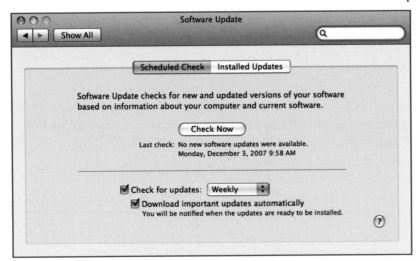

Figure 5-11: You can configure Software Update's behavior on the Scheduled Check tab of the Software Update pane in System Preferences.

5. To make Software Update automatically download important updates and then notify you about them, select the **Download Important Updates Automatically** check box. This check box is available only if you select the **Check For Updates** check box.

6. Open the **System Preferences** menu and click **Quit System Preferences** to close System Preferences.

Get System Information

To get quick information about your Mac, open the menu and click **About This Mac**. The About This Mac window will be displayed (see Figure 5-12), showing the version of Mac OS X (for example, 10.5.1) and your Mac's processor and memory.

If you need no more information, click the **Close** button (the red button) to close the About This Mac window. You can close the window and make Software Update automatically check for updates by clicking **Software Update**. But what you'll probably want to do is click **More Info** to launch the System Profiler

application, which presents detailed information on various aspects of your Mac's hardware and software.

Select the category of information in the Contents pane on the left. Figure 5-13 shows an example of the Network category for an aging PowerBook. After checking the information you need, open the **System Profiler** menu and click **Quit System Profiler** to close System Profiler.

*Figure 5-12: **The About This Mac window shows details of your Mac's version of Mac OS X, processor, and memory.***

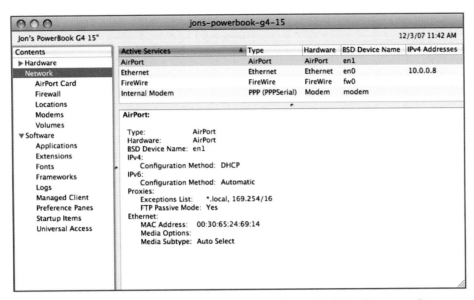

Figure 5-13: **Use System Profiler to check the details of your Mac's hardware or software.**

Set Energy Saver Options

Setting power options is most important on laptop Macs that run at least some of the time on batteries, but it's a good idea to configure suitable power options for desktop Macs as well to conserve power and keep your electricity bills down. Mac OS X's Energy Saver options provide several settings that allow you to manage your Mac's use of power.

1. Open the menu and click **System Preferences** to open the System Preferences window.

2. Click **Energy Saver** to display the Energy Saver pane. Figure 5-14 shows the Energy Saver pane for a portable Mac. The Energy Saver pane for a desktop Mac offers fewer controls: it doesn't have the Settings For drop-down list box or the Optimization drop-down list box, and the Sleep tab doesn't have the Show Details/Hide Details button.

3. If the Energy Saver pane is shown at its small size (smaller than in Figure 5-14), click **Show Details**. The pane will be displayed at its full size.

4. In the **Optimization** drop-down list box, select the setting that best describes the power configuration you want: Better Energy Savings, Better Battery Life, Normal, Better Performance, or Custom.

5. If your Mac is a laptop, choose **Power Adapter** or **Battery Power** in the **Settings For** drop-down list to specify which settings you want to configure. (Typically, you'll want different settings for when your laptop is plugged in and for when it's running on battery power.)

6. If the Sleep tab isn't displayed, click the **Sleep** tab.

7. Drag the **Put The Computer To Sleep When It Is Inactive For** slider to specify how long Mac OS X should wait before putting your Mac to sleep when it detects no input from the keyboard or mouse.

8. Select the **Put The Display(s) To Sleep When The Computer Is Inactive For** check box if you want to put the display or displays to sleep sooner than the computer. Drag the slider to specify the length of time. Putting the display to sleep soon is especially good for a laptop Mac running on battery power (the display uses a lot of power) or for an LCD monitor (the lamp eventually burns out).

NOTE

If your Mac laptop is plugged in, Mac OS X selects the Power Adapter item in the Settings For drop-down list box; if it's on battery power, Mac OS X selects the Battery Power item.

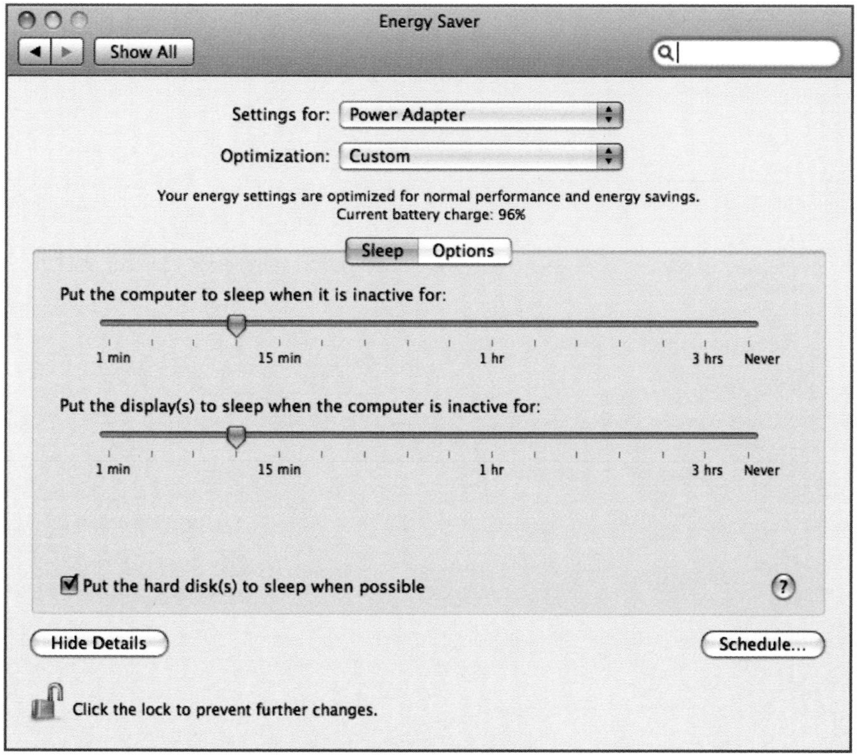

Energy Saver

Show All

Settings for: Power Adapter

Optimization: Custom

Your energy settings are optimized for normal performance and energy savings.
Current battery charge: 96%

Sleep | Options

Put the computer to sleep when it is inactive for:

1 min   15 min   1 hr   3 hrs   Never

Put the display(s) to sleep when the computer is inactive for:

1 min   15 min   1 hr   3 hrs   Never

☑ Put the hard disk(s) to sleep when possible

Hide Details   Schedule...

🔓 Click the lock to prevent further changes.

Figure 5-14: Configure power options on the Energy Saver pane in System Preferences. The Energy Saver pane shown here has battery-power settings because it is for a laptop Mac.

NOTE

For a laptop Mac, you can select the **Show Battery Status In The Menu Bar** check box to display a battery readout in the menu bar. This readout is usually helpful.

9. Select the **Put The Hard Disk(s) To Sleep When Possible** check box if you want Mac OS X to put the hard disk to sleep whenever it can. This saves power (and reduces noise) but decreases performance.

10. To choose other power options, click the **Options** tab. Figure 5-15 shows the Options tab for a laptop Mac. The Energy Saver pane for a desktop Mac doesn't have the Settings For drop-down list box or the Optimization drop-down list box. Also, the Options tab doesn't include the Processor Performance drop-down list box, but it may include an Allow Power Button To Sleep The Computer check box (depending on your Mac).

   • Choose whether to have your Mac wake from sleep when the modem detects a ring (to receive faxes) or wake via a prompt across an Ethernet network from an administrator.

   • Select the **Restart Automatically After A Power Failure** check box if you want your Mac to restart automatically after a power outage. This option is primarily useful for desktop Macs providing services (for example, sharing a printer or an iTunes music library) to other Macs. The battery in a laptop Mac normally allows it to ride out short power outages without a problem.

   • Choose whether to dim the display when a laptop Mac is running on battery power, and whether to reduce the display's brightness before putting the display to sleep.

   • In the Processor Performance drop-down list box, you can choose **Reduced** performance instead of Highest performance to increase battery life on a laptop Mac or to make action games designed for older, slower Macs run at a less frenetic pace.

11. For a laptop Mac, return to step 6, choose the other setting in the **Settings For** drop-down list box (Power Adapter or Battery Power), and choose suitable settings.

12. Open the **System Preferences** menu and choose **Quit System Preferences** to close System Preferences.

USE AN UNINTERRUPTIBLE POWER SUPPLY

The battery in a laptop Mac enables it to ride out power outages of up to several hours, depending on how fully the battery is charged and how much power the Mac is consuming.

Figure 5-15: You can configure your Mac to wake when the phone rings (to receive faxes) or when the network prompts it (for remote administration), to restart automatically after a power failure, and to change the processor performance.

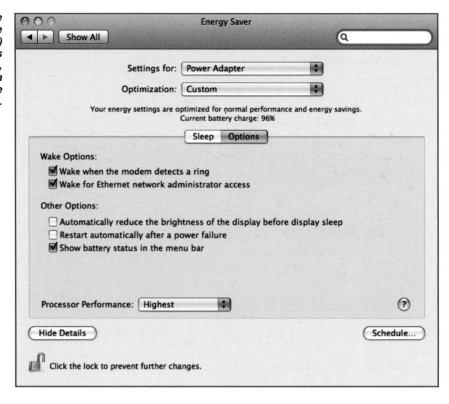

TIP

If you find that the underside of your laptop Mac gets uncomfortably hot, try using the **Reduced** Processor Performance setting to decrease the amount of heat being output. Alternatively, get a notebook fan.

TIP

Before buying a UPS, calculate how much power your Mac needs. The easiest way to calculate the power is to use a template such as the one at American Power Conversion Corp. (www.apcc.com/template/size/apc/; this web site requires your browser to accept cookies in order to work). Select a model that connects to your Mac and that supports software for shutting down your Mac automatically if you're not present to shut it down manually when a power outage occurs.

With a desktop Mac, you can use an uninterruptible power supply, or UPS, to prevent your Mac from crashing when the power goes out. Your Mac's power cord plugs into the UPS, which in turn plugs into a wall outlet. The UPS contains batteries that will supply power to your Mac for a short time (from 5 to 30 minutes), enough to get you through brief power interruptions or allow you to shut down your Mac "gracefully" (under control) on longer outages.

Some UPSs connect to your Mac via a USB (Universal Serial Bus) connection so that they can notify your Mac of power problems and even shut it down automatically if you're not there to do so yourself. Depending on the UPS, you may control it, either through the UPS tab in the Energy Saver pane of System Preferences (which appears only when a configurable UPS is connected) or via its own software.

Add and Remove Software

Today, almost all application and utility software comes in one of two ways: on a CD or DVD, or downloaded from the Internet.

If you get software on a CD or DVD, insert the CD or DVD in your optical drive. Mac OS X will mount the disc and display a window showing its contents, as in the example shown in Figure 5-16.

Most software that you download from the Internet is packed into a file called a *disk image*, which is then compressed to make it as small as possible. If you download a compressed disk image from the Internet by using Safari, Safari will save the compressed file to your desktop, uncompress the disk image automatically and save it to the desktop too, mount the disk image on your desktop, and open a window showing its contents. Figure 5-17 shows an example of a disk image on the desktop.

NOTE

For security reasons (preventing malware from installing itself without your approval), Safari may be set not to mount a downloaded disk image automatically. In this case, double-click the disk image to mount it.

UICKSTEPS

GETTING MAXIMUM BATTERY LIFE

If your Mac is a laptop, you will want the battery's charge to last as long as possible. Apple gives you various tools to help.

USE THE BATTERY STATUS MENU

First, put the battery status menu on your menu bar so that you can see the battery's status. Open the **Energy Saver** pane of System Preferences, click the **Options** tab, and select the **Show Battery Status In The Menu Bar** check box.

- The charging icon shows that the battery is charging. The time display shows the estimated time left to complete the charge. (0:28)

- When your laptop Mac is running on battery power, the display shows a battery icon with a black bar indicating approximately how much battery power is left. For more detail, click the icon, click **Show** on the menu, and choose **Time** to display the time left or **Percentage** to show the percentage left. (3:22)

Continued . . .

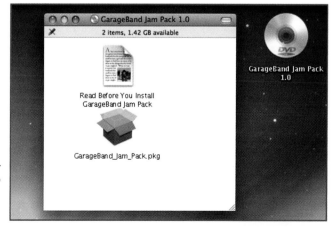

Figure 5-16: Mac OS X mounts a software CD or DVD so that you can install the applications it contains.

GETTING MAXIMUM BATTERY LIFE

(Continued)

REDUCE THE BRIGHTNESS OF THE DISPLAY

The display accounts for a large proportion of the power your laptop Mac consumes. To reduce the brightness of the display:

- Press **F1** on the keyboard to reduce the brightness one step at a time. (Press **F2** to increase the brightness.)

  –Or–

- Open the menu and click **System Preferences**, click **Displays**, click the **Display** tab, and drag the **Brightness** slider to the left.

If your laptop Mac supports automatic brightness adjustment, you can select the **Automatically Adjust Brightness As Ambient Light Changes** check box on the Display tab of the Displays pane to have Mac OS X automatically adjust the screen brightness for you. However, when you need to reduce the display's power draw as much as possible, turn this feature off so that you can make the display as dim as you can bear.

REDUCE PROCESSOR PERFORMANCE

If you don't mind sacrificing performance for battery life, select **Reduced** in the **Processor Performance** drop-down list box on the Options tab of the Energy Saver pane (see Figure 5-15) in System Preferences (open the menu and choose **System Preferences**).

AVOID POWER-HUNGRY APPLICATIONS

Any application that requires your Mac's optical drive to keep running will consume a lot of power. DVD Player is especially greedy, requiring power not just for spinning the DVD but also for rendering full-screen video. Playing CDs also consumes plenty of power.

Continued . . .

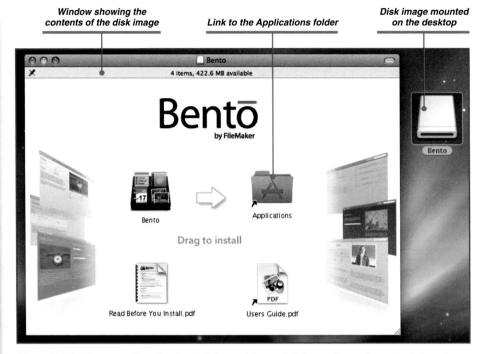

Window showing the contents of the disk image — **Link to the Applications folder** — **Disk image mounted on the desktop**

Figure 5-17: When you download a disk image file containing software from the Internet, Safari automatically displays a window showing its contents. Some software includes a link to the Applications folder so that you can drag the application there easily.

From a window such as this, you install the software in one of two ways: by dragging it to your Applications folder or by running the installer. Which technique you need depends on the software:

- If the software has a file named Install or Package (like the file in Figure 5-16), you must use the installer.
- If the software simply has a file with the application's name, you typically install it by dragging.
- If in doubt, read any instructions that came with the software, either as a leaflet accompanying a software disc or as a file that appears in the software's window.

QUICKSTEPS

GETTING MAXIMUM BATTERY LIFE

(Continued)

Even without the optical drive spinning, demanding applications consume much more power than less-demanding applications. For example, GarageBand makes your Mac work very hard, and iTunes' visualizations (complex moving images) make it work fairly hard. By contrast, TextEdit consumes minimal power, even when you're typing at full speed. For a rough guide to how much effort your laptop Mac is exerting, feel its underside. The hotter it is, the more power it's using. Factor the ambient temperature into your calculations.

SWITCH OFF HARDWARE FEATURES YOU'RE NOT USING

Switch off any hardware features you're not using, such as the AirPort wireless network (click the **AirPort** icon on the menu bar, and click **Turn AirPort Off**) or Bluetooth networking (click the **Bluetooth** icon on the menu bar, and click **Turn Bluetooth Off**).

USE HEADPHONES

When listening to audio on your laptop Mac, use headphones rather than your Mac's built-in speakers. Headphones require much less power to drive.

USE AGGRESSIVE POWER MANAGEMENT

Configure Energy Saver (see "Set Energy Saver Options," earlier in this chapter) to put your display, hard disk, and laptop Mac to sleep as quickly as makes sense. For example, you might make the display sleep after one minute and your Mac after ten minutes.

INSTALL SOFTWARE BY DRAGGING

If the window that contains the new software doesn't have the toolbar displayed (as in Figure 5-17), open the **View** menu and click **Show Toolbar**. Mac OS X will display the toolbar and the Sidebar.

1. Drag the icon for the software to your Applications folder in the Sidebar.
2. Click the **Applications** folder in the Sidebar to display its contents.
3. Double-click the icon for the software to run the software.
4. In the Sidebar, click the **Eject** icon next to the disk image to eject the disk image.

INSTALL SOFTWARE USING AN INSTALLER

Double-click the icon for the installer file to launch the installation routine, and then follow the displayed instructions. Figure 5-18 shows an example of the beginning of an installation routine.

After installing the software, eject the CD or DVD or unmount the disk image by dragging it to the Trash. If you downloaded the disk image from the Internet, you can now either move the disk image file to the Trash (drag it there) or move it to another folder for safe storage in case you need it again (for example, to install on another Mac). If there's a compressed file as well (which will typically have a .sit, .tar, .gz, or .tgz extension), drag this to the Trash too unless you want to keep it so that you can reinstall the software if necessary.

REMOVE SOFTWARE

1. Click the **Finder** icon on the Dock. A Finder window will open.
2. Click **Applications** in the Sidebar. The contents of the Applications folder will be displayed.
3. Drag the application or the folder containing it to the Trash.

Add Hardware

Most external hardware today is *Plug and Play*. This means you can plug it in to your Mac, usually via USB or FireWire, and immediately use it. When you first turn on your Mac after installing the hardware, Mac OS X may notify you that it has discovered the hardware; however, Mac OS X may simply install the *drivers* (the software that enables Mac OS X to communicate with the hardware) without comment.

Beyond being Plug and Play, most peripheral hardware that connects via FireWire or USB is *hot pluggable*: you can plug it in or remove it while Mac OS X is running, instead of having to shut down Mac OS X before installing the hardware. You don't need to warn Mac OS X before you plug in a hot-pluggable device, such as an iPod or memory-card reader, but you must eject the device (usually by dragging it to the Trash) before disconnecting it. If you don't, you may lose data, and Mac OS X will display a warning, like the example shown here. Click **OK** (there's nothing else you can do).

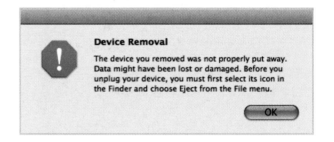

Figure 5-18: If an application has an installer file, run the installer to install the software.

NOTE

If you're short of disk space, you might prefer to keep a compressed file containing downloaded software instead of the disk image file. But you'll save the most space by deleting both the disk image and the compressed file.

Back Up and Restore Files with Time Machine

Time Machine is a new feature in Leopard that lets you recover files even after you have deleted them—and emptied the Trash. Time Machine uses the metaphor of going back in time to find the file or folder you want. You can then recover the file or folder to the present.

Understand How Time Machine Works

Here's the essence of how Time Machine works:

- You turn on Time Machine and tell Mac OS X which disk to use.

- It's best to use an external disk for your backups. This way, you avoid losing files if your Mac's hard disk goes wrong.

INSTALLING MANUFACTURER DRIVERS

Some hardware requires you to install drivers provided by the manufacturer. Typically, you'll either receive these drivers on a CD in the hardware box or have to download them from a web site:

- The **manufacturer** of the device is generally the best source of drivers for a current product.

- **Apple's Downloads site** (www.apple.com/downloads/macosx/drivers/) provides a collection of drivers for widely used devices.

- **Third-party driver sites** can be good sources of drivers for older hardware, although many older hardware devices that worked with earlier versions of Mac OS (such as System 8 and System 9) do not work with Mac OS X because nobody has written drivers for them. The best way to find driver sites is to search using a search engine such as Google (www.google.com) or Yahoo! (www.yahoo.com).

NOTE

Time Machine cannot back up files to your iDisk on the .Mac service. However, you can use the Backup utility (which you can download from the .Mac web site) to copy backup files to your iDisk.

- For the first backup, Time Machine backs up all the files on your Mac to the backup disk so that it can recover them if necessary.

- For each subsequent backup, Time Machine backs up the files that have changed but not any files that haven't changed.

- When you need to recover a file, you open Time Machine and go back to find the file you want.

Get an External Hard Disk for Time Machine

If you already have an external hard disk attached to your Mac, you're ready to use Time Machine. If not, buy an external hard disk. Follow these guidelines:

- **Connection type**   If your Mac has a FireWire 800 port, use this for the fastest connection. Otherwise, either FireWire 400 or USB 2.0 is fine. USB 1.*x* is too slow to be practical.

- **Capacity**   Ideally, the external hard disk should be big enough to save all the information on your Mac's hard disk—and have plenty of free space for new versions of files. For example, if your Mac has a 350GB hard drive, get a 500GB or 750GB external drive for Time Machine. (If your Mac's hard disk is only partly full, you can get away with a smaller Time Machine disk.)

- **Use**   Use this external hard disk only for Time Machine. Don't store any other files on it, because Time Machine will not back them up.

The first time you connect an external hard disk to your Mac, Mac OS X asks if you want to use it for Time Machine. Click the **Yes** button.

Turn On Time Machine and Choose Preferences

If you've turned on Time Machine and told Mac OS X which drive to use as described in the previous section, you're ready to use Time Machine. Otherwise, turn on Time Machine and choose preferences like this:

1. Open the menu and click **System Preferences** to open the System Preferences window.

2. In the System category, click the **Time Machine** icon to display the Time Machine pane.

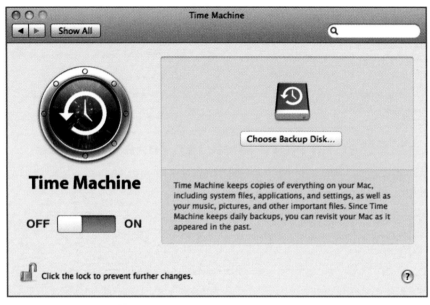

Figure 5-19: Turn on Time Machine to start backing up your Mac's files to the safety of an external disk.

3. If the On/Off switch is set to Off, as in Figure 5-19, click the **On** side to turn Time Machine on.

4. When you turn Time Machine on, Mac OS X displays a listing of the hard drives you can use for backup, as shown here.

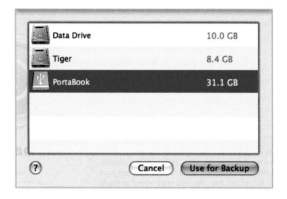

5. Click the drive you want to use, and then click the **Use For Backup** button.

6. Time Machine begins a 120-second countdown to starting its first backup.

7. If you want to back up all your Mac's files and let Time Machine delete old backups without warning you, simply let Time Machine complete the countdown and start the backup. If you want to exclude certain files or drives, or receive warnings about backups, click the **Options** button. Time Machine displays the Do Not Back Up sheet. Your Time Machine external backup drive is listed here, and you cannot remove it.

8. If you want Mac OS X to warn you before it deletes old backups to make space for new backups, select the **Warn When Old Backups Are Deleted** check box.

9. To add a drive or folder to the Do Not Back Up list, click the + button. On the sheet that appears, select the drive or folder, and then click the **Exclude** button.

10. When you've finished choosing items to exclude, click the **Done** button. Time Machine starts backing up your Mac, as shown in Figure 5-20.

11. There's no need to keep the System Preferences window open. To close it, open the **System Preferences** menu and click **Quit System Preferences**. You can then track the backup's progress via the Time Machine Backup window.

CAUTION

If Mac OS X displays a warning dialog box asking if you're sure you want to back up to the same disk as your original data is on, you'll normally want to click the **Choose Another Disk** button. You can click the **Use Selected Disk** button if you're determined to proceed, but you risk losing data if your Mac suffers a problem with the disk.

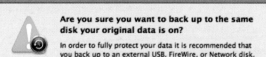

Are you sure you want to back up to the same disk your original data is on?

In order to fully protect your data it is recommended that you back up to an external USB, FireWire, or Network disk.

Choose Another Disk   Use Selected Disk

12. If possible, allow Time Machine to complete the first backup without interruption. However, if necessary, you can put your Mac to sleep, or shut it down. Time Machine resumes the backup when you reawaken or restart your Mac.

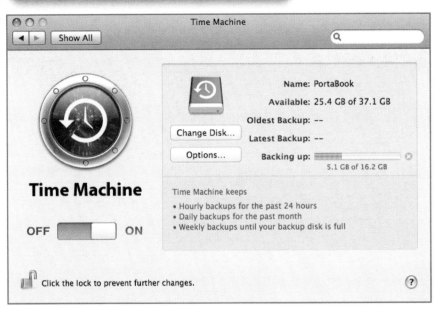

Figure 5-20: *Your first Time Machine backup may take several hours, because Time Machine copies every file. Subsequent backups copy only files that have changed, and thus are much faster.*

Recover Files Using Time Machine

Making backups regularly and easily is the main feature of the Time Machine process—but arguably being able to retrieve deleted or previous versions of files easily is even more important:

1. Open a **Finder** window to the folder that contained the file that's missing. (This step is optional, but it helps—and you'll probably do it anyway while looking for the file.)

2. Click the **Time Machine** icon on the Dock. Mac OS X will display a starry night sky across your desktop, with a series of Finder windows for the current folder receding into the distance. Figure 5-21 shows an example.

3. Click the Finder window you want. Mac OS X will display its contents. The bar at the bottom of Time Machine shows the date of the folder.

4. When you've located the file you want, click it, and then click the **Restore** button at the right end of the bottom bar. Time Machine will copy the file to the present-day version of the folder.

5. If the copied file will have the same name as an existing file, Time Machine warns you, as shown here. Click **Keep Original, Keep Both,** or **Replace**, as appropriate. If you choose Keep Both, Time Machine adds "(original)" to the name of the original file to distinguish it from the other version.

Figure 5-21: **Time Machine displays a progression of Finder windows and a timeline on the right. The bar at the bottom shows the date of the current folder—here, Today.**

Manage Disks

Mac OS X makes managing disks as straightforward as possible.

Add a Disk to Your Mac

You can add most disks to your Mac by simply inserting them or plugging them in. For example:

- Insert a CD or DVD in your CD drive or DVD drive. Mac OS X will mount it automatically, making its contents available to your Mac, and display an icon on the desktop for it. If the disc is a type for which you've chosen a default action, Mac OS X takes that action. For example, you can choose to have a DVD movie play automatically.

- Plug in a hot-pluggable drive such as a USB drive, a FireWire drive, a memory-card reader, or an iPod. Mac OS X will mount the drive automatically and display an icon for it on the desktop.

Remove a Disk from Your Mac

You can remove most kinds of disks from your Mac by dragging them to the Trash. If you find this concept peculiar or the action awkward, select the disk, open the **File** menu, and click **Eject Disk** *Name* (where *Disk Name* is the name of the disk). Some keyboards have an eject button in the upper-right corner for ejecting a disk from a CD or DVD drive.

Erase a Rewritable CD or DVD

After writing data to a rewritable CD or DVD, you must erase the disc's contents before you can write data to it again:

1. Activate the **Finder**.

2. Open the **Go** menu and click **Utilities**. A Finder window showing your Utilities folder will be displayed.

3. Double-click **Disk Utility**. Disk Utility will open.

4. In the list box on the left, click the entry for the disc. The title bar of the Disk Utility window shows the name of the disc you've clicked (rather than the words "Disk Utility").

5. If the Erase tab (see Figure 5-22) isn't displayed, click the **Erase** tab.

6. Select the **Quickly** option button if you want to erase the data quickly. If you want to make sure the disc is in good condition, select the **Completely** option button. (A complete erasure takes several times longer than a quick erase.)

7. Click **Erase**. Disk Utility will display a confirmation sheet, shown here.

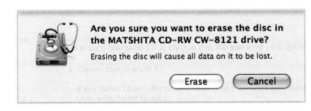

Are you sure you want to erase the disc in the MATSHITA CD–RW CW–8121 drive?

Erasing the disc will cause all data on it to be lost.

[Erase] [Cancel]

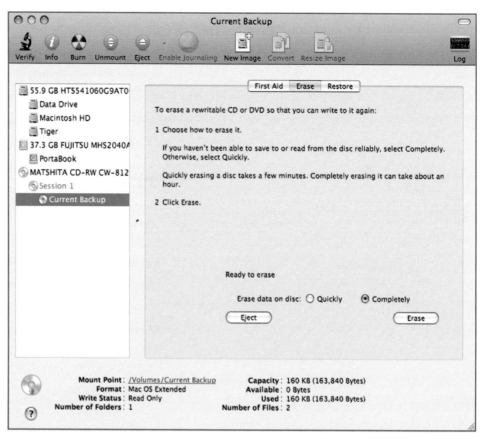

Figure 5-22: Use the Erase tab of Disk Utility to erase a rewritable disc so that you can use it again.

8. Click **Erase**. Disk Utility erases the disc.

9. The Finder displays a dialog box asking what you want to do with the disc. Click **Eject** to eject it, or select **Open Finder** in the **Action** drop-down list box and click **OK** if you want to write data to the disc immediately.

10. Open the **Disk Utility** menu and click **Quit Disk Utility** to close Disk Utility.

How to...

Chapter 6
Working with Documents and Pictures

In this chapter you will discover the many aspects of creating documents and pictures and how to install and use printers with documents and pictures. You will also learn how to set up and use Mac OS X's built-in fax capability with documents and pictures.

Create Documents and Pictures

To create documents and pictures, you normally use applications that run on Mac OS X rather than using Mac OS X's own components. For example, many Mac users run word processing applications, such as TextEdit (included with Mac OS X), Microsoft Word, or the OpenOffice.org word processor, to create text-based documents; and they use drawing applications and image-editing applications, such as Adobe Illustrator and Adobe Photoshop, to create and manipulate pictures.

QUICKSTEPS

ACQUIRING A DOCUMENT

The documents on your Mac got there because they were created with an application on your Mac, they were brought to your Mac on a disk or removable storage device, they were transferred across a local area network (LAN), or they were downloaded from the Internet.

CREATE A DOCUMENT WITH AN APPLICATION

1. Start the application. For example, start Microsoft Word by activating the **Finder**, opening the **Go** menu, clicking **Applications**, and then double-clicking the **Microsoft Word** icon in the Microsoft Office folder.

2. Create the document using the application's features. In Word, for example, type the document, formatting it with Word's formatting tools.

3. Save the document (again, in Word) by opening the **File** menu and choosing **Save**, choosing the name and folder for the document, and clicking **Save** (see Figure 6-1).

4. Close the application used to create the file (for example, open the menu that bears the application's name and click the **Quit** command).

IMPORT A DOCUMENT FROM A DISK

Use the Finder to bring in a document from a disk or another removable storage device:

1. Insert the disk in the appropriate drive on your Mac. For example, insert a CD or DVD in an optical drive, or connect a USB key or an iPod you're using in disk mode. Mac OS X will mount the disk and display it on your desktop.

Continued . . .

All new Macs, however, include iPhoto, a powerful but straightforward application for importing, editing, and exporting photos. iPhoto is included in iLife, Apple's set of multimedia applications that comes bundled with new Macs. At this writing, the current version of iLife is iLife '08. If you don't have iLife '08, or if you have an earlier version, you can buy iLife '08 from the Apple Store (http://store.apple.com) or a computer store.

Mac OS X provides strong features for bringing documents and pictures in from other computers, from the Internet, and from scanners and cameras.

Create a Picture

In computer terms, a picture file is a document that consists only of an image. You can create pictures or bring them into your Mac in the same way as any other document (see the "Acquiring a Document" QuickSteps).

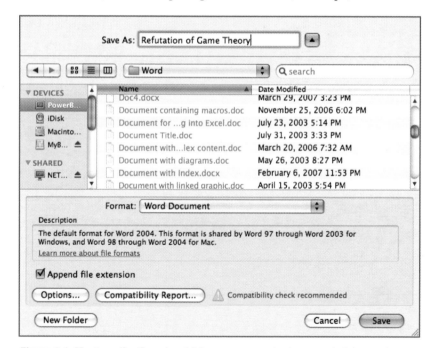

*Figure 6-1: **Most applications in which you can create documents let you choose where to save the files you create.***

ACQUIRING A DOCUMENT *(Continued)*

2. If Mac OS X doesn't automatically display a Finder window showing the contents of the disk, double-click the disk's icon on your desktop to open a Finder window.

3. Drag the file to the folder in which you want to store it. If the destination folder is in the Sidebar, simply drag the file there. Otherwise, drag the file to the Sidebar folder that contains the destination folder, wait for the Spring-Loaded Folders feature to open a window showing that folder, and then drag to the target folder, using the spring-loading to open other folders as necessary.

4. Click the **Close** button (the red button) or open the **File** menu and click **Close Window** to close the Finder window after you have copied the file.

5. Drag the disk's icon to the **Trash** icon on the Dock to eject the disk.

TRANSFER A DOCUMENT ACROSS A NETWORK

Use the Finder to bring in a document from another computer on your network:

1. Click the **Finder** icon on the Dock. Mac OS X will open a new Finder window (if none is open) or will display an existing window.

2. In the Shared area of the Source list, connect to the network drive that contains the document file you want so that the drive appears in the Sidebar. Click that network drive, and the detail pane will display its contents. See "Connect to a Shared Folder" in Chapter 10 for detailed instructions on connecting to a shared network drive.

3. Open the folder that contains the document file.

Continued . . .

For example, if you have a drawing application such as Adobe Illustrator installed on your Mac, you can create a picture by taking these general steps:

1. Open the application by clicking its icon on the Dock, or open a Finder window to the Applications folder and double-click the application's icon in that folder.

2. Use the New command to create a new file. For example, depending on the application, you might open the **File** menu and click **New**.

3. Create the picture using the tools in the application.

4. Save the document by opening the **File** menu and choosing **Save** or **Save As** (depending on the application), specifying the location and filename on the Save As sheet, and clicking the **Save** button.

5. Open the application's application menu and click **Quit** to close the application.

Install Cameras and Scanners

How you install a digital camera or scanner depends on whether the device is Plug and Play (you plug it in and it starts to function), what type of connection it has, and whether Mac OS X already has a driver for it.

INSTALL A USB CAMERA OR MEDIA READER

Many digital cameras can connect to your Mac via USB (Universal Serial Bus). If your camera doesn't connect via USB, chances are good that the camera has a storage card (such as a CompactFlash card, an SD card, or a Memory Stick card) that can be removed from the camera and inserted in a card reader that is connected to your Mac via USB.

When you connect a digital camera or a storage card containing photos via USB, Mac OS X recognizes the camera or storage card as a removable disk drive and mounts it on the desktop so that you can access its contents. If iPhoto (the photo-editing application included in the iLife multimedia suite) is installed on your Mac, Mac OS X also automatically starts iPhoto and switches it into Import mode so that you can easily import the pictures into your Library in iPhoto. (See "Transfer Pictures from a Camera," later in this chapter.) If iPhoto isn't installed on your Mac (which is rare but possible), Mac OS X opens a Finder window.

QUICKSTEPS

ACQUIRING A DOCUMENT (Continued)

4. Drag the document file to the folder in which you want to store it. Use the Spring-Loaded Folders feature if necessary.

5. Click the **Close** button (the red button) or open the **File** menu and click **Close Window** to close the Finder window after you have copied the file.

DOWNLOAD A DOCUMENT FROM THE INTERNET

Use Safari to bring in a document from a site on the Internet:

1. Click the **Safari** icon on the Dock. Safari will launch.

2. Go to the web site and web page from which you can download the document file.

3. Click the document file's link on the web page to begin downloading the file. Safari will automatically save the file to your Downloads folder.

4. Click the **Downloads** icon on the Dock and click **Show In Finder** to open a Finder window showing the Downloads folder.

5. Drag the file from the Downloads folder to the folder in which you want to store the file.

6. Open the **Safari** menu and click **Quit Safari** to close Safari.

TIP

If your scanner came with custom scanning software, use that software in preference to Image Capture, as it probably is designed to make better use of your scanner's capabilities. Also, you may not be able to use Image Capture.

INSTALL A SCANNER

Most recent scanners designed for the consumer market connect to your Mac via USB. Some more expensive scanners connect via FireWire, the high-speed data-transfer technology that Apple favors over USB. Mac OS X includes drivers for many popular models of scanners and for scanners that use the TWAIN scanning technology, but if you buy a new scanner, you will normally need to either use a driver included with the scanner or download the latest driver from the manufacturer's web site.

If the scanner came with a driver for Mac OS X or with custom scanning software and there are manufacturer's instructions for installing the scanner with Mac OS X, follow those instructions. Otherwise, use these instructions:

1. Install the driver or software.

2. Connect the scanner to your Mac.

3. Run the scanning software (if any).

If you don't have a driver for the scanner:

1. Connect the scanner to your Mac via the interface it uses—typically USB, but sometimes FireWire.

2. Turn on the scanner and put a document on its scanning surface.

3. Press the button on your scanner that starts the scanning operation.

4. If Mac OS X opens the Image Capture application, you're all set. If not, check the scanner manufacturer's web site to see if a driver for Mac OS X is available.

Scan Pictures Using Image Capture

Scanners enable you to take printed images and convert them to digital images on your Mac. The scanner must first be installed, as described in the previous section. To scan a picture using Image Capture, Mac OS X's default scanning application:

1. Turn on the scanner.

2. Place the document carefully on the scanning surface.

Drag across the overview to select the area you want to scan. Image Capture then enables the Scan button.

Size To Fit button, sizes the overview to fit in the window

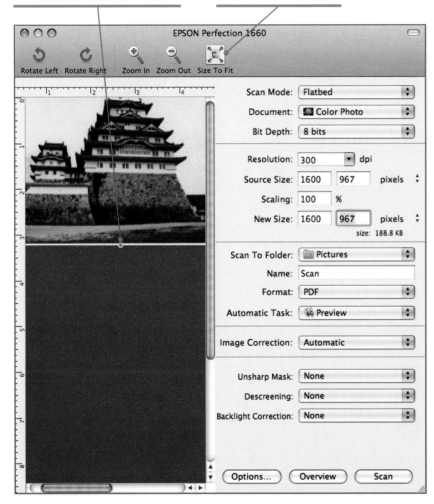

Figure 6-2: ***Image Capture enables you to scan documents using many popular models of scanners.***

3. Press the button on your scanner that starts the scanning operation. Either your scanner's software or Image Capture will open. The scanner will scan the document, and the overview (a preliminary scan) will appear in your software or in Image Capture. Figure 6-2 shows Image Capture.

4. To make the overview fit in the window, click the **Size To Fit** button.

5. Use the **Zoom In** and **Zoom Out** buttons if you need to zoom the picture, or use the **Rotate Left** and **Rotate Right** buttons to rotate it.

6. Drag across the preview to specify which part of it you want to capture.

7. Choose the scan mode, document type, and bit depth:

   - In the **Scan Mode** drop-down list, choose **Flatbed** for a document or image. Choose **Transparency** for a transparency or slide.

   - In the **Document** drop-down list, choose **Text, B/W Photo**, or **Color Photo**, as appropriate.

   - In the **Bit Depth** drop-down list, choose 1 Bit for text scanning, 8 Bits for modest-quality black-and-white or color scanning, and 16 Bits or a higher setting for higher-quality scanning. The settings available depend on your scanner. 24-bit scans give near-photographic quality.

8. Choose the resolution, size, and scaling:

   - In the **Resolution** drop-down list, choose the resolution in dots per inch (dpi). The higher the resolution, the larger the file size will be, and the more detail you will see. Try 150 dpi or 300 dpi for general-purpose scans, and increase the resolution if the quality of the results is not high enough.

   - On the **Source Size** line, specify the source size (in inches, centimeters, or pixels).

   - In the **Scaling** box, enter the percentage of any scaling needed, and Image Capture will indicate the resulting size in the New Size boxes.

9. Specify the folder, filename, and format for the document:

- In the **Scan To Folder** drop-down list, choose the folder.

- In the Name text box, type the name to give the file. The base filename is <u>Scan</u>, which is not especially helpful.

- In the **Format** drop-down list, choose the format to use: JPEG, TIFF, PNG, or PDF. JPEG provides moderate quality with variable compression and is good for web use. TIFF provides full quality and widespread compatibility and is good for general use. PNG provides full quality and good compatibility, but some computers cannot read PNG files. PDF is great for Macs, but users of other operating systems may need to install Adobe Acrobat Reader or another PDF reader to view your scanned PDF document.

- In the **Automatic Task** drop-down list, choose the program you want to associate with the scanned file. The default choice, **Preview**, works well, but you may prefer to use a more powerful application (such as Adobe Photoshop) if you have one.

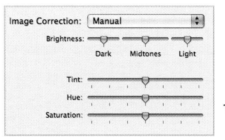

- In the **Image Correction** drop-down list, choose whether to use image correction: None, Automatic, or Manual. If you select Manual, Image Capture displays the Brightness, Tint, Hue, and Saturation sliders (which you drag to specify settings) and hides the Unsharp Mask, Descreening, and Backlight Correction drop-down lists.

10. If necessary, choose further settings:

- **Unsharp Mask**   Choose **Low, Medium**, or **High** to control the degree of "sharpness" in the picture. Increase the sharpness to produce more differentiation between colors.

- **Descreening**   If a scan produces a cross-hatched or speckled look, choose a different setting than None. Your options (in ascending order) are General, Newspaper (85 lpi), Magazine (133 lpi), and Fine Prints (175 lpi).

- **Backlight Correction**   Choose **Low, Medium**, or **High** if you need to adjust the lighting (for example, because the item you're scanning was underexposed).

11. Click **Scan**. Image Capture causes the scanner to scan the picture and then saves the file using the name and folder you specified. Image Capture then opens the file in the associated application so that you can check it. When you have done so, quit this application.

12. Open the **Image Capture** menu and click **Quit Image Capture** to close Image Capture.

Transfer Pictures from a Camera

As mentioned in "Install a USB Camera or Media Reader" (earlier in this chapter), when you connect your camera or its memory card via USB, Mac OS X automatically mounts the device on the desktop, opens iPhoto (if installed), and displays the contents of the device, as shown in Figure 6-3. If iPhoto is not installed, Mac OS X opens a Finder window.

Source list, shows your Library, albums, and devices

Viewing area, displays one or more pictures

Import buttons, click to start importing the pictures

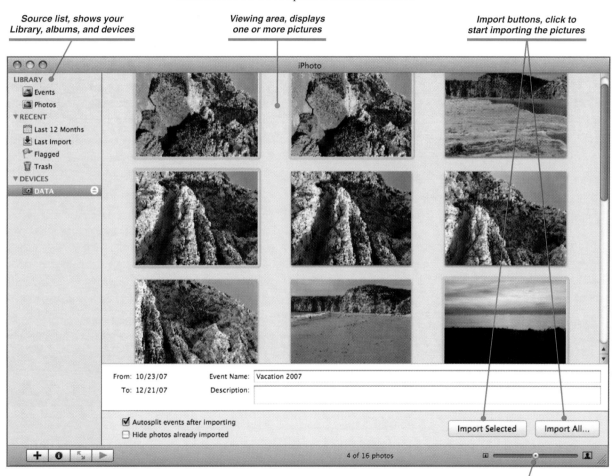

*Figure 6-3: **When Mac OS X detects you've plugged in a digital camera or a storage card that contains digital pictures, it automatically opens iPhoto and displays the contents of the device.***

Size slider, changes the size of pictures displayed in the Viewing area

To import the pictures:

1. In the Event Name text box, type the name for the set of photos you will import.

2. In the Description text box, type a description for the photos to help you identify them later. You can adjust the description for individual photos later.

3. Select the **Autosplit Events After Importing** check box if you want iPhoto to break the photos into different albums by the date and time they were taken.

4. Select the **Hide Photos Already Imported** check box if you want iPhoto to hide photos you've already imported so that you don't try to import them again.

5. If you want to import all the pictures, click the **Import All** button. If you want to import only one picture, click it to select it, and then click the **Import Selected** button. To import a range of pictures, select them using one of the methods described next, and then click the **Import Selected** button:

   ● Click the first picture, then hold down SHIFT and click the last picture. ⌘+click to add an individual picture to the current selection or to remove a picture from the selection.

   ● Drag across the range of pictures you want to select.

6. iPhoto will import the pictures, showing you a preview of the current photo and a readout of its progress. If any of the pictures are duplicates of pictures you've imported before (for example, because you left them on your camera after importing them), iPhoto displays the Duplicate Photo dialog box (see Figure 6-4). Select the **Apply To All Duplicates** check box if you want your decision to apply to all duplicate pictures rather than just the one currently displayed, and then click **Import** or **Don't Import**.

7. After importing all your pictures, iPhoto prompts you to delete them. Click the **Delete Originals** button or the **Keep Originals** button as appropriate.

Figure 6-4: **Choose whether or not to import pictures that are duplicates of pictures already in your Photo Library.**

TIP

You can also drag the pictures to a specific album. iPhoto will add the pictures to your Photo Library and will create references to them in that album so that they appear in the album.

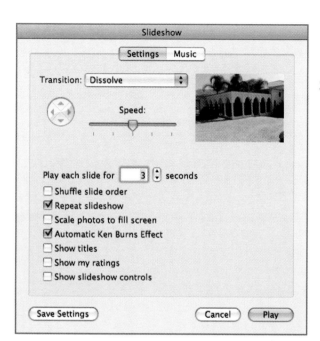

Figure 6-5: *The Slideshow dialog box lets you quickly start a slideshow with default settings or create a customized show with your preferred music.*

After importing the pictures either automatically or manually, eject the camera or memory card by clicking the **Eject** button next to its entry in the iPhoto Source list or in the Sidebar of a Finder window. You can then unplug the camera or memory card from your Mac without causing an error.

Sort Through Your Last Import Quickly

iPhoto stores details of the last batch of pictures you imported in the Last Import album, which appears in the Recent category in the Source list. After importing pictures, you can use Last Import and iPhoto's Slideshow feature to sort through them quickly, as follows:

1. Click **Last Import** in the Recent category in the Source pane. The last pictures you imported will be displayed.

2. Click **Play Slideshow** in the toolbar at the bottom of the window. The Slideshow dialog box will be displayed (see Figure 6-5).

3. Unless you want to see the slideshow over and over, make sure the **Repeat Slideshow** check box is cleared.

4. Clear the **Automatic Ken Burns Effect** check box to prevent iPhoto from panning and zooming over the photos while you review them. The Ken Burns Effect can be great for slideshows, but not when you're quickly sorting your last import.

5. Select the **Show Slideshow Controls** check box to make iPhoto display the slideshow controls throughout the slideshow.

6. Select the **Show Titles** check box if you want iPhoto to display the filenames of the pictures in the upper-left corner of each picture.

7. Click **Play**. iPhoto starts a full-screen slideshow of the pictures, using default settings.

8. To take an action, click a button on the Control bar (see Figure 6-6). The Control bar lets you navigate among pictures, rotate the current picture, assign a rating to the current picture (from no stars to five stars) by dragging along the line of five dots, or delete the current picture.

9. At the end of the slideshow, iPhoto displays its main window again. If you chose to repeat the slideshow, press **ESC** to stop it.

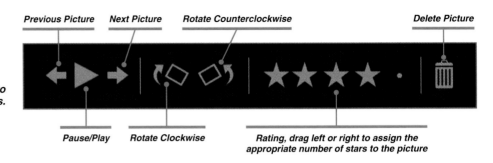

Previous Picture   Next Picture   Rotate Counterclockwise   Delete Picture

Figure 6-6: *Use the Control bar to rotate, delete, or rate pictures.*

Pause/Play   Rotate Clockwise   Rating, drag left or right to assign the appropriate number of stars to the picture

QUICKSTEPS

CROPPING PICTURES TO FIT YOUR DESKTOP

As explained in "Change the Desktop from iPhoto" in Chapter 2, you can quickly put pictures on your desktop from iPhoto. But for best effects, you may need to crop the pictures to the right dimensions first:

1. Click the **iPhoto** icon on the Dock. iPhoto will open.

2. In the Source list, click the album that contains the picture.

3. In the detail pane, **CONTROL**+click or right-click the picture you want to crop and click **Edit In Separate Window**. iPhoto will open the picture in an editing window.

4. Click the **Crop** button. iPhoto displays a cropping frame and controls on the picture (see Figure 6-7).

5. To constrain the crop to the display size, select the **Constrain** check box. In the Constrain drop-down list, select the item marked (**Display**) after the pixel size—for example, **1440 × 900 (Display)**.

6. To move the crop area, click in it and drag it.

7. Click the **Apply** button to crop the picture.

8. Click the **Done** button to close the editing window.

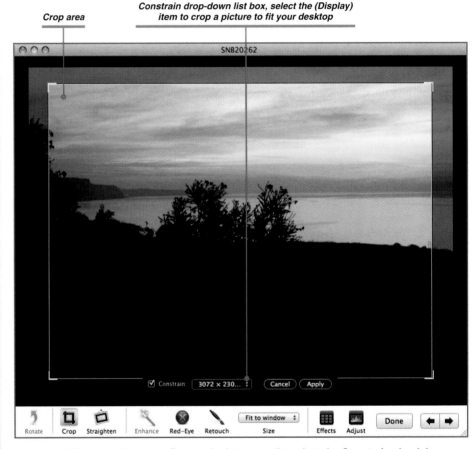

Crop area   Constrain drop-down list box, select the (Display) item to crop a picture to fit your desktop

Figure 6-7: *To crop a picture to fit your desktop exactly, select the Constrain check box, choose the size, and then click the Apply button.*

NOTE

iPhoto lets you edit a picture either in the main window or in a separate window. Editing in a separate window tends to be more flexible, as you can open two or more pictures for editing at the same time; but you may prefer editing in the same window to keep your screen uncluttered. To choose which editing method iPhoto uses when you double-click a picture, click **iPhoto I Preferences** and click the **General** button. In the **Edit Photo** drop-down list, choose **In Main Window**, **In Separate Window**, or **Using Full Screen**, as appropriate. Click the **Close** button (the red button) to close the Preferences window.

Edit and Manage Your Pictures with iPhoto

After culling the dud pictures from your imported group, you can edit the remaining pictures in iPhoto and sort them into albums.

EDIT A PICTURE

To edit a picture, CONTROL+click or right-click it and click **Edit In Separate Window**. iPhoto will open the picture in a separate window for editing (see Figure 6-8). You can then:

- Use the **Size** drop-down list to zoom the picture to a different size. Choose **Fit To Window** to display the picture at the largest possible size that fits into the window.

Figure 6-8: iPhoto provides easy but effective tools for editing your pictures.

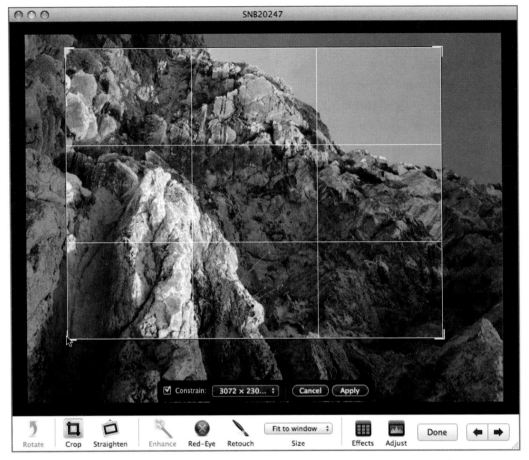

Figure 6-9: *To crop, click the Crop button. You can then drag a border or a cropping handle to change the selected area, or drag in the middle of the selected area to move the whole area.*

- Click the **Rotate** button to rotate the picture. OPTION+click the **Rotate** button to rotate the picture the opposite way.

- To crop a picture, click the **Crop** button. iPhoto displays cropping handles, controls, and a border around the picture (see Figure 6-9). If you want to constrain the picture to a particular size or dimensions, select the **Constrain** check box, and then choose the size or dimensions in the drop-down list. Click **Apply** when you're ready.

- To straighten the picture, click the **Straighten** button. iPhoto displays the Straighten slider, together with a grid on the screen to help you judge horizontal and vertical lines. Drag the slider to the right to rotate the picture gradually clockwise, or to the left to rotate the picture gradually counterclockwise.

- To enhance the picture, letting iPhoto automatically tweak the colors, click **Enhance** one or more times.

- To remove red-eye from flash pictures, drag a rectangle that includes the eyes but leaves some of the face selected, and then click **Red-Eye**. If you find iPhoto changes the skin color when you do this, try drawing a rectangle around one eye, clicking **Red-Eye**, and then repeating for the other eye.

- To apply an effect, such as Black and White, Sepia, or Edge Blur, click the **Effects** button, and then choose the effect from the Effects panel. Click the **Close** button (the X button) when you're satisfied with the result.

- To adjust the exposure, contrast, colors, or more, click the **Adjust** button. Use the controls in the Adjust panel (shown next) to change the picture, watching the effects

TIP

To apply the same adjustment to multiple pictures, use the Copy and Paste buttons in the Adjust panel. Set up the adjustment on one picture, then click the **Copy** button. Open the next picture, and then click the **Paste** button.

Adjust

0%   Levels   100%

Exposure: 0
Contrast: 0

Highlights: 0
Shadows: 0

Saturation: 50
Temperature: 0
Tint: 0

Sharpness: 0
Reduce Noise: 0

Reset   Copy   Paste

of the changes you make. Click the **Reset** button if you need to reset the picture to its original look. Click the **Close** button (the X button) when you've finished adjusting the picture.

- To temporarily remove the changes you've made, press **CONTROL**. Toggling the changes off like this helps you judge how successful they are.

- To undo a change, open the **Edit** menu and choose the **Undo** command. (The Undo menu item specifies what will be undone—for example, "Undo Enhance Photo.") You can undo multiple actions until you switch to another picture.

- To revert to the previous version of the picture, open the **Photos** menu and click **Revert To Previous**.

After editing the picture, click the **Done** button to close its window and return to the main window, or click the **Previous** button or the **Next** button to move to another picture.

WORK WITH ALBUMS

iPhoto stores all your pictures in the Photos item inside the Library category, so you can access any picture by selecting **Photos** under the Library category in the Source list. But what you'll typically want to do is arrange your pictures into albums for topics or occasions.

iPhoto lets you create either conventional albums, in which you select the pictures, or Smart Albums, in which iPhoto selects the pictures to match criteria you set.

To create a conventional album:

1. Open the **File** menu and click **New Album**. Type the name in the resulting sheet. If you've selected pictures to include in the new album, check the **Use Selected Items In New Album** check box. Click **Create**. iPhoto will add the album to the Source list.

2. To add a picture to the album, drag it from the Photos collection (or another album) to the destination album. iPhoto will add to the album a reference to the picture, which remains stored in the Photo Library but now appears in the album as well.

3. To display an album's pictures, click the album in the Source list.

4. To delete an album, select it in the Source list and press ⌘+**BACKSPACE**. iPhoto will display a confirmation dialog box. Click **Delete**. The photos remain in your Photo Library.

TIP

iPhoto also lets you drag to create a new album from pictures you've selected. Select the pictures, and then drag them into the Source list. iPhoto creates a new album and displays a text box around its title. Type the name for the album and press **RETURN**.

Smart Album name: Family Best

Match [all ⬦] of the following conditions:

| [Keyword ⬦] | [contains ⬦] | Family | ⊖ ⊕ |
| [My Rating ⬦] | [is ⬦] | ★★★★★ | ⊖ ⊕ |

(Cancel)　(OK)

To create a Smart Album:

1. Open the **File** menu and click **New Smart Album**. iPhoto will display the Smart Album panel (shown here with two conditions).

2. In the Smart Album Name text box, type the name for the album.

3. In the first row of controls, set up the first condition: for example, Keyword Contains Family.

4. If you want to add another condition, click the + button. iPhoto will add another set of controls. Use these to set the condition. Add other conditions as needed.

5. Near the top of the sheet, choose **Match All Of The Following Conditions** or **Match Any Of The Following Conditions**, as appropriate to your needs.

6. Click **OK**. iPhoto will automatically add matching pictures to the Smart Album.

Print Documents and Pictures

Before you can transfer your digital documents and pictures to paper, you must install and configure a printer.

Install a Printer

To install either a local printer or a network printer in Mac OS X, you use System Preferences. This section explains the process of installing a local printer separately from the process of installing a network printer, as there are several differences between the two processes.

Before installing a local printer, work through the following checklist.

CHECKLIST BEFORE INSTALLING A LOCAL PRINTER

A local printer is one that is attached to your Mac with a cable or a wireless connection. Make sure your printer meets the following conditions *before* you begin to install it in Mac OS X:

- It is plugged into the correct port on your Mac. Most inkjet printers and personal laser printers connect to your Mac directly via a USB cable. Most laser printers designed for multiple users connect via an Ethernet connection: both the printer and your Mac

TIP

You can also connect an Ethernet laser printer directly to your Mac by using either a regular cable or a *crossover* cable, a special cable that reverses the wires in the cable from their standard arrangement. If you use a regular cable, your Mac automatically changes the inputs on the Ethernet port to accommodate the incoming signal.

NOTE

Some printers connect to your Mac via a wireless connection. This arrangement is typically used for laptop Macs, for which it offers the most benefits, but it can be used with desktop Macs as well. In this case, "plugging the printer into your Mac" means that you should establish the appropriate wireless connection.

connect to the network's switch or router via standard Ethernet cables or a wireless AirPort, and they communicate through the switch or router.

- It is plugged into an electrical outlet.
- Fresh ink, toner, or ribbon is correctly installed.
- It is loaded with paper.
- You have installed the driver software if the printer's instructions require you to do so before connecting the printer.

INSTALL A LOCAL PRINTER

Installing a local printer is usually straightforward:

1. With the printer turned off, connect it to your Mac. Then make sure the other points in the above checklist are satisfied.

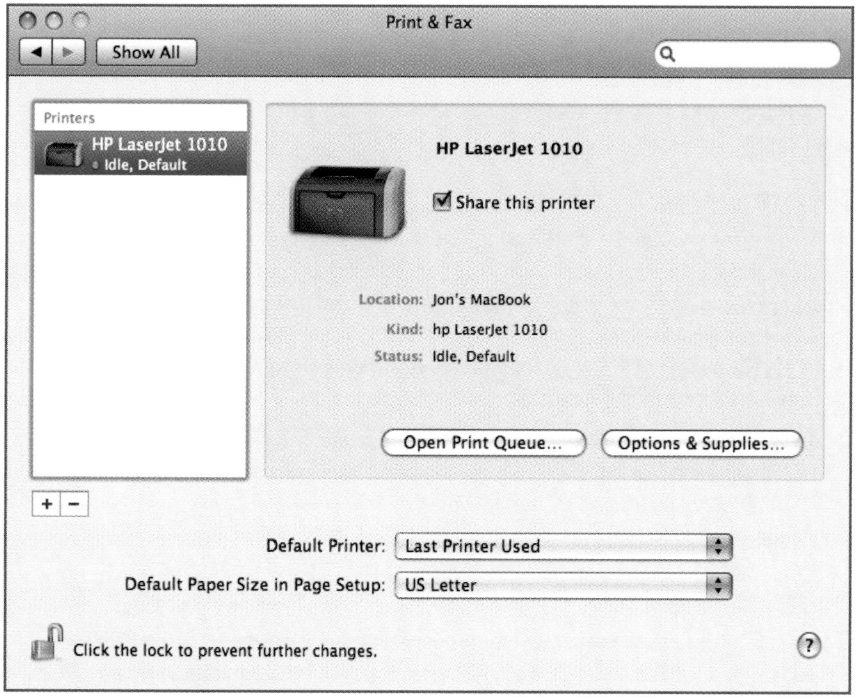

2. Turn on the printer.

3. Open the ⌘ menu and click **System Preferences** to open the System Preferences window.

4. Click **Print & Fax** to display the Print & Fax pane.
   - If the printer appears in the Printers list on the left, as in Figure 6-10, you need only choose sharing and default options, as discussed in this list.
   - If the printer doesn't appear in the Printers list, follow the procedure described in "Install a Network Printer," on the next page, to add it.

5. If you have multiple printers installed, click the printer you want to configure in the Printers list.

6. If you want to share the printer, select the **Share This Printer** check box. Otherwise, clear this check box.

7. In the **Default Printer** drop-down list, choose the printer you want to use as the default: this printer (listed by name), another printer (also listed by name), or Last Printer Used.

8. In the **Default Paper Size In Page Setup** drop-down list, choose the paper size you want to use as the default—for example, US Letter.

9. Open the **System Preferences** menu and click **Quit System Preferences** to close System Preferences.

Figure 6-10: **When you connect and turn on a printer, Mac OS X may recognize it immediately and list it on the Print & Fax pane in System Preferences. If not, click the + button to add the printer manually.**

You're ready to test your printer. Go to "Test the Printer," later in this chapter.

Network printers are not directly connected to your Mac but are available to you by being shared through the network to which your Mac is connected. There are three types of network printers:

- Printers connected to someone else's computer and shared by that computer
- Printers connected to a dedicated print server (a special-purpose computer whose function is to share and manage printers on a network) or a sharing device such as an Apple AirPort
- Printers directly connected to a network (these printers have a built-in print server)

To connect to a network printer:

1. Connect your Mac to the network if it's not already connected.
2. Open the menu and click **System Preferences** to open the System Preferences window.
3. Click **Print & Fax**. The Print & Fax pane will be displayed.
4. Click the + button. Mac OS X will display the printer setup window.
5. Specify the details of the printer:

   - To connect to a printer shared by a Mac, click the **Default** button to display the Default pane. In the Printer Name list box, click the printer's name, which appears as the name assigned to the printer by that Mac, an @ sign, and the Mac's name (see Figure 6-11). When you click the printer's name, Mac OS X automatically fills in the Name text box, the Location text box, and the Print Using drop-down list. Edit the name or location if necessary, and then click **Add**.

   - To connect to a line printer (typically on a corporate or college network), click the **IP** button to display the IP pane. Complete the Protocol, Address, and other information as instructed by the network's administrator, and edit the name and location to make clear which printer this is. Click **Add**.

   - To connect to a printer shared by a Windows computer, click the **Windows** button to display the Windows pane (see Figure 6-12). Click the workgroup, the computer, and then the shared printer. (Enter a user name and password for the Windows computer if requested and click **OK**. If you don't have a user name and password, try connecting as **Guest**.) Adjust the printer's name in the Name text box if needed,

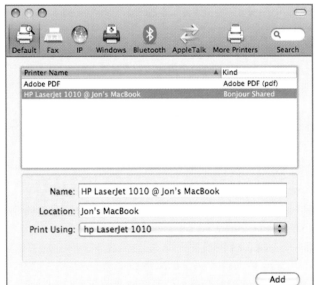

Figure 6-11: **Use the Default pane of the printer setup window to connect to a printer shared by another Mac.**

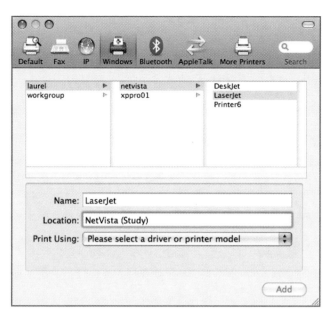

Figure 6-12: *Open the entry for the Windows computer that's sharing the printer (here, the computer called "netvista") so that you can select the printer and specify what model it is.*

and type a description in the Location text box if you will find it helpful. In the **Print Using** drop-down list, either accept the suggested driver, or click **Select A Driver To Use** and click the driver in the panel that appears. Click **Add**.

- To connect to a printer that's shared via the Bluetooth wireless networking protocol, click the **Bluetooth** button to display the Bluetooth pane. Select the printer in the Printer Name list, edit the name or description if necessary, and then click **Add**.

- To connect to a network printer shared using Apple's AppleTalk protocol, click the **AppleTalk** button to display the AppleTalk pane. In the left box, select the AppleTalk zone—for example, **Local Zone**. Select the printer by name in the list box. Edit the name or description if necessary, and then click **Add**.

6. The printer setup utility adds the printer to the Printers list on the Print & Fax pane of System Preferences. If this is the first printer you've added, the utility automatically makes the printer the default printer.

7. Open the **System Preferences** menu and click **Quit System Preferences** to close System Preferences.

8. Test the printer as described next.

TEST THE PRINTER

After adding your printer, test it by printing a document. For example:

1. Click the **iPhoto** icon on the Dock. iPhoto will open.

2. Select a picture you want to print.

3. Click **Print** on the toolbar at the bottom of the window. The Print sheet will open (see Figure 6-13).

4. On the left side, click **Standard** for the style of print.

5. Ensure the correct printer is selected in the Printer drop-down list.

6. Click **Print**. iPhoto sends the page to the printer, which prints it.

IDENTIFY A DEFAULT PRINTER

If you add two or more printers, you need to tell Mac OS X which is the default. To do so:

1. Open the menu and click **System Preferences** to open the System Preferences window.

2. Click **Print & Fax** to display the Print & Fax pane.

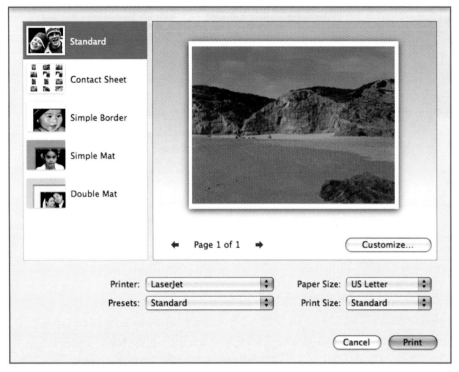

3. Click the **Default Printer** drop-down list, and then choose the printer you want. If you want Mac OS X to use the last printer you used, click **Last Printer Used**.

4. Open the **System Preferences** menu and click **Quit System Preferences** to close System Preferences.

Print to a PDF File

Instead of printing a document on a piece of paper, you can print it to a file in Adobe's Portable Document Format (PDF) format. There are two primary reasons for printing to a PDF:

- To create a file that you can take to a remote printer. For example, you might create a PDF file so that you can have it printed on a specialist item, such as a T-shirt, at a service bureau.

- To create a file that you can send to someone who is using a different computer platform (for example, Windows or Linux) and be confident that they will be able to not only open the document but also see it exactly as you laid it out.

Because Adobe has promoted the PDF format vigorously and has produced and distributed free versions of its Acrobat Reader software for all significant computer operating systems, almost anybody with an Internet connection should be able to open a PDF and view it as its creator intended.

To create a PDF file:

1. Open the file from which you want to create the PDF file in the appropriate application. For example, open **TextEdit** and open a document.

2. Open the **File** menu and choose **Print** to display the Print dialog box.

3. Choose printing options.

4. Click the **PDF** button, and then click **Save As PDF**. The application displays the Save dialog box (shown on the left in the upcoming Figure 6-15).

5. Enter the filename and choose the folder in which to save it.

CAUTION

The PDF format is widely used for sending high-resolution print jobs to professional printers. The PDF files that Mac OS X creates aren't suitable for this purpose: they're optimized to look great onscreen and to provide impressively high quality in a relatively compact file size, but they don't provide the super-high resolution that professional applications, such as Adobe Acrobat, deliver.

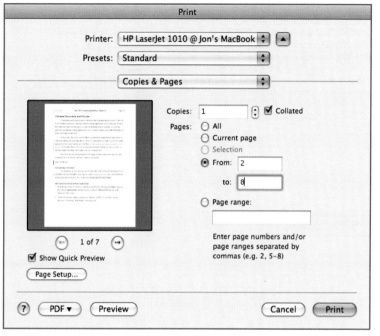

Figure 6-14: *The Print dialog box in Microsoft Word is similar to those in many applications.*

6. Enter other information, such as the title, author, subject, and keywords, as needed.

7. If you want to secure the PDF file against unauthorized opening, copying, or printing, click the **Security Options** button. In the PDF Security Options dialog box (shown on the right in Figure 6-15), choose the options you want, and then click **OK**.

8. Click **Save**.

9. Open the application's application menu and click the **Quit** command to close the application. For example, open the **TextEdit** menu and click **Quit TextEdit** to close TextEdit.

Print Web Pages

Printing web pages works the same way as printing from any other application:

1. Click the **Safari** icon on the Dock. Safari will open.

2. Browse to the page you want to print.

Figure 6-15: *The Save dialog box (left) lets you create a PDF file of a document. You can choose the folder in which to save the PDF. To lock the PDF file with passwords so that unauthorized users cannot modify it, click the Security Options button and set security options in the PDF Security Options dialog box (right).*

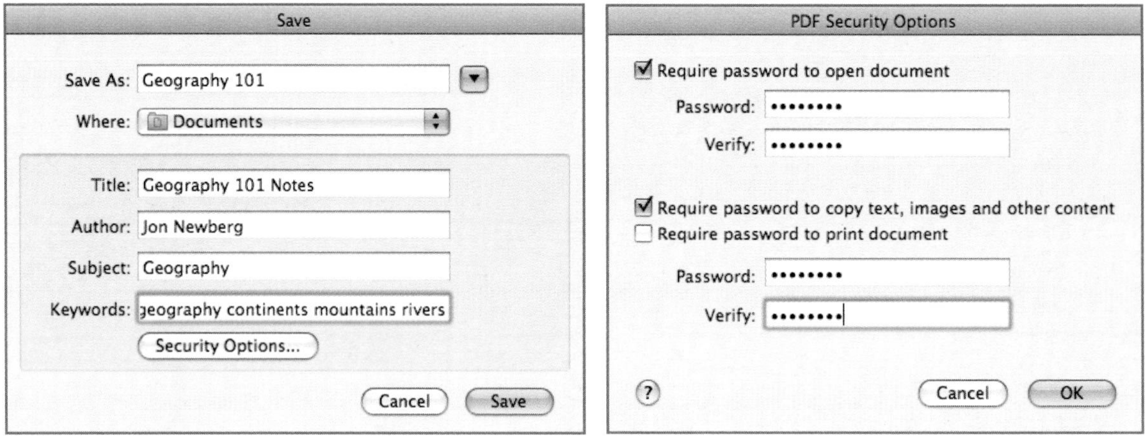

Save

Save As: Geography 101

Where: Documents

Title: Geography 101 Notes

Author: Jon Newberg

Subject: Geography

Keywords: geography continents mountains rivers

Security Options...

Cancel   Save

PDF Security Options

☑ Require password to open document

Password: ••••••••

Verify: ••••••••

☑ Require password to copy text, images and other content

☐ Require password to print document

Password: ••••••••

Verify: ••••••••

Cancel   OK

NOTE

On most operating systems, to create a PDF file, you need a custom application such as Adobe Acrobat—which, unlike Acrobat Reader, Adobe doesn't distribute for free. Apple, however, has built native support for PDF into Mac OS X, so you can create PDFs automatically from any application that supports printing.

NOTE

You cannot change the order in which print jobs are being printed by putting on hold the document that is currently being printed. You must either complete printing the current document or cancel it. You can, however, use hold to get around intermediate documents that are not currently printing. For example, suppose you want to print the third document in the queue immediately, but the first document is currently printing. You must either let the first document finish printing or cancel it. You can then pause the second document before it starts printing, and the third document will begin printing when the first document is out of the way.

3. Open the **File** menu, click **Print**, and select the printer and other options in the Print dialog box.

4. Click **Print** to print the page.

5. Open the **Safari** menu and click **Quit Safari** to close Safari.

Control Printing

When a document is printed, the *print job* (the information required to print the document) is sent to the printer, where it is stored temporarily in a holding area called the *print queue*. When the printer is ready, it starts to print the document. If further documents are sent to the printer while the printer is busy printing, they wait their turn in the print queue. You can control the print process by manipulating jobs in the print queue. For example, you might need to place a lower-priority print job on hold in order to get an urgent print job printed.

To control printing:

1. Open the menu and click **System Preferences** to open the System Preferences window.

2. Click **Print & Fax** to display the Print & Fax pane.

MANAGING FONTS

A *font* is a set of characters with the same design, size, weight, and style. A font is a member of a *typeface* family, all with the same design. The font 12-point Arial bold italic is a member of the Arial typeface family with a 12-point size, bold weight, and italic style.

Mac OS X comes with a good variety of fonts, which you can manipulate by using the Font Book application (see Figure 6-16).

1. Activate the **Finder**.
2. Click **Applications** in the Sidebar.
3. Double-click **Font Book**.

ADD FONTS

1. Activate the **Finder**.
2. Open the folder that contains the font file.
3. Double-click the font file. Mac OS X will open or activate Font Book, which will display a window showing the font.
4. Click **Install Font**. Font Book installs the font to your User font folder and displays its main window.
5. If you want the font to be available to all users of your Mac rather than just to you, drag the font to the **Computer** item under the All Fonts collection.

DISABLE FONTS

If you want to reduce temporarily the number of fonts you have available without deleting the fonts, you can *disable* the fonts:

1. Open **Font Book** and click the font in the Font list.
2. Click the **Disable** button (the button with the selected check box) at the bottom of the Font list. Font Book will display a confirmation dialog box.

Continued . . .

3. In the Printers list, click the printer you want to control. The main part of the sheet displays the printer's status:

- **Printing** indicates that the printer is currently printing.
- **Stopped** indicates that the printer has been stopped (for example, by an administrator).
- **Idle** indicates that the printer is functional but waiting for print jobs to be sent to it.

4. Click the **Open Print Queue** button. A window bearing the name of the printer will open.

5. To quickly stop all print jobs on the printer, click the **Pause Printer** button on the toolbar. (You might want to do this if you notice a problem with the printer.) You can then restart the jobs by clicking the **Resume Printer** button on the toolbar.

6. If necessary, you can control individual print jobs:

- To delete a job, select it and click **Delete**.
- To put a job on hold so that other jobs can print, select the job and click **Hold**.

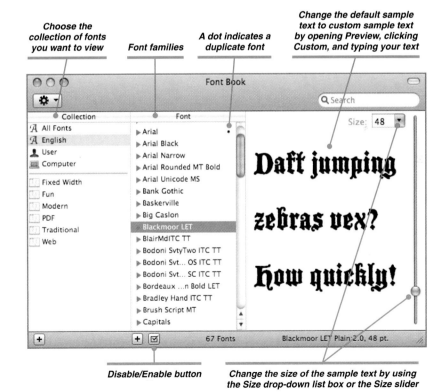

Figure 6-16: **Font Book lets you examine fonts, add them, and delete them.**

UICKSTEPS

MANAGING FONTS (Continued)

3. Click **Disable**. Font Book will disable the font and will display Off next to it in the Font list.

To enable a font you've disabled, click the font in the Font list and click the **Enable** button (the button with the cleared check box) at the bottom of the Font list.

DELETE FONTS

To delete a font that you are no longer using:

1. Open **Font Book** and click the font in the Font list.

2. Press DELETE. Font Book will display a confirmation dialog box.

3. Click **Remove**. Font Book will delete the font file.

If the font you have deleted is used in a document, that document will look strange if you open it. Apply a different font in place of the font you have deleted.

USE FONTS

Fonts are used or specified from within an application. In Microsoft Word, for example, you can select one or more characters and then open the Font menu or the Font dialog box (open the **Format** menu and click **Font**) to apply the font you want. Other applications use similar features to let you choose fonts. In many applications, the font list shows what the fonts look like instead of simply showing their names in a standard system font.

NOTE

If you've configured your Mac to go to sleep (see "Set Energy Saver Options" in Chapter 5), select the **Wake When The Modem Detects A Ring** check box on the Options tab of the Energy Saver pane if you want your Mac to be able to wake from sleep to receive faxes.

- To resume a job you've put on hold, select it and click **Resume**.
- To stop all jobs (for example, so that you can change the printer's cartridge), click **Pause Printer**.
- To restart all jobs after stopping them, click **Resume Printer**.

7. Close the printer window by clicking its application menu and choosing the **Quit** command. For example, on the HP LaserJet 1010 shown, open the **HP LaserJet 1010** menu and click the **Quit HP LaserJet 1010** command.

8. Open the **System Preferences** menu and click **Quit System Preferences** to close System Preferences.

Fax Documents and Pictures

Mac OS X includes the capability to send and receive faxes as part of the printing function and allows an application, such as Microsoft Word, to "print" to a remote fax by specifying the fax function as a printer. This service requires that your Mac have a fax modem and that you have connected a phone line to it.

Set Up Faxing

To set up faxing, you must first add your fax as a "printer," and then configure it:

1. Open the ⌘ menu and click **System Preferences** to open the System Preferences window.

2. Click **Print & Fax** to display the Print & Fax pane.

3. Click the **+** button. Mac OS X will open the printer setup utility window.

4. Click the **Fax** button to display the Fax pane.

5. In the Printer Name list, select your fax modem—for example, **Internal Modem**.

6. If you want, change the name and location to make them more descriptive.

7. Click **Add**. Mac OS X will close the printer setup utility window and add the modem to the Printers list on the Print & Fax pane.

8. Click the modem's entry in the Printer's list to display the controls for it (see Figure 6-17).

9. If you want to share the fax with other Macs on the network, select the **Share This Fax** check box.

10. If you plan to send faxes from this Mac, enter your fax number in the Fax Number text box.

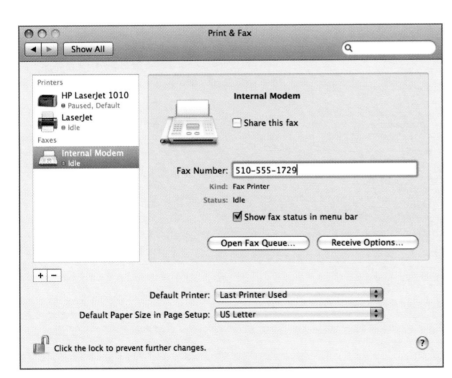

11. If you want to have a fax icon in the menu bar (which is usually helpful), select the **Show Fax Status In Menu Bar** check box.

12. To receive faxes on this Mac:

- Click the **Receive Options** button. Mac OS X will open the Receive Options sheet, shown here.
- Select the **Receive Faxes On This Computer** check box. Mac OS X enables the When A Fax Arrives group of controls.
- Specify the number of rings in the **Answer After** text box.
- To save the faxes you receive to a folder, select the **Save To** check box and specify the folder in the drop-down list box. The default location is the Shared Faxes folder—the Faxes folder in the /Users/Shared folder.

- To have Mac OS X automatically print each fax received, select the **Print To** check box and specify the printer in the drop-down list box. This setting makes your Mac behave like a fax machine for incoming faxes.
- To have Mac OS X automatically e-mail the faxes to an e-mail address, select the **Email To** check box and specify the address in the text box. Mac OS X saves the faxes as PDF files, which helps to keep them relatively compact.

13. Click **OK** to close the Receive Options sheet.

14. Open the **System Preferences** menu and click **Quit System Preferences** to close System Preferences.

Send a Fax

To send a fax:

1. Open the document you want to send. For example, open a word processing document in Microsoft Word.

2. Open the **File** menu and click **Print** to display the Print dialog box.

3. Click the **Printer** drop-down list, and then choose the modem's entry. Click **Fax** in the bottom toolbar. Mac OS X displays the Print sheet for faxing (see Figure 6-18).

4. In the To box, type either the fax number to use or the name of a person in your address book. If there's a match in your address book, Mac OS X completes the name and enters the fax number automatically. Add the dialing prefix if necessary.

*Figure 6-17: **After adding your modem to the Printers list, configure the fax properties on the Print & Fax pane.***

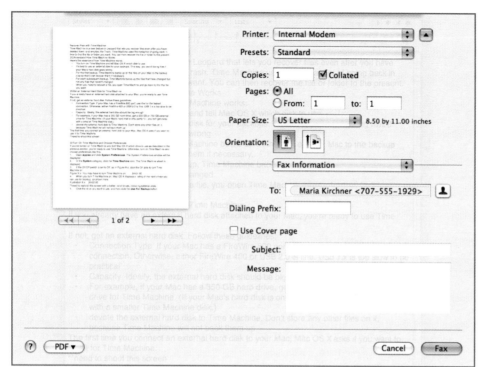

*Figure 6-18: **Specify the recipient of the fax in the Fax Information section of the Print sheet.***

5. To use a cover page, select the **Use Cover Page** check box. Type the subject in the Subject text box and the message in the Message text box. If you need to create a new paragraph in the Message text box, press **OPTION+RETURN** rather than **RETURN** on its own (pressing **RETURN** on its own "clicks" the Fax button).

6. Click the **Fax** button. Mac OS X removes the Print sheet from the display and starts the fax job in the background.

7. To see what's happening, click the modem's button on the Dock (the name reflects the name you've given the modem—for example, Internal Modem). Mac OS X displays the modem window, which shows the progress of the fax. If necessary, you can use the buttons on the toolbar to hold, resume, stop, and restart your faxes.

8. After the fax has been sent, open the application menu and click the **Quit** command to close the modem window.

Receive a Fax

When you've set up your Mac to receive faxes for you, it handles the process automatically, answering the phone after the number of rings you've specified, receiving the fax, and saving it, e-mailing it, or printing it, depending on your choices on the Print & Fax pane in System Preferences.

After receiving a fax, you can view it as follows:

1. Activate the **Finder**.
2. Open the folder in which you chose to save faxes—for example, the Shared Faxes folder.
3. Double-click the fax file. Mac OS X will open the file in Preview.
4. If the fax has multiple pages, click **Page Up** or **Page Down** on the toolbar to navigate from page to page.
5. Open the **Preview** menu and click **Quit Preview** to close Preview.

TIP

To create a long message in your cover page, type the message in another application, such as TextEdit, copy it, and paste it into the Message text box.

How to...

Chapter 7
Working with Multimedia

Multimedia is the combination of audio and video. Mac OS X makes it easy not only to play audio and watch video or DVDs on your Mac but also to record and edit audio and video. With the applications in the iLife suite that is included with most Macs, you are well equipped to work with audio and video. You can even create your own CDs and DVDs by using Mac OS X and the iLife applications. This chapter looks first at sound by itself, and then at video (which normally includes sound).

Work with Audio

Audio is sound. Mac OS X works with and uses sound in several ways, the simplest being to alert you to various events, such as when you dump an object into the Trash, receive an e-mail message, or try to take an action that isn't possible. "Change Sounds," in Chapter 2, shows you how to customize the use of sound for these purposes.

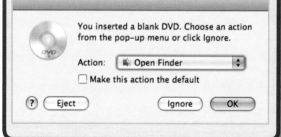

QUICKSTEPS

CONFIGURING ACTIONS FOR CDS AND DVDS

To choose what Mac OS X does when you insert a CD or DVD:

1. Open the menu and click **System Preferences** to open the System Preferences window.

2. Click **CDs & DVDs**. The CDs & DVDs pane will be displayed (see Figure 7-1).

3. Use the five drop-down lists to choose what Mac OS X should do when you insert a blank CD, a blank DVD (if your Mac has a DVD burner), a music (audio) CD, a picture CD, or a video DVD.

4. Open the **System Preferences** menu and click **Quit System Preferences** to close System Preferences.

The When You Insert A Blank CD and the When You Insert A Blank DVD drop-down lists offer an Ask What To Do choice that makes Mac OS X display a dialog box asking you what to do (as in the example here). From this dialog box, you can choose which action to take with the CD or DVD.

The second use of sound is to entertain or inform you—allowing you to listen to music or lectures from CDs, Internet radio, or another Internet site. This use of sound is the subject of this section, together with the third use of sound—to express yourself audibly.

Play CDs

Playing an audio CD is as easy as inserting the CD in an optical drive. When you insert an audio CD, Mac OS X takes the default action for CDs, which is to launch iTunes (or activate iTunes if it's already running) so that you can play the CD or copy it to your Mac's hard disk. You can change Mac OS X's default actions for optical discs; see the "Configuring Actions for CDs and DVDs" QuickSteps on this page.

How you insert a CD or DVD depends on the optical drive in your Mac:

- In a slot-loading optical drive (such as those used on most Macs), you simply slide the CD or DVD into the slot until the mechanism grabs the disc and pulls it in the rest of the way.

- In a tray-style drive (such as those used on eMacs and some older iMacs), press the **EJECT** button on your keyboard or (in some Macs) the **Eject** button on or near the drive itself to make the tray appear, put the disc in the tray, and then press the same button to close the drive.

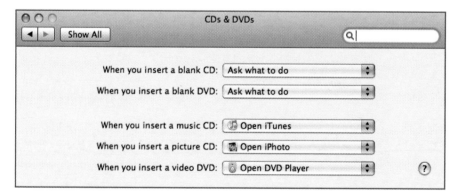

Figure 7-1: **Use the CDs & DVDs pane in System Preferences to tell Mac OS X how to handle CDs and DVDs you insert.**

After you insert the CD, iTunes will automatically look it up in the Gracenote CDDB (CD Database) if your Mac is connected to the Internet. If the CD is widely distributed, iTunes will display a listing of tracks on the CD along with their titles and artists.

Would you like to import the CD "High Time" into your iTunes library?

☐ Do not ask me again

No   Yes

If iTunes prompts you to import the CD into your iTunes Library, as shown here, click **No** if you just want to play the CD. Click **Yes** if you want to import the CD's songs as digital audio files (see "Copy CDs to Your Mac," later in this chapter, for details).

iTunes will select all tracks to play (the check marks on the left of the song titles). Click the **Play** button in the upper left and the first track will begin to play. On your screen iTunes should look like Figure 7-2, shown with a CD inserted and playing.

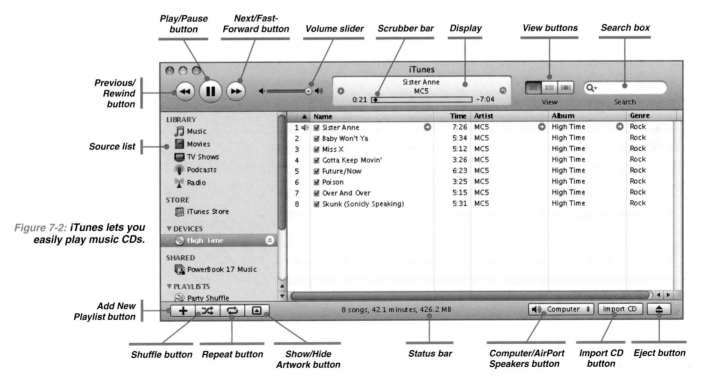

Figure 7-2: *iTunes lets you easily play music CDs.*

You can easily control iTunes:

- Click the **Play/Pause** button to start the selected song playing and to pause play (Play becomes Pause after you start playing a track).

- Click the **Previous/Rewind** button to move to the previous song. Click **Previous/Rewind** and hold down the mouse button to rewind through the current song.

- Click the **Next/Fast Forward** button to move to the next song. Click **Next/Fast Forward** and hold down the mouse button to fast forward through the current song.

- The **Scrubber bar** displays a diamond that you can drag to move quickly through the current song.

- Drag the **Volume slider** to change the volume iTunes is outputting. (The volume control on your Mac controls the overall volume output.)

- The **Search** box allows you to type the criterion for selecting just the songs that you want to play.

- The **View** buttons allow you to switch among viewing the songs as a list (the left button), by albums (the middle button), or using Cover Flow (the right button). For a CD, you can use only the list view.

- The **Source list** allows you to switch among different sources of music and video: your Library (which contains Music, Movies, Radio, and other items), Store (Apple's online media store), Devices (such as your CD drive), Shared (music and video shared by other iTunes users on your network), and Playlists (which includes iTunes built-in playlists, such as Party Shuffle, and playlists you've created).

- Click the **Add New Playlist** button to create a new playlist, or OPTION+click the **Add New Playlist** button to create a new Smart Playlist, one that selects songs that match criteria you set.

- Click the **Import CD** button to copy the CD in your optical drive to your Mac. (See "Copy CDs to Your Mac," later in this chapter.)

- Click the **Shuffle** button to randomize the order of the songs. Click it again to restore the normal order.

- Click the **Repeat** button once to repeat all the songs in the current CD or playlist. Click it again to repeat just the current song. Click it a third time to turn off repeating.

- Click the **Show/Hide Artwork** button to toggle the display of the picture or pictures associated with the current song or other item. Songs and videos you download from the iTunes Store typically have artwork. For other items, you can add your own pictures manually. Click the Artwork pane to display the artwork in a separate window, as shown here.

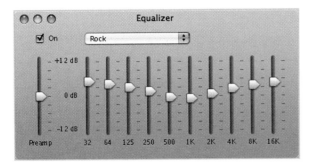

- If you have an AirPort (Apple's wireless network device) that can play audio, you can click the **Computer/AirPort Speakers** button to direct the audio to your Mac's speakers, the speakers connected to the AirPort, or both.

- Open the **Window** menu and choose **Equalizer** to display the Equalizer window (shown here), in which you can apply both preset equalizations and custom equalizations to change the sound of the songs. Click the **Close** button (the red button) to close the Equalizer window when you've finished using it.

- Open the **View** menu and choose **Turn On Visualizer** to display visualizations, automatically generated graphics to accompany the music. To control the size of the visualizations, open the **iTunes** menu, click **Preferences**, click the **Advanced** tab, and click the **General** subtab. In the **Visualizer Size** drop-down list, choose **Small, Medium,** or **Large**. Select the **Display Visualizer Full Screen** to display your chosen size of visualizations full screen. Click **OK** to close the Preferences dialog box. To turn off visualizations, open the **View** menu and choose **Turn On Visualizer**.

Control the Volume

You can control your Mac's audio volume in several ways:

- Turn the physical volume control on your receiver or speakers.

- If your Mac's keyboard includes volume keys, press them to change your Mac's overall output volume. For example, on most laptop Macs, you can press **F3** (without pressing the **FN** key) to mute the sound, press **F4** to reduce the volume, and press **F5** to increase the volume. You will find similar keys on many Apple desktop keyboards.

- Click the **Volume** icon on the menu bar and drag the slider to set the volume.

- Drag the **Volume** slider in iTunes itself. Changing the volume in iTunes changes iTunes' output volume but doesn't change your Mac's overall output volume. So if, for example, you turn the volume in iTunes up to its maximum setting but your Mac's overall output volume is set very low, the music output will be low.

- Drag the **Output Volume** slider in the Sound pane in System Preferences (open the menu and click **System Preferences**, and then click **Sound**). This is the least convenient method of changing the volume unless System Preferences is already open.

Listen to Radio Stations

iTunes' Radio feature lets you listen to radio stations around the world that broadcast their programs across the Internet, either in addition to conventional broadcasting or instead of it. Internet radio works best over a broadband connection that delivers at least 128 Kbps (see Chapter 4 for details of Internet connections), but you can also listen to lower-quality radio broadcasts over a dial-up connection.

To use iTunes' Radio feature:

1. Click the **iTunes** icon on the Dock to open iTunes (if it's not running) or activate it (if it is running).
2. Click **Radio** in the Library category in the Source list. iTunes will display the available categories of radio stations.
3. Click the **right-pointing gray triangle** on a category to expand it (see Figure 7-3). Click the resulting **down-pointing gray triangle** to collapse the category again.
4. Double-click a radio station to start it playing.
5. Click the **Stop** button to stop the radio stream.

You can also open MP3 audio streams that iTunes doesn't list. To do so, open the **Advanced** menu and click **Open Stream**, type or paste the stream address in the Open Stream dialog box (shown here), and click **OK**. Add the stream to a playlist so that you can access it more easily next time.

Buy Music from the iTunes Store

If you're planning to buy music online for use with the Mac, your first stop should be Apple's iTunes Store, which is tightly integrated with iTunes. The iTunes Store offers a wide selection of music—more than five million songs at this writing—for around $0.99 a song.

**Stop button,
click to stop the
radio stream**

**Click to expand
a collapsed
category**

**Click to collapse
an expanded
category**

**Stream column, lists the
categories and identifies
the radio station by name**

**Bit Rate column, shows the
data-transmission speeds
of the radio stations**

**Add New
Playlist button**

Figure 7-3: iTunes' Radio feature enables you to listen to Internet radio stations.

To use the iTunes Store, click **iTunes Store** in the Store category of the Source list.
iTunes will access the iTunes Store and display its home page. From here, you
can browse or search to find songs that interest you. Double-click a song to play
a 30-second preview of it and help you decide whether you want to buy it.

Before buying an item, you'll need to create an Apple account or an AOL screen
name and specify the details of the credit card with which you want to pay.
When you click a Buy link, the iTunes Store walks you through the process of
creating an account.

LOCATING MUSIC ON THE INTERNET

Apart from Internet radio and the iTunes Store, there are many other sources of music on the Internet. Some locations, such as the GarageBand.com site (www .garageband.com), provide legal audio files for free download; others provide illegal audio files for free download; and an ever-increasing number of online music stores sell legal audio files for download.

At this writing, online music stores of interest to iTunes users include:

- **eMusic** (www.emusic.com) offers more than two million songs for download in the MP3 format. eMusic focuses on subscription plans rather than individual sales.

- **Amazon.com** (www.amazon.com) has a download service that offers songs in the MP3 format. Amazon sells songs individually, but you can buy as many as you like.

- **RealPlayer Music Store** (www.real.com/musicstore) sells files in the AAC format that iTunes prefers. However, you must use the RealPlayer software (which is free) to access the RealPlayer Music Store.

- **Amie Street** (http://amiestreet.com) sells songs offered by artists directly (without record companies). Each song's pricing depends on its popularity: it starts off being free, and the price rises as more people download it.

Copy CDs to Your Mac

iTunes gives you the ability to copy songs from your CDs to your hard disk, to build and manage a library of music, and to copy this material to recordable CDs or recordable DVDs. To copy from a CD:

1. Insert the CD from which you want to copy songs. Mac OS X will automatically open iTunes. If iTunes doesn't automatically display the CD's contents, click the CD's entry in the Source list.

2. If you have an Internet connection, iTunes will automatically connect to the Gracenote CDDB (CD Database) music server and download the CD's details, such as song titles and artist information.

3. iTunes will automatically select the check boxes for each song on the CD. Clear the check boxes for any songs you don't want to copy.

CAUTION

Other major online music stores, such as Napster (www.napster.com), sell files in the protected WMA format. You cannot use these files with iTunes unless you use a Windows computer to burn them to CD, and then copy the CD using iTunes. (This maneuver, while effective, is not only always tedious but also usually illegal.)

TIP

Copying songs from a CD to digital files on your computer is usually much quicker than playing the CD in real time. Although iTunes stores the songs in a compressed format, the song files take up a lot of space on your hard disk if you create a large music library. You can adjust the settings by opening the **iTunes** menu, clicking **Preferences**, and then clicking the **Importing** button to display the Importing pane. iTunes' default settings are to use the AAC (Advanced Audio Coding) format and the 128 Kbps bitrate, which delivers high audio quality at an acceptably compact file size. For higher audio quality, choose a higher bitrate; for smaller files, choose a lower bitrate. For the highest quality audio in compressed files, use the Apple Lossless Encoder format.

Figure 7-4: iTunes lets you copy songs from CDs to compressed files on your hard disk so that you can build a music library.

4. Click **Import CD** in the lower-right corner. iTunes will start copying the audio from the CD (see Figure 7-4) and storing it in compressed audio files on your hard disk.

5. When the copying is finished, click the **Eject** button to eject the CD.

6. If you've finished using iTunes, open the **iTunes** menu and click **Quit iTunes** to close it.

NOTE

The material on most CDs and DVDs is owned and copyrighted by some combination of the composer, the artist, the producer, and/or the publisher. Copyright law prohibits using the copyrighted material in ways that are not beneficial to the copyright holders, including giving or selling the content without giving or selling the original CD or DVD itself. iTunes provides the ability to copy copyrighted material to your hard disk and then to a recordable optical disc or a portable player (such as an iPod) with the understanding that the copy is solely for your own personal use and that you will not sell or give away copies.

CAUTION

To prevent people from violating copyright law, some CDs (and most DVDs) are protected to make copying difficult. Such CDs typically carry a warning such as "Copy Protected," or a notice such as "Will *not* play on PC or Mac." Don't put such CDs in your Mac, because it may be unable to eject them. Even if the copy protection doesn't work and your Mac can copy the CD, it's illegal to do so because of provisions in the Digital Millennium Copyright Act (DMCA).

TIP

When playing a playlist, you can randomize the order of the songs by clicking the **Shuffle** button once.

TIP

You can also create a *smart playlist*—a playlist that automatically selects its own contents based on criteria you set. Open the **File** menu, click **New Smart Playlist**, and then work in the Smart Playlist dialog box. You can create one or more conditions to match, set a limit on the number of songs, and choose whether to use live updating to automatically update the playlist as your Library changes.

Organize Music

Once you have copied several CDs and have, perhaps, downloaded other songs to your hard disk, you will want to organize them. iTunes' Library feature helps by automatically indexing the songs you add to your Music Library. To view your Music Library, click Library in the Source list.

The easiest way to browse through your Music Library is to use the Browser panes at the top of the window (see Figure 7-5). You can toggle the display of the Browser panes by clicking the Browse button (shown here) in the lower-right corner when the Library is displayed.

Browser panes, click the artist or album you want to display

View buttons

Figure 7-5: **The Library in iTunes provides a way to manage the songs and other items on your Mac.**

Add New Playlist button

Browse button

You can also combine songs into a new playlist so that you can play songs from different CDs in your preferred order. To create a new playlist:

1. Click the **Add New Playlist** button. iTunes will add a new entry in the Source list and display an edit box around it.

2. Type the name for the playlist and press **RETURN**.

3. Browse to each desired song in turn, and then drag it to the playlist.

4. Click the playlist to display its contents.

5. If you want, drag the songs into a different order.

6. Click the first song, and then click the **Play** button to start playing the playlist.

Make an Audio CD

Once you have created a playlist (see the previous section), you can burn it to a writable or rewritable CD or to a DVD. You can create either an audio CD—one that you can play in most CD players—or an MP3 CD, a CD that contains only MP3 files and that will play only in a computer CD drive or an MP3 CD player. You can also create a data CD or data DVD to back up your music in case your Mac's hard drive gets corrupted or stops working.

To create an audio CD:

1. In the Source list, click the playlist you want to burn to CD.

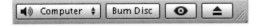

2. Click the **Burn Disc** button in the lower-right corner of the iTunes window.

3. iTunes will prompt you to insert a disc.

4. Insert a blank CD. iTunes will prompt you to click Burn Disc.

5. Click **Burn Disc**. iTunes will burn the CD and will select it in the Source list.

6. Click **Eject** to eject the CD.

The resulting CD should be playable in most music CD players and all computer CD drives.

NOTE

The iPhone follows a similar setup procedure to the iPod, but you must also activate the iPhone with AT&T before you can use the iPhone. You carry out activation using iTunes.

Copy Music to an iPod or iPhone

If you have an iPod or iPhone, you can synchronize its contents automatically with those of your Library. By doing so, you can put your entire Library on your iPod or iPhone so that you can listen to the music or watch the videos anytime or anywhere. If your Library is too large to fit on your iPod or iPhone, you can put selected playlists or selected items on the iPod or iPhone.

The first time you connect your iPod to your Mac via the supplied USB cable, the iPod Setup Assistant will be displayed. Type the name for your iPod in the The Name Of My iPod Is text box, select the **Automatically Sync Songs And Videos To My iPod** check box and the **Automatically Sync Photos To My iPod** check box if you want to use automatic updating, and then click **OK**.

Mac OS X will then launch iTunes and will update your iPod automatically (see Figure 7-6). When iTunes displays the message, "iPod Update Is Complete," click the **Eject** button to "eject" the iPod. You can then unplug the iPod from your Mac and start using it.

iPod's or iPhone's entry in Source list, click to display the device's contents and control screens

Eject button

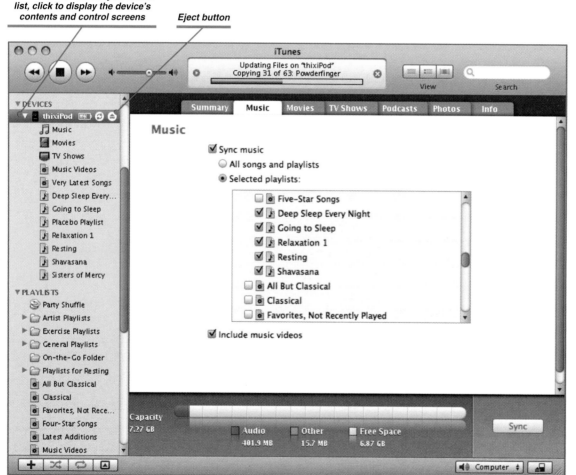

Figure 7-6: You can copy your Library automatically to an iPod or iPhone so that you can take your songs, videos, and other items with you.

TIP

For more information on GarageBand, see *How to Do Everything with GarageBand* (McGraw-Hill) or visit Apple's GarageBand site (www.apple.com/ilife/garageband/).

Compose Your Own Music with GarageBand

If you have iLife, you can use the GarageBand application (see Figure 7-7) to compose your own original music. You can:

- Use prerecorded loops to build tracks quickly
- Play software instruments by using a MIDI (musical) keyboard that you attach to your Mac via USB

Figure 7-7: *GarageBand lets you compose original music by using prerecorded loops and recording your own performances.*

- Record physical instruments that you plug into your Mac or that you record via microphones plugged into your Mac
- Mix your music to professional standards and export it to iTunes

Work with Video

Mac OS X lets you play video from a DVD using the DVD Player application or from a file by using QuickTime Player or iTunes. Mac OS X also allows you to capture and edit videos from a DV camcorder using iMovie. This section provides a brief introduction to these topics.

Play DVDs

Playing DVDs is as easy as playing CDs: simply insert a DVD in your Mac's DVD drive, and Mac OS X will open DVD Player and start the DVD playing automatically.

Use the Controller (shown here in the configuration in which it appears when you're running DVD Player full screen) to control the playback as you would use a remote control. To change the size of the video window, open the **View** menu and click **Half Size, Normal Size, Maximum Size, Fit To Screen**, or **Enter Full Screen**.

Record and Edit Video with iMovie

If you have a digital video camcorder, you will probably want to use iMovie (one of the applications in the iLife suite) to record video from your camcorder to your Mac so that you can manipulate it and create movies with it.

To record and edit video with iMovie, follow these general steps:

1. Open iMovie. Click the **iMovie** icon on the Dock. (If your Dock doesn't contain an iMovie icon, activate the **Finder**, open the **Go** menu, click **Applications**, and then double-click the **iMovie** icon.)

2. Create a movie project. In iMovie's opening dialog box, click the **Create A New Project** button. Specify the filename, location, and video format for the project in the Create Project dialog box, and then click **Create**.

QUICKSTEPS

WATCHING VIDEO FILES WITH QUICKTIME PLAYER

If you have video as a computer file rather than on a DVD, you can watch it by using QuickTime Player, which is included with Mac OS X:

1. Activate the **Finder.**

2. Open the **Go** menu and click **Applications**. Mac OS X will open a Finder window showing the contents of the Applications folder.

3. Double-click the **QuickTime Player** icon. A QuickTime Player window will open.

4. Open the **File** menu and click **Open File**. Use the Open dialog box to select the file you want to play, and then click **Open.**

5. Use the play controls at the bottom of the QuickTime Player window (see Figure 7-8) to control playback. To change the window size, open the **View** menu and use one of the size commands: Half Size, Actual Size, Double Size, Fit To Screen, or Enter Full Screen.

6. When you have finished watching, open the **QuickTime Player** menu and choose **Quit QuickTime Player** to close QuickTime Player.

TIP

Mac OS X automatically associates most types of video file with QuickTime Player, so you can also open a video file by double-clicking it in a Finder window.

3. Import video. Connect your DV camcorder to your Mac via the FireWire cable, and then turn your DV camcorder on. iMovie will automatically detect it and switch from Edit mode to Camera mode. You will see a blue screen saying "Camera Connected." Click the Import button to import the video. iMovie will import the video, playing it on the monitor and breaking the video into separate clips at the breaks in the timecode on the tape.

4. Review and trim your video clips. Double-click a clip in the Clips area to view it. Use the controls to trim the clips to length—for example, cutting out the boring parts and mistakes.

5. Arrange clips into a movie. Drag a clip to the clip viewer to make it part of the movie.

6. Add transitions and effects. iMovie provides audio effects, video effects, transitions, and titles, which can add visual excitement and a professional look to your movie.

7. Share the movie. When you've finished and saved the movie, use the options on the Share menu to share it with others. For example, you can send it to other people via e-mail, put it on your iWeb site, or burn it to DVD.

*Figure 7-8: **QuickTime Player can play back many types of video files.***

Create a DVD with iDVD

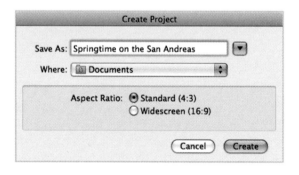

iDVD, one of the applications included in iLife, lets you create DVD projects and (provided your Mac has a DVD burner such as a SuperDrive) burn them to DVD. If your Mac doesn't have a DVD burner, you can create a DVD project on it and then transfer it to another Mac for burning.

To create a DVD project, follow these general instructions:

1. Click the **iDVD** icon on the Dock. (If your Dock doesn't contain an iDVD icon, activate the **Finder**, open the **Go** menu, click **Applications**, and then double-click the **iDVD** icon.) iDVD will display its opening screen.

2. Click the icon for the project type you want to create or open:

   - **Create A New Project** Click this button to create a new iDVD project that gives you full rein for customization. You can add your own content to the project, either from existing files or by importing it directly from a DV camcorder, and arrange it as you like. In the Create Project dialog box (shown here), name your project, choose the folder in which to store it, choose between **Standard** and **Widescreen** aspect ratios, and then click **Create**.

   - **Open An Existing Project** Click this button to open an iDVD project you've previously created and on which you now want to resume work. In the Open dialog box that appears, click the project, and then click **Open**.

   - **Magic iDVD** Click this button to use the Magic iDVD feature to create a DVD from one or more existing movie files (either in iDVD or on a hard drive). After you've chosen the movie files, and photos if you want to include them, iDVD does most of the hard work for you.

   - **OneStep DVD** Click this button to capture video from your DV camcorder and burn it to a DVD without editing it. Normally, you'll want to do this only when you have finished content on your DV camcorder—for example, if you're using your DV camcorder to transfer already edited footage from one computer or device to your Mac. Otherwise, you'll usually be better advised to edit your digital video footage in iMovie before burning it to DVD.

3. If you're creating a new iDVD, choose a theme for it:

- When creating a new project, drag the theme from the right panel to the main area of the window (see Figure 7-9). Then click the **Buttons** button in the lower-right corner of the iDVD window and choose the style of buttons to use for the DVD.

- When creating a Magic iDVD, click the theme in the Choose A Theme list box (see Figure 7-10).

4. Add content to your project:

- If you're creating a new project, add content to your project by clicking the **Media** button in the lower-right corner of the iDVD window, and then using the panel to drag movies, photos, and audio to the drop zones marked in the main area of

Add button   Show The DVD Map button   Preview DVD Playback button

Figure 7-9: When creating a new iDVD project, add a theme to it. Next, click the Buttons button, and then choose the style of buttons you want.

the window. Click the **Show The DVD Map** button to view a map of the DVD's layout. Click the **Add** button to add a submenu, movie, or slideshow to the DVD.

- If you're creating a Magic iDVD, use the Audio tab, Photos tab, and Movies tab on the right side of the interface to drag movies to the **Drop Movies Here** boxes and photos and audio to the **Drop Photos Here** boxes (see Figure 7-10). Drop audio on a box to add it to the slideshow of the photos you've dropped. When you've finished, click the **Create Project** button to create the project.

5. Click the **Preview DVD Playback** button to preview the DVD. Go back and make any changes that are needed.

6. Click the **Burn** button, insert a recordable DVD when instructed, and follow the prompts to burn it.

*Figure 7-10: **The Magic iDVD feature of iDVD provides a simplified interface that lets you create a DVD easily with few decisions.***

Chapter 8
Controlling Security

Controlling computer security is a complex subject because of the many different aspects that need protection. In this chapter, you'll see how to control who can use a particular Mac, control what a user can do, monitor users via parental controls, protect data stored on the Mac, and protect your Mac from attacks from malefactors across the Internet. You'll also learn how to transfer user accounts from another Mac or another volume.

Control Who Is a User

Controlling who is a user of a Mac means to identify the users to the Mac, giving users a secure way of logging in to the Mac while preventing others from using it. This is the process of adding and managing users and passwords.

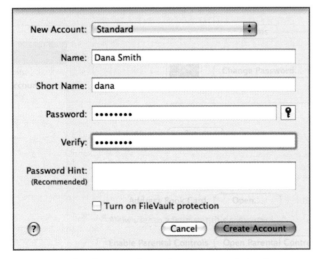

Figure 8-1: **The first step in setting up a user is to choose the account type, name the account, and set a password. You can also choose whether to turn on FileVault (see the discussion later in this chapter).**

Set Up a User

If you have multiple people using a single Mac, the best protection is to set up separate user accounts that require each user to sign on. To set up a user account, follow these general steps. For some account types, you will then need to take further steps, as explained later in this chapter.

1. While logged on as an administrator, open the menu and click **System Preferences** to open the System Preferences window.

2. Click **Accounts**. The Accounts pane will be displayed.

3. If the lower-left corner shows the closed-lock icon and the message "Click the lock to make changes," click the lock, type your user account name in the authentication dialog box that appears, type your user account password, and then click **OK**.

4. Click the + button in the lower-left corner. Mac OS X will open a sheet for creating a new user account (see Figure 8-1).

5. In the **New Account** drop-down list, choose the account type: Administrator, Standard, Managed With Parental Controls, or Sharing Only. See the "Understanding User Accounts" QuickSteps for details on the account types.

6. Type the user's full name in the Name text box and press **TAB**. Mac OS X will enter a lowercased version of the name, without spaces or punctuation, in the Short Name text box.

7. Change the short name as needed, but leave it in lowercase and without spaces or punctuation, and then press **TAB**.

8. Type the password to be used for the new account in the Password and Verify text boxes.

9. If the user will need a password hint, type one in the Password Hint text box. A password hint compromises the Mac's security, so it's best not to create a hint.

10. If necessary, choose further options for the user. For example, when setting up a Managed With Parental Controls user, follow the instructions in "Use Parental Controls to Limit What a User Can Do," next.

11. Open the **System Preferences** menu and click **Quit System Preferences** to close System Preferences.

UNDERSTANDING USER ACCOUNTS

To help you control security on your Mac, Mac OS X offers four kinds of user accounts: Administrator, Standard, Managed With Parental Controls, and Sharing Only.

ADMINISTRATOR ACCOUNTS

Administrator accounts are for users who manage a Mac. Administrators can:

- Install new applications in the Applications folder (so that they're available to all users)

- Create, delete, and modify user accounts

- Access, change, or even delete other users' files

- Unlock other users' files encrypted with FileVault (discussed later in this chapter)

- Change all settings in System Preferences (Standard users can change only some settings)

Every Mac must have at least one Administrator account. Mac OS X automatically makes the account used to install the OS an Administrator account—so if you installed Mac OS X, you will have an Administrator account.

STANDARD ACCOUNTS

Standard accounts are the next grade down after Administrator accounts. A Standard user can:

- Create and manipulate files and folders in his or her Home folder and its subfolders, but not in other folders

- Change some settings in System Preferences, but not major settings such as Startup Disk (which controls the disk your Mac starts from), Network, or Energy Saver

Continued . . .

NOTE

If your Mac is set to use Automatic Login (logging in your user account automatically on bootup), Mac OS X prompts you to turn it off when you create another user account. Normally, you'll want to click the **Turn Off Automatic Login** button so that each user must actively log in before they can use the Mac.

Automatic login is turned on. Do you want to turn it off?

If automatic login remains on, you must log out to allow this user to log in to their own account. The computer will automatically log in as user "jon" after a restart or shutdown.

(Turn Off Automatic Login)   (Keep Automatic Login)

Use Parental Controls to Limit What a User Can Do

In Mac OS X, the main way of controlling what a user can do is by assigning the user the appropriate type of account. As explained in the "Understanding User Accounts" QuickSteps in this chapter, Administrator users can take any action on a Mac, and Standard users essentially have freedom within their own user accounts.

For a user who might be irresponsible, you may need to implement restrictions. You can do so by setting up a Managed With Parental Controls account. For a user who finds the standard Mac OS X interface too complex, you can set the account to use Simple Finder, a stripped-down version of the Finder.

To control what a Managed With Parental Controls account can do:

1. With System Preferences open, click the **Accounts** icon, and then click the account name in the left list. (If you've just created the user account, the account will already be selected.)

2. Select the **Enable Parental Controls** check box.

UNDERSTANDING USER ACCOUNTS

(Continued)

MANAGED WITH PARENTAL CONTROLS ACCOUNTS

If a Standard account gives a user too much freedom, you can give the user a Managed With Parental Controls account, for which you can specify the applications a user can run or the actions he or she can take. In a Managed account, you can also apply a stripped-down version of the Finder called Simple Finder.

SHARING ONLY ACCOUNTS

A Sharing Only account lets the user access your Mac remotely to share items such as files. The user is not allowed to log on directly at the Mac.

MATCH ACCOUNT TYPE TO USER

Before creating a user account, consider what the user will need to be able to do:

- If the user will manage the computer, create an Administrator account.

- If the user must be restricted from taking particular actions, create a Managed account.

- If the user (for example, a child) will benefit from having fewer choices available, create a Managed account and apply the Simple Finder.

- Otherwise, create a Standard account.

If in doubt, err on the side of caution when creating accounts. You can change an account from one type to another if you need to.

3. Click the **Open Parental Controls** button to display the Parental Controls pane.

4. In the left list box, click the user name to display the Parental Controls.

5. On the System tab (see Figure 8-2), choose systemwide settings:

- Select the **Use Simple Finder** check box if you want to apply the Simple Finder.

*Figure 8-2: **Mac OS X's Parental Controls enable you to set limits on the actions a user can take—for example, for their own protection.***

- Select the **Only Allow Selected Applications** check box if you want to prevent the user from running certain applications. In the Check The Applications To Allow list box, clear the check box for each application you don't want the user to use.

- Select or clear the **Can Administer Printers** check box, the **Can Burn CDs And DVDs** check box, the **Can Change Password** check box, and the **Can Modify The Dock** check box as appropriate. (The Can Modify The Dock check box is unavailable if you select the Use Simple Finder check box.)

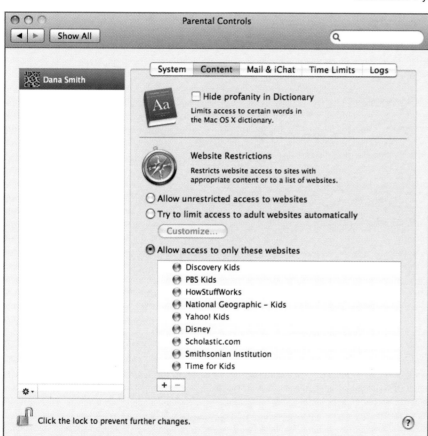

6. Click the **Content** tab (shown in Figure 8-3 with choices made), and then choose content restrictions:

- Select the **Hide Profanity In Dictionary** check box if you want to bowdlerize the dictionary.

- To allow the user free rein on the Web, select the **Allow Unrestricted Access To Websites** option button.

- If you want to prevent the user from accessing adult web sites, select the **Try To Limit Access To Adult Websites Automatically** option button. Click the **Customize** button, and use the resulting sheet to build a list of allowed sites and blocked sites. When you've finished, click **OK**.

- If you want to limit the user to accessing only certain sites, select the **Allow Access To Only These Websites** option button. Click the + button to add to the list a site you've bookmarked in Safari or a folder of bookmarks. To remove a site, click it, and then click the – button.

7. Click the **Mail & iChat** tab (shown in Figure 8-4 with choices made), and then choose whether to limit these two applications:

- Select the **Limit Mail** check box, the **Limit iChat** check box, or both, as appropriate.

- If you select either check box, build a list of allowed e-mail and instant messaging contacts in the **Only Allow Emailing And Instant Messaging With** list box. To add a contact, click the + button and use the resulting sheet. To remove a contact, click the contact, and then click the – button.

*Figure 8-3: **Parental Controls also let you hide profanity in the Dictionary and restrict the web sites the user can access.***

Figure 8-4: *You can restrict a Managed With Parental Controls user to an approved list of e-mail and instant messaging contacts.*

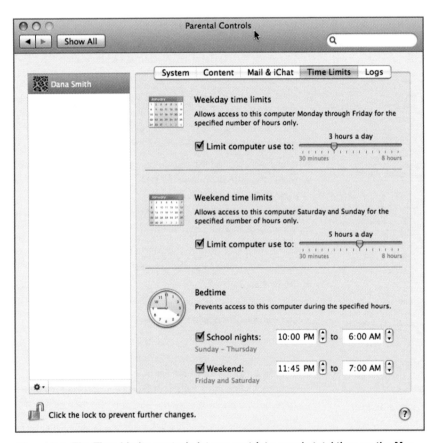

Figure 8-5: *The Time Limits controls let you restrict a user's total time on the Mac and prevent them from using it when they should be asleep.*

- If you selected the **Limit Mail** check box, select the **Send Permission Requests To** check box if you want Mac OS X to alert you (or another administrator) when the user tries to contact someone who's not on the list. Type your e-mail address (or that of the administrator for the Mac) in the text box.

8. Click the **Time Limits** tab (see Figure 8-5), and then set time limits:

   - In the Weekday Time Limits area, select the **Limit Computer Use To** check box, and then drag the slider to the number of hours you want to permit.

   - In the Weekend Time Limits area, select the **Limit Computer Use To** check box, and then drag the slider to the appropriate number of hours.

   - In the **Bedtime** area, select the **School Nights** check box and the **Weekend** check box, and then use the boxes to specify the times when the user may not use the Mac.

9. Click the **lock icon** to secure the changes you've made.

10. Open the **System Preferences** menu and click **Quit System Preferences** to close System Preferences.

Review the Parental Control Logs

Mac OS X makes the Parental Controls as set-and-forget as possible, but to monitor the managed users effectively you should periodically view the lists of web sites the users have visited (or tried to visit), the applications they've tried to use, and the contacts they've been chatting with. To do so, you use the Logs tab of the Parental Controls sheet:

1. Open the menu, click **System Preferences**, and then click **Parental Controls** to open the Parental Controls pane.

Figure 8-6: ***After setting Parental Controls, you should review the logs to see if you need to adjust the settings or the user's attitude toward them.***

2. In the left list box, click the name of the user whose logs you want to review.

3. Click the **Logs** tab to display its contents. Figure 8-6 shows an example.

4. In the **Log Collections** list box, select the log you want to view: Websites Visited, Websites Blocked, Applications, or iChat.

5. In the **Show Activity For** drop-down list, choose the period you want: Today, One Week, One Month, Three Months, Six Months, One Year, or All.

6. In the **Group By** drop-down list, select the way you want Mac OS X to group the data. One choice is **Date**. The other depends on the log you chose: Website, Application, or Contact.

7. In the log, click a sideways triangle next to an item you want to expand. You can then click an item and use the buttons that Mac OS X displays to control what the user can do with it. For example:

   - For a blocked web site, click the **Allow** button to let the user access this site in future. Click the **Open** button to open the site in Safari so that you can evaluate it before deciding.

   - For an allowed web site or application, click the **Restrict** button if you want to prevent the user from viewing or using it again. Click the **Open** button if you want to open the web site or application.

8. When you've finished checking the logs, open the **System Preferences** menu and click **Quit System Preferences** to close System Preferences.

Decide Whether to Use the Simple Finder for a User Account

As you saw earlier in this chapter, you can force a Managed With Parental Controls user to use the Simple Finder. Figure 8-7 shows the Simple Finder. These are the main differences from the regular Finder:

- The Dock contains a minimal set of icons: a Finder icon, a My Applications icon for displaying a window containing those applications to which the user has been granted access, a My Documents icon for displaying the user's documents, a Shared icon for displaying the contents of the /Users/Shared/ folder, and a Trash icon. Icons for applications the user opens also appear.

- The user can open only one Finder window at a time and cannot resize that window.

- The menu contains only the Force Quit, Sleep, and Log Out commands.

Customize a User Account

Each user account can be unique, with the user's own Dock, desktop, color scheme, and screen saver.

CHANGE THE PICTURE

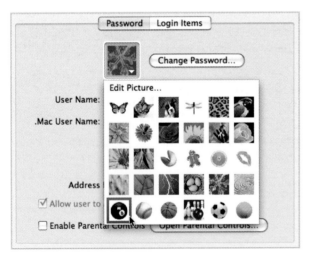

Most users like to choose a custom picture to represent their account instead of using the default picture that Mac OS X assigns when you create the account. The user's picture appears on the login screen (providing your Mac is using the login screen that lists user names), as the default picture in iChat, and on the user's entry in Address Book.

To change the picture:

1. Open the menu and click **System Preferences** to open the System Preferences window.

2. Click **Accounts**. The Accounts pane will be displayed.

3. In the list box on the left, click your account.

4. On the Password tab, click the picture button (the button that is the picture) to display a panel of pictures, as shown here.

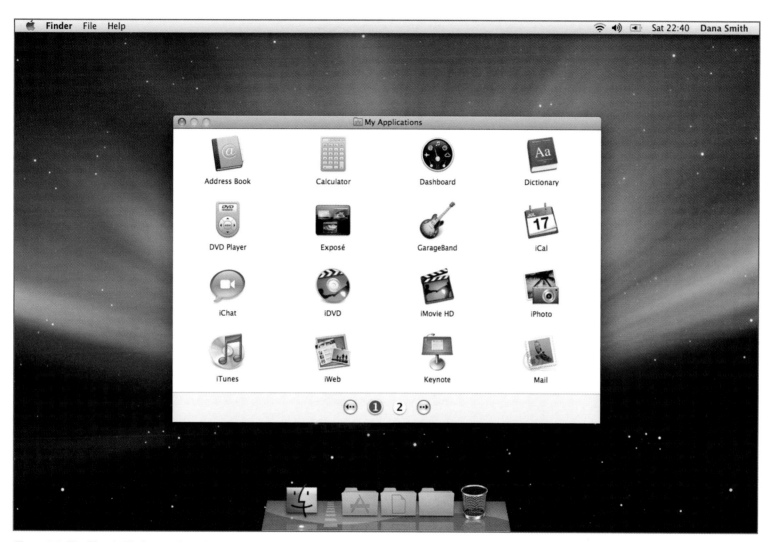

Figure 8-7: *The Simple Finder provides the user with a reduced set of windows and applications.*

QUICKSTEPS

RESETTING A LOST PASSWORD

If you forget the password for an Administrator account, you can reset it by using the Reset Password utility on the Mac OS X DVD:

1. Insert the Mac OS X DVD in your Mac's optical drive.

2. Restart your Mac. Hold down **C** at the startup sound to boot from the DVD. Mac OS X will start the installation process automatically.

3. On the initial screen, choose your language (for example, **English**), and then click the **arrow button** to proceed.

4. When the Welcome screen appears, open the **Utilities** menu and click **Reset Password**.

5. In the Select The Mac OS X Disk Which Contains A Password To Reset list, click the drive Mac OS X is installed on—for example, **Macintosh HD**.

6. Click the **Select A User Of This Volume To Reset Their Password** drop-down list, and then click the user's name.

7. Type the new password for the user in the two text boxes.

8. Optionally, type a password hint. (This is seldom a good idea.)

Continued . . .

5. Specify the picture to use:

   - Click the desired picture in the panel.

   - Click **Edit Picture** to display the Images window (shown in Figure 8-8), which shows the current picture. Change the picture by dragging another picture to the window or clicking **Choose** and using the resulting dialog box to select the picture, or connect a webcam and then click the **Take Video Snapshot** button to take a picture using it. Drag the slider to change the size of the picture as needed, and drag in the central square to make it display the part of the picture you want. Then click **Set**.

6. Open the **System Preferences** menu and click **Quit System Preferences** to close System Preferences.

*Figure 8-8: **You can change the picture for your account by using the Images window from the Accounts pane.***

CHOOSE STARTUP ITEMS

All users can choose applications, files, and folders to open automatically on login by using the Login Items tab of the Accounts pane in System Preferences. See "Start Applications Automatically When You Log In" in Chapter 5 for details.

CHANGE USER TYPE

Sometimes you may need to change a user's account type to give that user further privileges or to reduce the scope of actions permitted. To change user type:

1. Open the menu and click **System Preferences** to open the System Preferences window.

2. Click **Accounts**. The Accounts pane will be displayed.

3. In the list box on the left, click the user's name.

4. To change a Standard user or a Managed With Parental Controls user to an Administrator user, select the **Allow User To Administer The Computer** check box. For a Managed With Parental Controls user, Mac OS X warns you that Parental Controls will be turned off and asks you to confirm the decision.

RESETTING A LOST PASSWORD

(Continued)

9. Click **Save**. Mac OS X will display the Password Saved dialog box.

10. Click **OK**.

11. Open the **Reset Password** menu and click **Quit Reset Password**.

12. Open the **Mac OS X Installer** menu and click **Quit Mac OS X Installer**. Mac OS X will display the Are You Sure You Want To Quit The Installer? dialog box.

13. Click **Quit**. Mac OS X will restart from the hard disk.

14. Log in using your new password.

15. Drag the Mac OS X installation DVD to the **Trash** to eject it.

If your Mac restarts from the CD and displays the Installer again, choose your language, then open the **Mac OS X Installer** menu and click **Quit Mac OS X Installer**. In the Are You Sure You Want To Quit The Installer? dialog box, click **Startup Disk**. In the Choose Startup Disk dialog box, click the entry for your hard disk (for example, **Mac OS X, 10.5.1 On Macintosh HD**), and then click **Restart**.

NOTE

You can disable automatic login on the Security pane in System Preferences. See "Choose Tight Security Settings," later in this chapter.

5. To change an Administrator user to a Standard user, clear the **Allow User To Administer The Computer** check box.

6. To change a Standard user to a Managed With Parental Controls user, select the **Enable Parental Controls** check box, click the **Open Parental Controls** button, and then choose the appropriate controls. See "Use Parental Controls to Limit What a User Can Do," earlier in this chapter, for details.

7. To change a Managed With Parental Controls user to a Standard user, clear the **Enable Parental Controls** check box.

8. Open the **System Preferences** menu and click **Quit System Preferences** to close System Preferences.

Change Mac OS X's Login Procedure

To change Mac OS X's login procedure:

1. Open the menu and click **System Preferences** to open the System Preferences window.

2. Click **Accounts**. The Accounts pane will be displayed.

3. Click **Login Options** at the bottom of the left list box. The login options are displayed (see Figure 8-9).

4. Choose login options:

   - Choose whether to log in a specified user account automatically. In the **Automatic Login** drop-down list, choose the account you want to log in automatically. Choose **Disabled** if you want Mac OS X to display the login screen so that a user can log in manually. Automatic login is useful when you're the only person who uses your Mac, but it makes security experts turn pale with horror.

   - Choose how to display the login screen by selecting the **List of Users** option button or the **Name And Password** option button in the Display Login Window As area. Prompting for the user name is better for security, but is usually less convenient—especially if someone forgets their login name.

   - Select the **Show The Restart, Sleep, And Shut Down Buttons** check box if you want to display these controls on the login screen. Security is the usual reason for removing these controls: with default settings, a malefactor can restart your Mac from the login screen, reboot from a FireWire hard disk he or she plugs in, and circumvent your security.

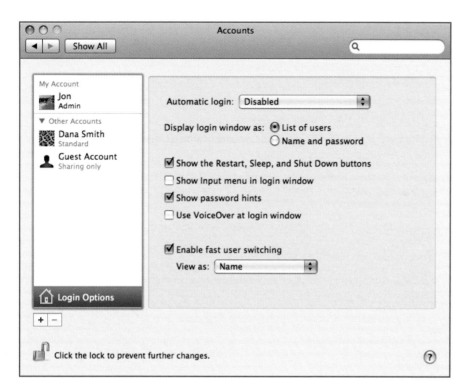

Figure 8-9: *Use the login options to control how Mac OS X handles login.*

- Select the **Show Input Menu In Login Window** check box if you want users to be able to switch among input methods in the login window—for example, to switch between US keyboard layout and Dvorak keyboard layout.

- Select the **Show Password Hints** check box if you want Mac OS X to display a user's password hint (assuming they have one) if the user enters their password wrong three times in succession.

- Select the **Use VoiceOver At Login Window** check box if you want Mac OS X to use the VoiceOver (voice announcement) feature in the login window. This is useful if some users of your Mac need help accessing the Mac.

- Select the **Enable Fast User Switching** check box if you want to use Fast User Switching. If you select this check box, choose **Name**, **Short Name**, or **Icon** in the **View As** drop-down list. (See the next section for details on Fast User Switching.)

5. Open the **System Preferences** menu and click **Quit System Preferences** to close System Preferences.

Turn On Fast User Switching

Fast User Switching enables two or more users to be logged into the same Mac at the same time. Only one user's session (windows and applications utilized by that user) is displayed at a time; any other user's session is hidden until he or she switches to it.

Fast User Switching enables you to let someone else use your Mac for a while without requiring that you shut down all your applications and log out. In a family or small-office situation, Fast User Switching can save a lot of logging on and off and reduce aggravation. Fast User Switching also has several disadvantages:

- Fast User Switching increases demands on your Mac, particularly its RAM. If your Mac is short of RAM, using Fast User Switching will probably make applications run more slowly.

NOTE

You can't change a user account when that user is logged in with another session (on a Mac that uses Fast User Switching).

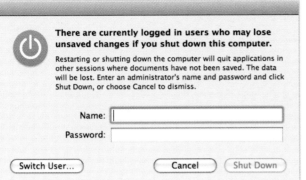

There are currently logged in users who may lose unsaved changes if you shut down this computer.

Restarting or shutting down the computer will quit applications in other sessions where documents have not been saved. The data will be lost. Enter an administrator's name and password and click Shut Down, or choose Cancel to dismiss.

Name: [   ]

Password: [   ]

(Switch User...)   (Cancel) (Shut Down)

- While most applications run happily in separate user sessions at the same time, others have problems. Mac OS X is smart about handling iTunes and DVD Player, but other audio and video players may cause problems.

- If a user shuts down your Mac, you can lose unsaved changes in your applications. Mac OS X reduces the chance of loss by warning the user that other user sessions are active and providing the choice of either canceling the shutdown or supplying an administrator name and password before effecting the shutdown, as shown at left.

To turn on Fast User Switching:

1. Select the **Enable Fast User Switching** check box on the Login Options screen (shown earlier in Figure 8-9).

2. Mac OS X displays a warning to make sure that you understand how Fast User Switching works.

Warning
This feature will allow other users to stay logged in and continue running software in the background while you're using this computer. This feature should only be enabled if you trust the other users of this computer.

(Cancel) (OK)

3. Click **OK**. Mac OS X displays the current user's name (yours at the moment) next to the Spotlight icon at the right end of the menu bar.

You can then use Fast User Switching to switch quickly from one user account to another by clicking the user name at the right end of the menu bar, clicking the name of the desired user, and entering the password if prompted for one.

Protect Stored Data

You can protect your stored data by locking files against accidental deletion, by encrypting your Home folder using FileVault, by choosing tight security settings in System Preferences, and by locking your Mac with a firmware password.

QUICKSTEPS

SHARING FILES AND FOLDERS WITH OTHER LOCAL USERS

Mac OS X provides two easy ways to share files and folders with other users of your Mac:

- Place the files and folders in your ~/Public folder, the Public folder inside your Home folder. (To display your Home folder, activate the **Finder**, open the **Go** menu, and click **Home**.) Others can then view the files and folders but not change them.

- Place the files and folders in the /Users/Shared/ folder, which all users can access and change. Similarly, you can access and change the files that other users have placed in this folder.

ACCESSING THE SHARED FOLDER

To access the /Users/Shared/ folder:

1. Click the **Finder** icon on the Dock. A Finder window will be displayed.

2. Click **Macintosh HD** in the Sidebar. The contents of your Mac's hard disk will be displayed.

3. Open the **Users** item by clicking it or double-clicking it (depending on the Finder view you're using). The contents of the Users folder will be displayed.

4. Open the **Shared** item by clicking it or double-clicking it.

GAINING EASY ACCESS TO THE SHARED FOLDER

To provide easy access to the /Users/Shared/ folder via the Finder, drag the **Shared** folder to the Sidebar to create an entry for it there.

Continued . . .

Lock Files Against Accidental Deletion

To protect a file or folder against being accidentally deleted, you can lock it. To do so:

1. Activate the **Finder** and navigate to the folder or file.
2. Click the folder or file to select it.
3. Open the **File** menu and click **Get Info**. The Info window for the folder or file is displayed.
4. Select the **Locked** check box.
5. Click the **Close** button (the red button) to close the Info window.

When you've locked a folder or file, Mac OS X displays a lock icon at the lower-left corner of its icon. If you try to delete a locked folder or file, Mac OS X displays an error dialog box (as shown below). Click **Stop** if you want to keep the item; click **Continue** if you want to delete it.

Encrypt Your Home Folder with FileVault

When security is vital, you can use the FileVault feature to automatically encrypt all the objects stored in your Home folder using a security protocol that's extremely hard to crack.

DECIDE WHETHER TO USE FILEVAULT

FileVault is turned off by default because, while it's extremely secure, if you forget your password, you can lose access to your own files—permanently. Before turning on FileVault, evaluate whether you really need it. If your Mac

CAUTION

Once you encrypt your files with FileVault, the *only* way to retrieve your files is with the password. If you forget or lose your password, you have effectively lost your files.

CAUTION

When you log in, FileVault decrypts your files and folders so that you can use them. This means that if anyone else can access your Mac while you are logged in, your files have no protection. It also means that using Fast User Switching can be dangerous: if you leave your user session open while another user works on the Mac, your files remain decrypted (because you are still logged in, although another user is active) and are vulnerable to attack. For this reason, it's best to turn off Fast User Switching if you use FileVault.

contains secret or sensitive information, and if the risk of losing your Mac is even moderately high (for example, because you have a laptop Mac), consider FileVault. If your Mac contains only mundane information, FileVault probably isn't worth the effort.

Apart from the potential for losing your files, FileVault's other main disadvantage is that it slows down your Mac a little. If your Mac is slow anyway, you may find FileVault's added burden a problem. If your Mac normally runs quickly, you may not notice the difference.

FileVault also prevents you from recovering individual files and folders using Time Machine. Instead, you can restore your entire system if necessary. This limitation too may deter you from using FileVault.

When you log in, FileVault decrypts your folders and files so that you can use them. When you log out (or shut down your Mac), FileVault encrypts the folders and files again. This means that FileVault ensures that your folders and files are secure only when you're logged out. If you leave your Mac running without logging out, anyone can access your folders and files, because they have been decrypted using your credentials.

SET A MASTER PASSWORD FOR YOUR MAC

Before you turn on FileVault, you must create a master password for your Mac. The master password enables an administrator to turn off FileVault for any user of the Mac. So if a user who isn't an administrator forgets his or her FileVault password, the administrator can use the master password to rescue that user's files.

To set the master password:

1. Open the menu and click **System Preferences** to open the System Preferences window.
2. Click **Security**. The Security pane will be displayed.
3. Click the **FileVault** tab to display its contents (see Figure 8-10).

As with password hints for user accounts, creating a password hint to the master password reduces your security—but with all your Mac's files potentially at stake if users forget their FileVault passwords, you may feel that the risk a hint entails is warranted. If so, make the hint oblique enough that it helps only you, not anyone looking to break into your Mac.

If you're having difficulty thinking up a suitable password, click the button with the key icon, and then use the Password Assistant window. You can choose the type of password you want—for example, **Memorable** or **Letters & Numbers**—and see how high the password rates on the hard-to-break scale.

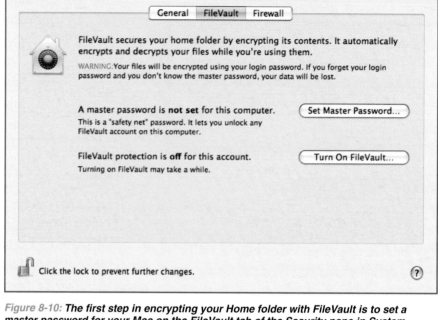

Figure 8-10: *The first step in encrypting your Home folder with FileVault is to set a master password for your Mac on the FileVault tab of the Security pane in System Preferences.*

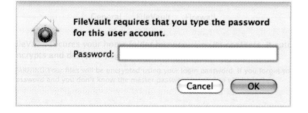

4. Click **Set Master Password**. Mac OS X will display the sheet shown in Figure 8-11.

5. Type the password in the Master Password text box and in the Verify text box, and enter a reminder in the Hint text box if you want to.

6. Click **OK**. Leave System Preferences open so that you can turn on FileVault.

TURN ON FILEVAULT

After setting the master password, you can turn on FileVault:

1. If any other user is logged in to your Mac using Fast User Switching, get them to log out.

2. Click **Turn On FileVault**. FileVault will prompt you for your password.

3. Type your password and click **OK**. FileVault will display a warning dialog box to ensure that you understand the consequences of what you're doing.

A master password must be created for this computer to provide a safety net for accounts with FileVault protection.

An administrator of this computer can use the master password to reset the password of any user on the computer. If you forget your password, you can reset the password to gain access to your home folder even if it's protected by FileVault. This provides protection for users who forget their login password.

Master Password: [   ] 🔑

Verify: [   ]

Hint: [   ]

Choose a password that is difficult to guess, yet based on something important to you so that you never forget it. Click the Help button for more information about choosing a good password.

(?)   (Cancel) (OK)

*Figure 8-11: **Set a master password for your Mac so that you can recover your files if you forget your account password.***

You are ready to turn off FileVault protection.

Once you turn off FileVault, you will be logged out and FileVault will decrypt your entire home folder. Depending on how much information you have, this could take a while. You will not be able to log in or use this computer until FileVault finishes.

(Cancel) (Turn Off FileVault)

4. Select the **Use Secure Erase** check box if you want Mac OS X always to erase files securely when you empty the Trash. Secure erase overwrites the files to make them unrecoverable, so it takes longer than regular deletion, but it is a good security measure.

5. Select the **Use Secure Virtual Memory** check box if you want Mac OS X to encrypt the hard-disk space it uses for virtual memory. This too is a good security measure, but it will make your Mac run somewhat more slowly.

6. Click **Turn On FileVault**. Mac OS X will log you out so that FileVault can encrypt your Home folder. You will see the FileVault screen and a progress readout while FileVault works.

7. When FileVault has finished encrypting your Home folder, Mac OS X will display the login screen. Log in as usual.

TURN OFF FILEVAULT

If you decide that FileVault doesn't suit you, turn it off:

1. Open the menu and click **System Preferences** to open the System Preferences window.

2. Click **Security**. The Security pane will be displayed.

3. Click the **FileVault** tab to display its contents.

4. Click **Turn Off FileVault**. FileVault will prompt you for your password.

5. Type your password and click **OK**. FileVault will display a confirmation message box.

6. Click **Turn Off FileVault**. Mac OS X will log you out so that FileVault can decrypt your Home folder. You'll see a FileVault screen during the decryption.

7. When FileVault has finished decrypting your Home folder, Mac OS X will display the login screen. Log in as usual.

Choose Tight Security Settings

The Security pane of System Preferences offers five options for tightening security on your Mac:

● Requiring a password when waking the Mac from sleep or when the screen saver is running

● Disabling automatic login

TIP

If you use a password for waking your computer from sleep or for interrupting the screen saver, configure your Mac to start the screen saver after a short interval of inactivity (or by using a hot corner) as discussed in "Pick a New Screen Saver" in Chapter 2, or configure it to go to sleep quickly (see "Set Energy Saver Options" in Chapter 5).

● Requiring a password to unlock secure system preferences

● Automatically logging out an inactive account

● Using secure virtual memory

To tighten your security settings:

1. Open the menu and click **System Preferences** to open the System Preferences window.

2. Click **Security**. The Security pane will be displayed.

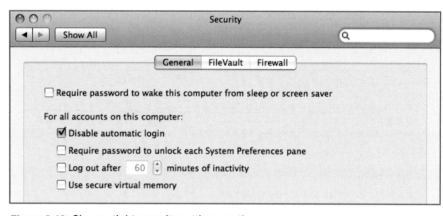

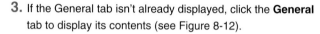

Figure 8-12: ***Choose tight security settings on the General tab of the Security pane in System Preferences.***

3. If the General tab isn't already displayed, click the **General** tab to display its contents (see Figure 8-12).

4. Select the **Require Password To Wake This Computer From Sleep Or Screen Saver** check box to make Mac OS X prompt for a password when anyone wakes it from sleep or interrupts the screen saver. Requiring the password delays your resuming work (or play) but is a good security measure.

5. Select the **Disable Automatic Login** check box if you want to prevent any account from logging in automatically.

6. Select the **Require Password To Unlock Each Secure System Preference** check box if you want to ensure that sensitive system preferences are kept locked.

7. Select the **Log Out After *NN* Minutes Of Inactivity** check box if you want Mac OS X to log each user out automatically after they leave the keyboard and mouse inactive for a specified length of time. The shorter length of time you set, the more security this setting offers.

8. Select the **Use Secure Virtual Memory** check box if you want Mac OS X to encrypt the hard-disk space it uses for virtual memory. This security measure protects you against more advanced threats than the others discussed here (against serious attackers rather than people casually accessing your Mac), but it will make your Mac run somewhat more slowly.

9. Open the **System Preferences** menu and click **Quit System Preferences** to close System Preferences.

CAUTION

A firmware password provides serious security, but if you forget your password, you're in serious trouble—you can't change the startup disk again. If you use a firmware password, make sure you don't forget it.

TIP

If you want to be able to use Firmware Password Utility without having the Mac OS X DVD present, copy Firmware Password Utility from the DVD to your Mac's Utilities folder (or another folder that you find more convenient).

Firmware Password Utility

The firmware password is used to prevent others from starting your computer with a different disk. This makes your computer even more secure.

☑ Require password to change firmware settings

Password: ●●●●●●●●●●●●●●●●
Type a password or phrase

Verify: ●●●●●●●●●●●●●●●●
Retype the password or phrase

Cancel   OK

Figure 8-13: **You can set a firmware password to prevent anyone else from starting your Mac using a different disk (such as a hard drive–based iPod or a FireWire disk), a CD, or DVD.**

Lock Your Mac with a Firmware Password

To prevent other users from using a FireWire disk or a CD or DVD to boot your Mac, you can protect it with a firmware password—a password required to start using the firmware (the permanently installed software) on your Mac.

To apply a firmware password:

1. Insert your Mac OS X installation DVD in your optical drive. A Finder window will open showing the DVD's contents.
2. Press ⌘+**SHIFT**+**G** to open a Go To The Folder box.
3. Type the path <u>Volumes/Mac OS X Install DVD/Applications/Utilities/</u> and then click **Go**. Mac OS X reveals the Applications folder and the Utilities folder, which were hidden, and displays the contents of the Utilities folder.
4. Double-click **Firmware Password Utility**. The first Firmware Password Utility window will be displayed.
5. Click **Change**. The Firmware Password Utility window shown in Figure 8-13 will be displayed.
6. Select the **Require Password To Change Firmware Settings** check box.
7. Type the password in the Password text box and the Verify text box.
8. Click **OK**. Mac OS X displays the authentication dialog box.
9. Type your password (the password for your Mac OS X account) and click **OK**. Firmware Password Utility will display a message box telling you that the settings were successfully saved and that they will take effect when you restart your Mac.
10. Open the **Firmware Password Utility** menu and click **Quit Firmware Password Utility** to close the application.
11. Restart your Mac (for example, open the menu and click **Restart**, and then click **Restart**).

After you apply the firmware password, when anyone tries to start your Mac from a disk other than your regular disk, Mac OS X will prompt for the firmware password.

To remove the firmware password:

1. Run Firmware Password Utility from the Mac OS X DVD as before. Alternatively, if you copied Firmware Password Utility to your hard disk, run it from there.
2. Clear the **Require Password To Change Firmware Settings** check box.

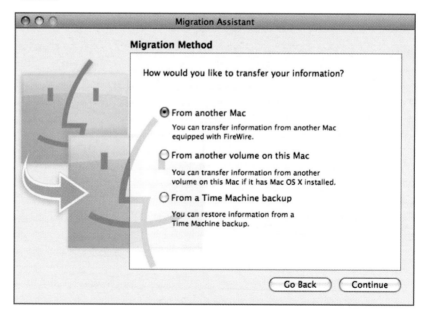

TIP

Mac OS X's firewall is usually worthwhile, but it can get in your way both in a local network and with Internet traffic. If, after turning on the firewall, you find that you are having network problems either locally or on the Internet, you may need to turn off the firewall again.

QUICKSTEPS

TRANSFERRING USER ACCOUNTS FROM ANOTHER MAC OR VOLUME

Mac OS X provides Migration Assistant for transferring user accounts from one Mac to another via a FireWire cable, from a hard drive, or from a Time Machine backup. To transfer an account, follow these steps:

1. Activate the **Finder**, open the **Go** menu and click **Utilities**, and then double-click the **Migration Assistant** item. The first screen of Migration Assistant will appear.

2. Click **Continue**. Migration Assistant displays the authentication dialog box.

3. Type your Administrator password, and then click **OK**. Migration Assistant will display the Migration Method screen (see Figure 8-14).

4. Choose the transfer means you want:

   • Select the **From Another Mac** option button if your user accounts are on another Mac—for example, your old Mac. Connect that Mac to this Mac via a FireWire cable.

Continued . . .

3. Authenticate yourself.

4. Open the **Firmware Password Utility** menu and click **Quit Firmware Password Utility** to close the application.

5. Restart your Mac (for example, open the menu and click **Restart**, and then click **Restart**).

Turn On the Firewall

Mac OS X includes a firewall that you can use to help prevent hackers from getting into your computer while you are online. If your Mac connects directly to the Internet, you should ensure that the firewall is turned on. If your Mac connects to the Internet through a shared Internet connection that already uses a firewall, you probably don't need to turn your firewall on. (For example, many Internet routers and Internet-sharing hardware devices include a firewall.)

1. Open the menu and click **System Preferences** to open the System Preferences window.

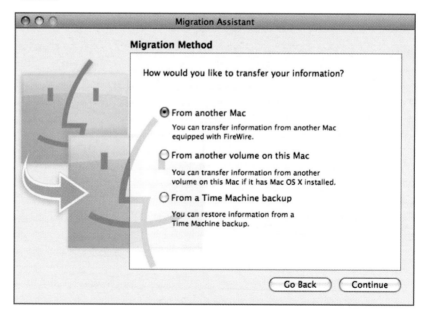

*Figure 8-14: **Migration Assistant lets you transfer one or more accounts from another Mac, from another volume on the same Mac, or from a Time Machine backup (useful after a hard-disk disaster).***

TRANSFERRING USER ACCOUNTS FROM ANOTHER MAC OR VOLUME

(Continued)

- Select the **From Another Volume On This Mac** option button if your user accounts are on another hard disk volume on the same Mac. For example, you may have installed Leopard on a different volume from Tiger, and now you're ready to transfer your Tiger accounts to Leopard.

- Select the **From A Time Machine Backup** option button if you're restoring the information from a backup you created using Time Machine.

5. Click the **Continue** button. Mac OS X will display the Select The System To Transfer screen.

6. Select the system or backup that contains the user accounts, and then click **Continue**. Migration Assistant will display the Select User Accounts To Transfer screen.

7. Clear the check box for each user account you don't want to transfer, and then click **Continue**. Migration Assistant displays the Select The Items To Transfer screen.

8. Select the **Applications** check box if you want to transfer the applications.

9. Select the **Files And Folders** check box if you want to transfer the user's files and folders. (You will usually want to do this.)

10. Click **Continue**. Mac OS X displays the Select Computer Settings To Transfer screen.

Continued . . .

2. Click the **Security** icon. The Security pane will be displayed.

3. Click the **Firewall** tab (see Figure 8-15).

4. Choose which incoming connections you want to allow through the firewall:

- Select the **Allow All Incoming Connections** option button if you want your Mac to allow all connections. This setting ensures that your Mac can respond to all requests but may expose it to threats.

- Select the **Allow Only Essential Services** option button if you want to allow only essential system services (such as remote login) that you've told your Mac to use. To allow or block another service, click the + button, use the resulting sheet to select the application or utility, and then click **Add**. In the entry that Mac OS X adds to the list box, choose **Allow Incoming Connections** (the default) or **Block Incoming Connections**, as appropriate. To remove a service, click it, and then click the – button.

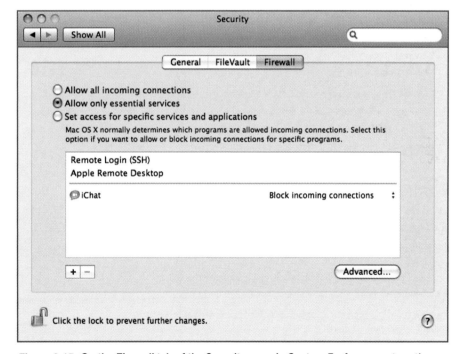

Figure 8-15: *On the Firewall tab of the Security pane in System Preferences, turn the firewall on and control the services that can poke holes through the firewall.*

QUICKSTEPS

TRANSFERRING USER ACCOUNTS FROM ANOTHER MAC OR VOLUME

(Continued)

11. Select the **Network Settings** check box if you want to transfer the accounts' network settings. (This is usually a good idea.)

12. Select the **Time Zone** check box if you want to transfer the accounts' time zone. (You may already have chosen the time on your new Mac or installation of Mac OS X.)

13. Select the **Sharing Settings** check box if you want to transfer the accounts' sharing settings. These can be useful, but you may prefer to take your move to a new Mac or installation of Mac OS X to streamline your sharing settings—especially if you're moving from Tiger to Leopard, which has more flexible settings.

14. Click **Transfer**. Migration Assistant transfers the files and settings, and then notifies you when it has finished.

NOTE

In Stealth mode, your Mac does not respond to any uninvited network traffic. This is a great way of protecting your Mac from unwanted attention, but it may also cause your Mac to turn away legitimate traffic as well as malevolent probing.

• Select the **Set Access For Specific Services And Applications** option button if you want to allow or block particular services or applications. To allow or block a service, click the + button, use the resulting sheet to select the application or utility, and then click **Add**. In the entry that Mac OS X adds to the list box, choose **Allow Incoming Connections** (the default) or **Block Incoming Connections**, as appropriate. To remove a service, click it, and then click the – button.

5. If you want to turn logging on or off or enable stealth mode, click **Advanced**. On the resulting sheet (shown here), select the **Enable Firewall Logging** check box or the **Enable Stealth Mode** check box, as appropriate. If you turn on logging, click **View Log** to open the log file to see its contents. Click **OK**.

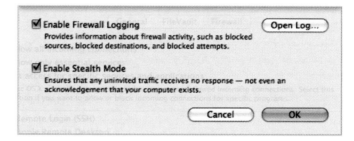

6. Open the **System Preferences** menu and click **Quit System Preferences** to close System Preferences.

Chapter 9
Setting Up Networking

Networking is the sharing of resources and information between two or more connected computers—at home, within an organization, or around the world. In this chapter, you will see how to connect to a local area network, or LAN, which is generally confined to a single residence, a building, or a section of a building.

Plan a Network

Mac OS X lets you connect two or more computers for many purposes:

- **Exchanging information**, such as sending a file from one computer to another
- **Communicating**, for example, sending e-mail among network users
- **Sharing information** by having common files accessed by network users
- **Sharing network resources**, such as printers and Internet connections

Networking includes both connecting computers to transfer information and the means of transferring information between the computers. This is the function of the networking hardware and software in your Mac and the protocols, or standards, they use.

Select a Type of Network

Today the majority of LANs use the *Ethernet* standard, which determines the type of network hardware and software needed by the network, and *TCP/IP* (Transmission Control Protocol/Internet Protocol), which determines how information is exchanged over the network. With this foundation, you can then choose between using a peer-to-peer LAN and a client/server LAN.

PEER-TO-PEER LANS

All computers in a *peer-to-peer LAN* are both servers and clients, which means they share in both providing and using resources. Any computer in the network may store information and provide resources, such as a printer, for the use of any other computer in the network.

Peer-to-peer networking is an easy first step to networking, as you can create such a network simply by joining computers together, as shown in Figure 9-1. You do not need to buy extra computers or make significant changes to the way an organization is using computers, yet you can share resources (such as the printer in Figure 9-1), transfer files and communications, and access shared information.

Peer-to-peer LANs tend to be used in smaller organizations that do not need to share a large central resource, such as a database, or to have a high degree of security or central control.

Each computer in a peer-to-peer LAN is autonomous and is often networked with other computers simply to transfer files and share expensive equipment or services (such as a fast Internet connection). Putting together a peer-to-peer LAN with Macs

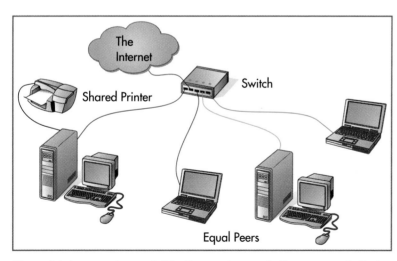

Figure 9-1: *In a peer-to-peer LAN, all computers are both servers and clients.*

is very easy and inexpensive: because all Macs have Ethernet networking built in, you need buy only the cables and the switch or router.

CLIENT/SERVER LANS

Each computer in a *client/server LAN* performs one of two distinct functions. Each is either a server or a client:

- *Servers* manage the network, store information to be shared on the network, and provide the shared resources to the network.

- *Clients*, or *workstations*, are the users of the network and are normally desktop or laptop computers.

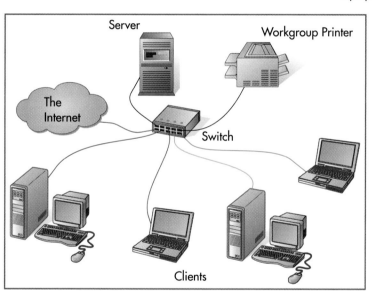

Figure 9-2: *In a client/server LAN, one or more computers are servers and the rest are clients.*

To create a network, the clients and server(s) are connected together, often with additional stand-alone network resources (such as printers), as shown in Figure 9-2.

The management functions provided by the server include network security, managing the permissions needed to implement security, communications among network users, and management of shared files on the network.

Servers generally are more capable than clients in terms of having more memory, faster (and possibly more) processors, larger (and maybe more) disk drives, and special data-storage peripherals, such as high-capacity, high-speed tape drives (for backing up large amounts of data). Servers generally are dedicated to their function and are normally not used for everyday client tasks, such as word processing, spreadsheets, or e-mail.

Clients generally are less capable than servers and, in some cases, may not even have a disk. Clients usually are normal desktop and laptop computers that perform the typical functions of those types of machines, in addition to being part of the network. Clients can also be "mini-servers" by sharing some or all of their disk drives or other resources. The principal difference between peer-to-peer networks and client/server networks is the presence of a dedicated server and the degree to which the network is centrally managed.

Mac OS X is designed to work with Mac OS X Server, Apple's network operating system, to form a client/server network operating environment, with Mac OS X Server performing the server functions and Mac OS X being the client. Mac OS X can also work with other network operating systems, such as Windows Server 2008, Windows Server 2003, Windows 2000 Server, UNIX, or Linux.

Several Mac OS X workstations can operate easily in a peer-to-peer network, either a Mac OS X–only network or one that includes computers running other network operating systems (such as Windows). This arrangement works well for home networks, home-office networks, and the smallest of office networks. Beyond a dozen or more computers, peer-to-peer networks tend to become too complex to perform effectively: the added effort of providing services to multiple computers slows down each peer computer. At this point, a client/server network becomes a better choice, because the server provides the services and centralizes the management functions.

Simple client/server networks, such as those used in many small offices or organizations, may use a single server for all services and management functions. Larger and more complex client/server networks are organized into logical units called *domains* for management purposes, with one or more servers set up as *domain controllers* to run the other servers.

In a large organization, a domain-based structure provides many benefits— most importantly, a central registry for all users so that one registration provides access to all the computers and resources in the domain. Domains, however, are very complex and require significant expertise to set up and manage. For that reason, this book focuses on setting up and using a peer-to-peer network and on connecting to shared resources on a client/server network.

Select a Network Standard

Mac OS X supports the two predominant networking standards, wired Ethernet and wireless, additionally offering the option of creating small networks using FireWire. These standards determine the type of hardware you need.

QUICKSTEPS

SELECTING WIRED ETHERNET HARDWARE

Hardware used in a wired Ethernet network includes a network connection, switch or router, and cabling. Many brands are available, with the lower end of the market competing on price. To ensure that your network is reliable and that you can get support when you need it, stick with name-brand products from companies that are likely to be around for a while. Respected brands include 3Com, D-Link, Linksys (now a division of networking giant Cisco Systems), and NETGEAR.

SELECT A NETWORK CONNECTION

All Macs come with an Ethernet network connection built in, so you will normally not need to add a network adapter to a Mac. (Rarely, a Mac may need two Ethernet connections.) If you haven't identified the jack, look for one that resembles a telephone jack but is wider and is marked with the symbol <...>.

SELECT CONNECTING DEVICES

The best connecting device for your network is a *switch* or *router*, a connection box into which you connect a cable for each computer or other networked device that is part of the network. The switch routes data around the network as needed.

The switch or router needs a port for each Mac, PC, or other device, but you can plug one switch or router into another switch to increase the number of ports on your network. If you plan to do this, choose switches that are designed to stack one on top of the other for neatness and for speed (their interconnecting bus is faster than a wire connection).

Continued . . .

USE WIRED ETHERNET

The wired Ethernet standard comes in several forms based on speed and cable type. These are the three most common standards:

- **10BaseT** provides a network that operates at the regular Ethernet speed of 10 Mbps (megabits, or millions of bits, per second).
- **100BaseT**, or Fast Ethernet, provides a network that operates at 100 Mbps.
- **Gigabit Ethernet** provides a network that operates at speeds of up to 1 Gbps (gigabit, or billion bits, per second).

At this writing, Gigabit Ethernet equipment is becoming affordable enough for home use, where previously it was used mainly in corporate networks. Most Macs include Gigabit Ethernet network adapters, so you can use Gigabit Ethernet, Fast Ethernet, or regular Ethernet, as you choose.

For most home, home-office, and small-office networks, a Fast Ethernet network is fast enough. However, if you want to be able to stream video across the network, or transfer large files quickly, Gigabit Ethernet is a better choice.

A wired Ethernet network (Gigabit, Fast, or regular Ethernet), shown in Figure 9-3, has the following three major components.

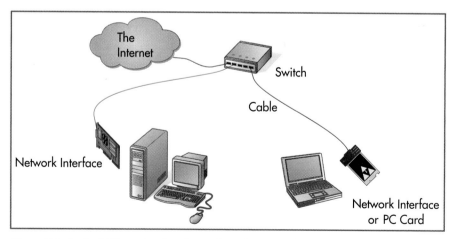

*Figure 9-3: **A wired Ethernet network consists of a network connection on your computer, a switch or router into which other computers are connected, and a cable connecting the two.***

SELECTING WIRED ETHERNET HARDWARE *(Continued)*

Instead of a switch or router, you can use a *hub*, an older style of connection box that doesn't work as efficiently. The only reason to use a hub nowadays is if you have an old one that you want to reuse to avoid buying new equipment. If not, buy a switch or router.

SELECT CABLING

At this writing, Category 5 enhanced ("Cat 5e") cable is the best choice for your network. Cat 5e works for Gigabit Ethernet, Fast Ethernet, and regular Ethernet. If you want to future-proof your network, consider Category 6 cable instead, which will support even faster network speeds.

Cat 5e and Cat 6 cables come in various colors and in lengths of up to 100 feet with the connectors molded on. Alternatively, you can buy a spool of cable (typically 1000 feet) and a crimping tool, cut the cables to the lengths you need, and crimp connectors on yourself.

NOTE

A **router** joins two different networks—for example, joining a LAN to the Internet. Often a router is combined with a switch, either in a single device or in separate devices, to join several computers to each other and to the Internet.

- The **network connection** on your Mac connects it to the network.
- A **switch** or **router** joins several computers together to form the network.
- An **unshielded twisted pair (UTP)** cable with a simple RJ-45 connector (like a telephone connector, only bigger) joins the network connection to the switch. The most widely used types of UTP cable are Category 5 enhanced ("Cat 5e") and Category 6 ("Cat 6").

Ethernet networks are very easy to set up (see "Set Up a Network," later in this chapter), have become pervasive throughout organizations, and typically cost less than $30 per computer on the network.

WIRELESS LANS

Wireless LANs (WLANs) replace the cable used in a wired network with small radio transceivers (combined transmitters and receivers) at the computer and at the switch or router. There are several wireless standards at this writing, with further standards being developed to provide faster data transmission and greater security:

- **802.11n** is a standard that will support speeds of up to about 300 Mbps. At this writing, 802.11n, also called Wireless-N, is a draft standard—it has not been ratified yet. However, manufacturers are releasing Draft-N wireless network equipment. Draft-N equipment from one manufacturer may not work at 802.11n speeds with Draft-N equipment from another manufacturer.

- **802.11g** is a standard that supports speeds of up to 54 Mbps. Also called Wireless-G and generally referred to as *Wi-Fi*, 802.11g is widely used, and is backward compatible with 802.11b (discussed next).

- **802.11b** is a standard that supports speeds of up to 11 Mbps. Generally referred to as *Wi-Fi*, 802.11b is still very widely used, especially in public wireless networks.

- **802.11a** is a standard that supports speeds of up to 54 Mbps. However, 802.11a is not compatible with 802.11b or 802.11g and is not widely used.

A WLAN has two components (see Figure 9-4):

- An **access point** is connected to the wired Ethernet network via a switch or connected to the Internet via a router. It uses one or more transceivers to communicate wirelessly with cards installed in or attached to computers using the WLAN.

QUICK**FACTS**

UNDERSTANDING WI-FI

The term "Wi-Fi" can be confusing, because it's used in different ways. At this writing, it is widely used to mean either 802.11b or 802.11g. Technically, Wi-Fi means that a product has been certified by the Wi-Fi Alliance as conforming to Wi-Fi standards and thus is interoperable with other Wi-Fi–certified products.

For example, Apple's AirPort cards are Wi-Fi certified for 802.11b, whereas the AirPort Extreme cards are Wi-Fi certified for 802.11b *and* 802.11g. This means you can take an AirPort- or AirPort Extreme–equipped laptop Mac into any office, airport, or other building with a Wi-Fi standard wireless system and be able to connect to the WLAN if it is open or if you have the appropriate permissions and passwords.

In many airports, hotels, and coffee shops, you see signs for Wi-Fi *hotspots*, wireless networks that you can connect to using standard Wi-Fi equipment.

CAUTION

Lessened security is also a potential downside with wireless networks if they're not configured properly. For example, if you don't turn on encryption and don't force users to use passwords, your neighbor might be able to connect to your network or examine your network traffic. Even with encryption, passwords, and other security turned on, a wireless network is less secure than a wired network. This is because, with a wired network, an attacker must usually have direct access to the physical network to attack it. By contrast, using a high-gain antenna, an attacker can attack a wireless network from a distance—even from several miles away.

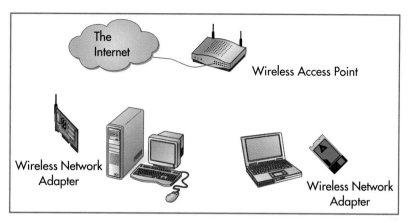

Figure 9-4: *A wireless network consists of a card in your computer and an access point that is connected to a wired network, the Internet, or both.*

- An **adapter** is installed in or plugs into your computer and has a transceiver built in to communicate wirelessly to an access point within its range. For laptop computers, built-in adapters are increasingly common (for both Macs and PCs). For desktop computers, adapters are typically either installed in the computer as a PCI card or attached to the computer via USB.

If the access point is connected to a switch or router on a wired network, the wireless computers within the range of the access point operate on the network in exactly the same way, except for being a little slower, as they would operate with a cable connection. A WLAN has some significant benefits over a normal wired LAN:

- You do not have the expense of cabling and the even higher expense of installing and maintaining cabling.
- Adding users to and removing them from the network is extremely easy.
- Users can move easily from office to office.
- Users can roam within an area—for example, carrying their laptops to a meeting.
- Visitors can easily connect to the network.

Wireless network connections now cost little more than wired network connections, so the main downside of a wireless network is its lower transmission speeds. When a wireless network is busy (such as when many

9

computers are connected to it), transmission speeds tend to drop far below the theoretical maximum speeds. Despite these drawbacks, WLANs are enjoying great popularity, with many systems being sold for both homes and offices.

USE FIREWIRE

Instead of wired or wireless Ethernet, you can network Macs quickly and easily by using the FireWire capabilities built into all recent Macs. FireWire allows data transfer at extremely high speeds—up to 400 Mbps for regular FireWire and up to 800 Mbps for FireWire-800, the latest generation of FireWire devices.

The catch is that the maximum length of any FireWire cable is 4.5 meters, or about 15 feet. Even if you use a FireWire hub, all the computers on the network will probably need to be in the same room; and for best results, the number of computers on the network should be small.

Set Up a Network

When you installed Mac OS X, the installation routine installed and configured a full set of networking services using your input (for example, for your Internet connection) and system defaults. These default settings typically provide an operable networking system, enabling you to plug your Mac into an Ethernet network or connect to a wireless network (if your Mac has an AirPort card installed) and start using the network, with a minimum of further configuration.

This section walks you through creating a network using the four means you're most likely to use: wired Ethernet, wireless using an access point, wireless without an access point, and FireWire. It then shows you how to check that your network configuration is working and how to make key changes to it.

Set Up an Ethernet Network

To create an Ethernet network, you need a Cat 5e or Cat 6 Ethernet cable for each computer that will be connected, and a switch or router with enough ports for each computer or other device that you will connect.

> **NOTE**
>
> If your Mac has Bluetooth built in (or added on), you can also use Bluetooth to create a network among Macs. Bluetooth has slow data-transfer rates and limited range, so you probably won't want to use it for networking Macs unless all the other networking options are unavailable—in which case, it will suddenly become much more attractive. Bluetooth is primarily intended for transferring data among personal devices, such as mobile phones and PDAs, or between a personal device and a computer (for example, a Mac).

If you want, you can leave your Mac running while you connect it to an Ethernet network; if you prefer, you can shut your Mac down first. If you're connecting PCs to the network as well, it's best to shut them down before connecting them.

1. Plug one end of an Ethernet cable into your switch or router and the other end into your Mac.
2. Repeat the process for each of the other Macs that will be part of the network.
3. Turn on the power for the switch or router.
4. If you have shut down your Macs or PCs, turn them on.

Set Up a Wireless Network Using an Access Point

To create a wireless network using an access point, you need a wireless adapter in each Mac and an access point. The wireless adapters and the access point must be compatible with each other:

- Use all Draft-N 802.11n products from the same manufacturer if you want Wireless-N speeds. If your Mac includes a Draft-N AirPort card, your best bet is to get a Draft-N AirPort from Apple as well.
- Use all Wi-Fi–certified 802.11g products if you want 54 Mbps speeds.
- Use either a mixture of Wi-Fi–certified 802.11g products and Wi-Fi–certified 802.11b products or all Wi-Fi–certified 802.11b products if 11 Mbps is good enough.

INSTALL THE HARDWARE

If the wireless adapters aren't installed in the Macs, install them first. Then set up your access point by following the instructions that come with it. A typical setup process for an access point involves connecting your computer to it using an Ethernet cable so that you can communicate via a wired network in order to configure the wireless network. Configuration typically also includes:

- Specifying the name, or service set identifier (SSID), of the wireless network—often simply a descriptive text name (for example, Wireless1).
- Choosing whether to use encryption. If your access point offers a choice, choose Wi-Fi Protected Access version 2 (WPA-2) or Wi-Fi Protected Access (WPA) over Wired

CAUTION

When you mix wireless standards in a wireless network, you usually end up with the slowest speed for parts of the network or for all of it. For example, if you add a device using 802.11b to an otherwise 802.11g network, the whole network drops down to the 802.11b speed. However, some Draft-N equipment can maintain both Draft-N speeds with Draft-N equipment and 802.11g speeds with 802.11g equipment simultaneously.

TIP

If you're not sure whether your Mac has an AirPort card, open the menu and click **About This Mac**. In the About This Mac window that opens, click **More Info** to launch System Profiler. In the left column, expand the **Network** category if it's collapsed, and see if an AirPort Card entry appears. Open the **System Profiler** menu and click **Quit System Profiler** to close System Profiler.

SELECTING WIRELESS HARDWARE

Hardware for a wireless network includes a wireless adapter and a wireless access point.

SELECT A WIRELESS SPEED

For a new wireless network using Macs, you'll typically want to choose Apple's implementation of the 802.11n draft standard to get the fastest data rates available. For example, the AirPort Extreme Base Station with Gigabit Ethernet uses Draft-N. The faster rate is especially important if you're building a multiuser network, as each computer has to share the capacity with all the other computers on the network at any given time.

Even if your Mac has 802.11g rather than Draft-N, Apple's Draft-N equipment is a good choice. Apple has a strong record of ensuring backward compatibility with its earlier Macs—as indeed it should.

If you'll need only to connect to public Wi-Fi networks, such as those in airports and coffee shops, 802.11g equipment—or even 802.11b—should be adequate. It is likely to be several years before public Wi-Fi networks upgrade to 802.11n.

SELECT A WIRELESS ADAPTER

All current laptop Macs and iMacs include built-in wireless adapters. You can install wireless adapters on all other Macs, from the Mac mini through to the Mac Pro, either as a build option at the time of purchase or afterward.

Your first choice for a wireless adapter in a Mac should be an Apple AirPort card using the fastest wireless technology compatible with the Mac—at this writing, draft 802.11n or 802.11g.

Continued . . .

Equivalent Privacy (WEP), an older standard that includes known compromises; but even WEP is better than no encryption at all.

- Choosing whether to restrict the network to a specified list of wireless adapters (identified by their Media Access Control number, or MAC number) or to leave it open to any wireless adapter within range. Restricting the network to a list is a good security move for detecting casual interlopers, but determined hackers can learn an approved MAC number by "sniffing" (eavesdropping on) a transmission, and then set their computer to "spoof" (fake) that number when the genuine device isn't using it.

TURN YOUR AIRPORT ON

If your AirPort is off, you can turn it on in either of two ways:

- If the AirPort icon is displayed on the menu bar, click it to open the menu, and click **Turn AirPort On**.

–Or–

- Open the menu, click **System Preferences**, and then click **Network**. In the left panel, click **AirPort**, and then click the **Turn AirPort On** button (see Figure 9-5).

CONNECT TO THE WIRELESS NETWORK

When you turn your Mac's AirPort on, Mac OS X will automatically identify wireless networks that it can connect to. To choose a wireless network:

- If the AirPort icon is displayed on the menu bar, click it to open the menu, and then click the network on the menu.

–Or–

- Choose the network in the **Network Name** drop-down list in the AirPort category in the Network pane in System Preferences. Then open the **System Preferences** menu and click **Quit System Preferences** to close System Preferences.

If Mac OS X prompts you to enter the password for the network, enter it in the Password text box. Select the **Show Password** check box if you want to see the letters you're typing (this is usually helpful if nobody else is watching your screen).

QUICKSTEPS

SELECTING WIRELESS HARDWARE

(Continued)

Your other option is to install a third-party wireless adapter: a PCI card (in a full-size desktop Mac), a PC Card (in a laptop Mac), or a USB adapter (on any Mac). Because Apple's AirPort cards have most of the market, the selection of third-party wireless adapters with Mac drivers is relatively thin. (By comparison, the selection of third-party wireless adapters with drivers for Windows Vista and Windows XP drivers is huge.) Generally, an AirPort card is the best choice, especially if you also choose an AirPort as your access point.

SELECT A WIRELESS ACCESS POINT

Wireless access points come in simple versions that plug into a wired Ethernet network and in more sophisticated versions, called "wireless broadband routers," that terminate a DSL or cable Internet connection. When choosing a wireless access point, you can choose between these two types. You can also choose the speed of the access point.

Apple's AirPort and AirPort Extreme cards work with any wireless access point. But if you're selecting a wireless access point for a Mac network, an AirPort or AirPort Extreme access point is likely to be your best choice, as it is designed to work seamlessly with Mac OS X and with AirPort cards.

An AirPort access point works with any wireless adapter that uses the same network standard. For example, you can connect Windows PCs that have 801.11g adapters to a wireless network via an 802.11g AirPort access point. Similarly, you can connect a Mac via an AirPort card to a non-AirPort wireless access point.

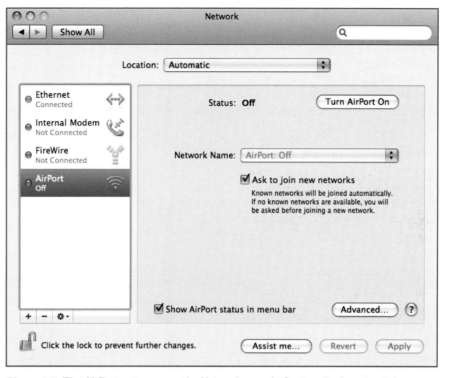

*Figure 9-5: **The AirPort category on the Network pane in System Preferences lets you turn your AirPort on, select a network, and choose other settings.***

Select the **Remember This Network** check box if you want to add the password to your Keychain. Then click **OK**.

CONNECT TO A CLOSED NETWORK

If the wireless network's access point is configured not to broadcast its SSID (for security), the network won't appear in the AirPort menu or in the Network Name drop-down list box on the Network pane in System Preferences. Such a network is called a *closed* network. You'll need to know the network's name, security type, and password before you can access it.

1. Click **Join Other Network** in the **AirPort** menu or in the **Network Name** drop-down list on the Network pane in System Preferences. Mac OS X will display the Closed Network dialog box.

2. Choose the type of security (for example, **WPA Personal**, **WPA Enterprise**, or **WEP Password**) in the **Security** drop-down list box.

3. Type the network name, your user name (for some security types only), and the password. (If you've connected to this closed network before, you can select the network in the Network Name drop-down list box. Otherwise, you'll need to type it.)

4. Select the **Remember This Network** check box if you want Mac OS X to store your password.

5. Click **Join**.

UNDERSTANDING TCP/IP ESSENTIALS

Networking protocols are sets of standards used to package and transmit data over a network. The protocol determines how the information is divided into packets (units) for transmission, how it is addressed, and what is done to ensure it is transferred reliably.

To transmit data between your Mac and another computer, Mac OS X uses TCP/IP, the networking protocol used on the Internet. TCP/IP is a powerful protocol and very complex. Mac OS X makes TCP/IP configuration as straightforward as possible, masking most of the ugly details from your sight. Yet it helps if you understand a few essentials about TCP/IP.

First, there are two main versions of the Internet Protocol: version 4 (usually called IPv4) and version 6 (usually called IPv6). IPv4 is still used most widely in North America and in much of the world, so this section discusses it. IPv6 is the new version, is widely used in China and other rapidly developing economies, and will eventually take over from IPv4.

IP ADDRESSES

TCP/IP identifies the different computers (actually, the different network interfaces—more on this in a moment) on a network by using addresses called *IP addresses*. In IPv4, an IP address takes the form of four groups of three decimal numbers separated by periods—for example, 192.168.0.1. The first group (here, 192) defines the largest unit; the second group defines the unit within that unit; the third, another unit within the second unit; and the fourth, another unit within the third. In layperson's terms, each of the numbers can go up to 255. (This is a generalization and ignores some exceptions.)

Continued . . .

SET YOUR PREFERRED ORDER OF WIRELESS NETWORKS

If your Mac connects to multiple wireless networks, tell your Mac your order of preference for the networks:

1. Open the menu and click **System Preferences** to open the System Preferences window.

2. Click **Network**. The Network pane will be displayed.

3. Select **AirPort** in the left list box.

4. Click the **Advanced** button to display the AirPort sheet. Make sure the **AirPort** tab is selected, as in Figure 9-6.

5. In the Preferred Networks list, set your preferred order by dragging the networks up and down so that the network you want to use first appears at the top.

6. If necessary, add other networks to the list. Click the + button below the list box, specify the details in the Enter The Name Of The Network dialog box, and then click the **Add** button.

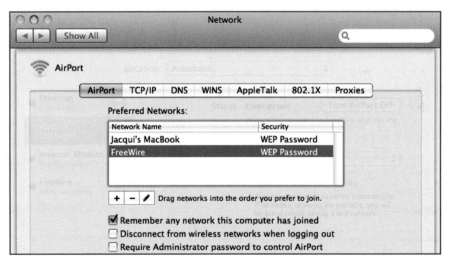

Figure 9-6: **Tell your Mac the order in which you want it to connect to wireless networks when they're available.**

UNDERSTANDING TCP/IP ESSENTIALS *(Continued)*

For identification, each IP address must be unique on the network it's being used on, so each network interface on a network is assigned a different IP address. Most Macs come with several ways to connect to another computer or network: the network connection, the FireWire port, the internal modem, and maybe an AirPort card.

You can use two or more connections at the same time, so one Mac can have two or more IP addresses at once. These IP addresses can be on the same network, but they'll typically be on different networks. For example, when your Mac is connected directly to the Internet (rather than through a shared broadband connection), it has one IP address on the Internet and another IP address on your local network.

The Internet functions as a single huge TCP/IP network, so each computer on the Internet must have a unique IP address. When you connect your broadband router or your Mac to the Internet, your ISP assigns it an IP address from the block of IP addresses allocated to the ISP. For a typical dial-up connection, the IP address is *dynamic*, meaning that it is likely to be different each time you establish the connection: the ISP allocates one of the addresses assigned to its modem pool. For a typical broadband connection, the IP address is *static*, meaning that you keep the same IP address all the time (your ISP reserves the IP address for you).

NETWORK ADDRESS TRANSLATION

To reduce the number of computers directly connected to the Internet, many networks use a process called Network Address Translation (NAT). In NAT, one computer (or a special-purpose device, such as a router)

Continued . . .

7. Choose other options as needed:

- Select the **Remember Any Network This Computer Has Joined** check box if you want Mac OS X to remember all networks. This setting is handy if you use several networks, but turn it off if you connect to many public networks on a one-time basis.

- Select the **Disconnect From Wireless Networks When Logging Out** check box if you tend to use a network for a session and then move on. If you use a wireless network at home, leave this check box cleared so that you can stay connected even when you log out.

- Select the **Require Administrator Password To Control AirPort** check box if you want to prevent non-Administrator users from configuring the AirPort.

8. When you've finished setting your order of preference for wireless networks and choosing options, click **OK**.

9. Open the **System Preferences** menu and click **Quit System Preferences** to close System Preferences.

DISCONNECT FROM A WIRELESS NETWORK

To disconnect from a wireless network, turn your Mac's AirPort off:

- If the AirPort icon is displayed on the menu bar, click it to open the menu, and click **Turn AirPort Off**.

–Or–

- Open the menu and click **System Preferences**, click **Network**, and select **AirPort** in the left list box. Click the **Turn AirPort Off** button. Open the **System Preferences** menu and click **Quit System Preferences** to close System Preferences.

Set Up a Computer-to-Computer Wireless Network

If you don't have an access point, you can set up a *computer-to-computer* wireless network by using a Mac as a "software access point." This capability means that one Mac starts broadcasting an SSID and other Macs can join the network. Computer-to-computer networks work well for small numbers of computers, but if you plan to add more than a half-dozen computers to your wireless network, an access point will give you better results.

UNDERSTANDING TCP/IP ESSENTIALS (Continued)

is connected to the Internet and has an IP address on the Internet. The NAT computer shares the Internet connection with the other computers on the internal network as required, funneling Internet requests and replies through its IP address. This process is often compared to the mailroom in a building, through which all incoming and outgoing mail is directed.

GET AN IP ADDRESS

IP addresses can be allocated either manually or automatically. Manual allocation is handy for some situations (such as when you need a particular computer to keep the same IP address), but automatic allocation is the norm for most networks because it is more efficient. Most automatic allocation is performed by a DHCP (Dynamic Host Configuration Protocol) server, either at your ISP (for an Internet connection) or on your local network.

When your Mac detects that no DHCP server is available, it falls back on Automatic Private IP Addressing (APIPA). APIPA assigns an IP address in the address range 169.254.0.0 through 169.254.255.255 and checks that no other computer on the network is using that IP address (and if one is, changes the IP address until it is unique on the network).

NOTE

Mac OS X can't use WPA on a computer-to-computer wireless network at this writing, so 128-bit WEP is the best choice for security.

To set up a computer-to-computer wireless network:

1. Turn on your Mac's **AirPort** (as described in the previous section).

2. Display the **Create A Computer-To-Computer** sheet:
   - If the AirPort icon is displayed on the menu bar, click it to open the menu, and then click **Create Network**. Mac OS X displays the Computer-To-Computer dialog box, which is shown in Figure 9-7 with all its options displayed.
   - Otherwise, open the menu and click **System Preferences**, click **Network**, and select **AirPort** in the left list box. Choose **Create Network** in the **Network Name** drop-down list box. Mac OS X displays the Computer-To-Computer sheet.

3. Type the name for the network in the Name text box.

4. Choose the wireless network channel in the **Channel** drop-down list box. In most cases, the best choice is **Automatic (11)** unless you know you need to use another channel to avoid conflicts with an existing wireless network.

5. If you want to protect the network with a password (which is usually a good idea), select the **Require Password** check box. The lower part of the Computer-To-Computer dialog box or sheet will appear.

Figure 9-7: **Create a computer-to-computer wireless network in the Computer To Computer dialog box.**

GETTING A BLOCK OF IP ADDRESSES

The block of IP addresses you use with the Internet Protocol depends on whether the computers to be assigned the addresses will be private or public.

GET PRIVATE IP ADDRESSES

If the computers will be operating only on an internal network, they are *private* and need be unique only on the internal network. Four blocks of IP addresses have been set aside and can be used by any organization for its private, internal needs:

- 10.0.0.0 through 10.255.255.255 (typically used for large networks)
- 169.254.0.0 through 169.254.255.255 (used for APIPA)
- 172.16.0.0 through 172.31.255.255 (typically used for medium-sized networks)
- 192.168.0.0 through 192.168.255.255 (widely used for small networks)

GET PUBLIC IP ADDRESSES

Computers that are connected directly to the Internet are *public* and thus need a globally unique IP number. Your ISP will probably provide the IP addresses you need. For a larger block, you may have to go to one of the three Internet registries:

- American Registry for Internet Numbers (ARIN), at www.arin.net/, which covers North and South America, the Caribbean, and sub-Saharan Africa
- Réseaux IP Européens (RIPE), at www.ripe.net/, which covers Europe, the Middle East, and northern Africa
- Asia Pacific Network Information Center (APNIC), at www.apnic.net/, which covers Asia and the Pacific

6. In the **Security** drop-down list, choose the length of password to use for the WEP key. Choose **128-Bit** over 40-Bit (More Compatible) unless a wireless adapter that you'll use on another computer on the network is limited to 40-bit WEP.

7. In the Password and Verify text boxes, type a password of the length specified by the readout at the bottom of the dialog box: 13 ASCII (regular text) characters for 128-bit WEP, 5 ASCII characters for 40-bit WEP.

8. Click **OK**. Mac OS X creates the AirPort network. If the AirPort icon is displayed in the menu bar, you will see the symbol for a computer-to-computer network, as shown here: 📶

You can now join other Macs to the network as described in "Connect to the Network," earlier in this chapter. To tear down your computer-to-computer network, click **Turn AirPort Off** on either the **AirPort** menu or the Network pane in System Preferences on the Mac that created the network.

Set Up a FireWire Network

As explained earlier in this chapter, FireWire offers you the option of setting up a small but very fast network among Macs. Because each FireWire cable is limited to 4.5 meters (15 feet), the computers must be physically close to each other, even if you use a FireWire hub to connect two cables and so double the cable length.

If you need to connect only two Macs, all you need is a six-pin to six-pin FireWire cable. To connect three or more Macs, you need a FireWire hub with enough ports and a cable to connect each Mac to the FireWire hub.

CREATE THE FIREWIRE NETWORK

With the Macs running, connect them to each other using FireWire cables. Use a FireWire hub if necessary. If the hub requires power (rather than drawing it from one of the Macs), connect its power adapter. Then perform the following steps on each Mac in turn:

1. Open the menu and click **System Preferences** to open the System Preferences window.

2. Click **Network**. The Network pane will be displayed.

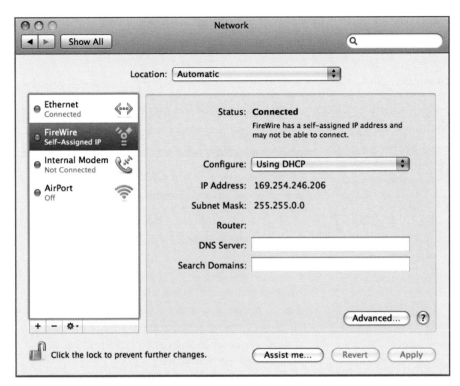

Figure 9-8: *If all your computers are close together, you can create a fast network using FireWire.*

3. In the left list box, select **FireWire** to display the controls for configuring a FireWire connection (see Figure 9-8).

4. Use the controls to set up the TCP/IP configuration for the network. Here is an example of using a manual configuration:
   - In the **Configure** drop-down list, select **Manually**.
   - In the IP Address text box, type the IP address—for example, **10.0.0.3**.
   - In the Subnet Mask text box, type the corresponding subnet mask for the IP address—for example, **255.255.255.0**.
   - In the Router text box, type the IP address of the router you're using (for example, your DSL or cable modem)—for example, **10.0.0.2**.
   - In the DNS Server text box, type the IP address of your ISP's domain name server.
   - Click **Apply** to apply the changes.

5. Open the **System Preferences** menu and click **Quit System Preferences** to close System Preferences.

Change Your Network Configuration

The Network pane of System Preferences lets you change your network configuration. The previous sections have shown you specific examples of the changes you'll typically need to make in order to implement a particular network (for example, a FireWire network). This section shows you how to get an overview of your network connections, change the order of your network connections, and specify which method Mac OS X should use to get an IP address.

Start by displaying the Network pane of System Preferences:

1. Open the menu and click **System Preferences** to open the System Preferences window.

2. Click **Network** to display the Network pane.

NOTE

AirPort appears on the Network pane only if your Mac has an AirPort card. FireWire may not appear until you create a configuration for FireWire networking, as described in "Set Up a FireWire Network," earlier in this chapter.

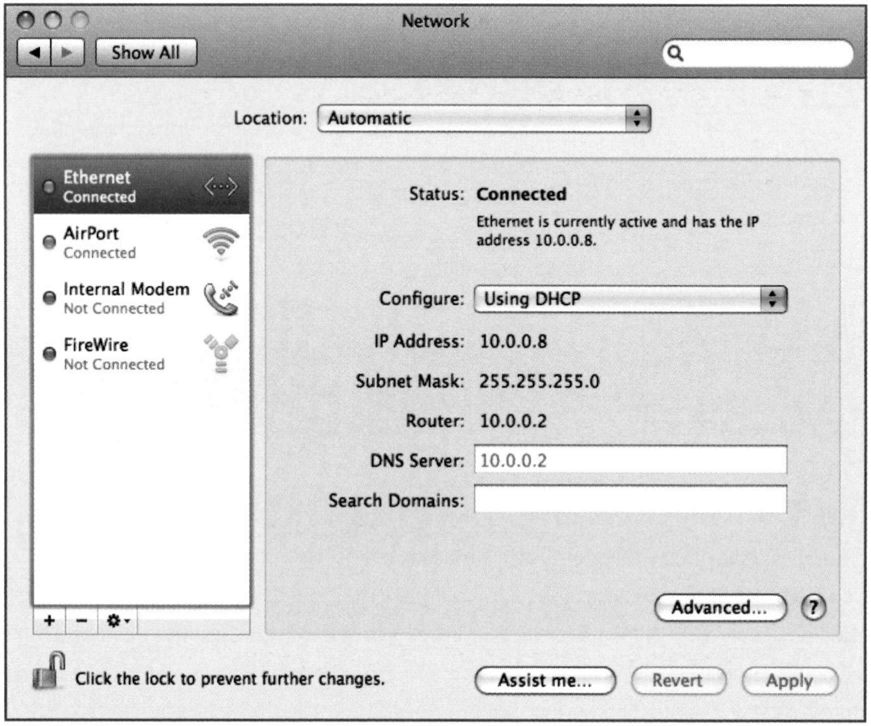

Figure 9-9: ***The Network pane in System Preferences gives you a quick overview of your Mac's network connections.***

GET AN OVERVIEW OF YOUR MAC'S NETWORK CONNECTIONS

To get an overview of your Mac's network connections, simply view the list on the Network pane. Figure 9-9 shows an example of the Network pane with two connections.

To see the details of a connection, click it in the left list box. You can then use the controls to configure it or (depending on the connection type) turn it off.

CHANGE THE ORDER OF NETWORK CONNECTIONS

If your Mac has established multiple network connections via different network interfaces, you must tell Mac OS X the order in which to use the interfaces:

1. Open the Network pane of System Preferences if it's not already displayed.
2. If you don't want to use any of the network connections that appear in the left list box, click the network connection, click the **Action** drop-down button (the cog-wheel below the left list box), and then choose **Make Service Inactive**. (To turn the connection back on again, repeat this action, but choose **Make Service Active**.)
3. Click the **Action** drop-down button, and then choose **Set Service Order**. Mac OS X will display the Service Order sheet.
4. Drag the items in the list box into the order in which you want to use them for connecting to a network.
5. Click **OK** to close the Service Order sheet.
6. Click **Apply** to apply your changes.

SPECIFY HOW MAC OS X SHOULD GET AN IP ADDRESS

To specify how Mac OS X should get an IP address:

1. Open the Network pane of System Preferences if it's not already displayed.
2. In the left list box, click **Ethernet**, **AirPort**, or **FireWire** as appropriate. This example uses Ethernet.

CAUTION

Remember that private ranges of IP addresses work only with computers on their own subnets and with IP addresses from the same range. You can tell what the subnet is from the subnet mask. For example, with a subnet mask of 255.255.255.0, all computers in the network must have IP addresses with the same first three numbers, varying only in the last number. For example, computers with the IP addresses 192.168.104.1 and 192.168.104.2 are on the same subnet.

3. Click the **Configure** drop-down list, and then click the appropriate item:

- Click **Using DHCP** to have Mac OS X request an IP address automatically from a DHCP server (possibly your DSL router).
- Click **Using DHCP With Manual Address** to supply the Mac's IP address yourself but allow the DHCP server to supply the subnet mask, router, and DNS server.
- Click **Using BootP** to have Mac OS X request the TCP/IP address information as your Mac starts up. (BootP is used more in corporate networks than in home or small-office networks. Don't use it unless a network administrator tells you to.)
- Click **Manually** to specify an IP address manually. Type the IP address, the subnet mask, and the router details in the text boxes that Mac OS X displays.

4. Click **Apply**.

After you've finished working on the Network pane, open the **System Preferences** menu and click **Quit System Preferences** to close System Preferences.

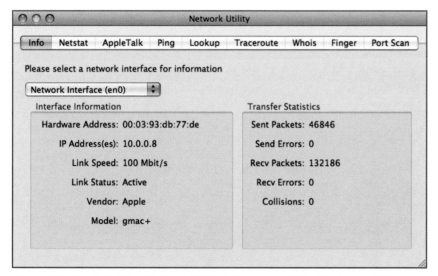

Figure 9-10: *The Info tab of Network Utility lets you check the IP address, link speed, and status for a network interface.*

Check Network Interface Status and Connections

To check the status of a network interface or find out if a network connection is working, launch Network Utility:

1. Activate the **Finder**.

2. Open the **Go** menu and click **Utilities**. The Utilities folder will be displayed.

3. Double-click **Network Utility**. Network Utility will open.

You can then use Network Utility as discussed in the following sections.

CHECK THE STATUS OF A NETWORK INTERFACE

To check the status of a network interface:

1. Click the **Info** tab button in Network Utility to display the Info tab (see Figure 9-10).

2. Select the network interface in the **Please Select A Network Interface For Information** drop-down list box:

- **Network Interface (en0)** is the Ethernet adapter.

- **Network Interface (en1)** is the AirPort card (and appears only if your Mac has an AirPort card).
- **Network Interface (fw0)** is your Mac's FireWire connection.

3. The Interface Information area displays the following information:

- The **Hardware Address** (also called the MAC, or Media Access Control, address) is an address encoded into the physical network adapter—for example, 00:0a:95: a2:77:96. This address doesn't change.
- The **IP Address** is the IP address currently assigned to the network interface—for example, 192.168.0.209.
- The **Link Speed** is the speed of the network connection in megabits per second, which Mac OS X lists as Mbit/s rather than Mbps: 1000 Mbit/s for Gigabit Ethernet, 400 Mbit/s for FireWire, 100 Mbit/s for Fast Ethernet, 54 Mbit/s for 802.11g, 11 Mbit/s for 802.11b, and 10 Mbit/s for regular Ethernet (10BaseT).

CHECK A CONNECTION TO ANOTHER COMPUTER

To check a connection to another computer:

1. Find out the computer's IP address. (If the computer is a Mac, you can use the technique described in the previous section).

2. Click the **Ping** tab button in Network Utility to display the Ping tab (see Figure 9-11).

3. Type the other computer's IP address in the Please Enter The Network Address To Ping text box.

4. Select the **Send Only *NN* Pings** option button and type a low number (such as 3 or 5) in the text box.

5. Click **Ping**. The Ping utility sends data packets to the specified address and displays its results. The example in Figure 9-11 shows responses from the address that was pinged, with the Statistics section showing that 5 packets were sent and 5 packets received, indicating that the connection is working. If Ping gets no response and the Statistics section indicates a "100% packet loss," you know the connection isn't working.

After you've finished using Network Utility, open the **Network Utility** menu and click **Quit Network Utility** to close the application.

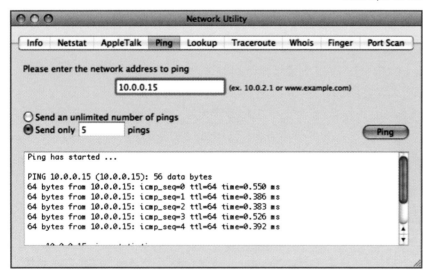

Figure 9-11: Use the Ping tab of Network Utility to test the TCP/IP connection to another computer.

How to...

Chapter 10
Using a Network

Networking brings a vastly enlarged world of computing to your Mac, giving you access to all the computers, printers, and other devices to which you are connected and have permission to access.

Using a network and its resources is no harder than accessing the hard disk, printer, or Internet connection that is directly connected to your Mac. Your network connection can be either wired or wireless. You'll seldom notice the difference between the two, other than that the hardware is different and that a wireless network may perform more slowly than a wired network.

In this chapter, you'll see how to access other computers and printers over a local area network (LAN), how to let others access your Mac and its resources, and how to access your Mac remotely, either across a LAN or over the Internet.

NOTE

A "share" or "network share" is a folder or drive on a computer on your network that has been deliberately shared by the user or administrator so that you can access it.

Access Network Resources

To access files and folders on a network, you typically connect to shared folders, mounting them on your Mac so that you can use them as if they were local folders. You can print on network printers in the same way as you can print on local printers, and you can access the Internet via the network.

Connect to a Shared Folder

You can connect to a shared folder either directly from the Sidebar in a Finder window (if the computer sharing the folder is listed) or by using the Connect To Server dialog box.

CONNECT TO A SHARED FOLDER FROM THE SIDEBAR

To connect to a shared folder from the Sidebar:

1. Activate the **Finder** and open a Finder window. For example, open the **Go** menu and click **Computer**.

2. If the Shared category in the Sidebar is collapsed, click the sideways gray triangle to expand it.

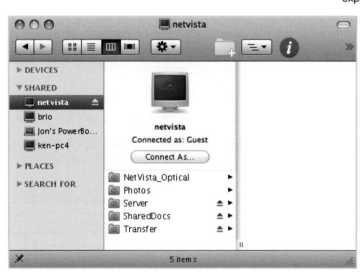

3. Under the Shared category, click the name of the computer sharing the folder.
   - If you see a list of shared folders, as shown here, you have successfully connected to the computer as the Guest user or by using previously stored credentials. You can start using the shared folder. Skip the remaining numbered steps in this list.
   - If you see the message Connection Failed, you need to supply other credentials. Follow the remaining numbered steps in this list.
   - If the computer sharing the folder isn't listed, connect using the Connect To Server dialog box instead. See the next section.

4. Click **Connect As** to open the dialog box.

5. Choose how to connect:
   - If you have a user account on the computer sharing the folder, select the **Registered User** option button. Type your user name for that computer in the Name text box and your password in the Password text box. Select the **Remember This Password In My Keychain** check box if you want Mac OS X to store your credentials for future use.

QUICKSTEPS

CONNECTING AUTOMATICALLY TO A SHARED FOLDER AT LOGIN

If you always need to connect to the same shared folders, you may want to make Mac OS X connect to them automatically when you log in. To do this:

1. Connect to the shared folder as described in "Connect to a Shared Folder." Save the password for the connection in your Keychain.

2. Open the menu and click **System Preferences** to open the System Preferences window.

3. Click **Accounts**. The Accounts pane will be displayed.

4. Click your account in the left list box.

Continued . . .

- If you don't have a user account on the computer sharing the folder, try to connect as a guest user. Select the **Guest** option button. Mac OS X hides the name and password controls.

6. Click **Connect**.

- If your credentials or the guest request is accepted, Mac OS X connects and displays the connection type. You can then click a shared folder to access its contents.

- If your credentials or the guest request is denied, Mac OS X tells you. You can then try to connect with different credentials.

When you have finished accessing the shared folder, click **Disconnect** to disconnect it. Alternatively, click the **Eject** button next to the sharing computer's name in the Source list.

CONNECT TO A SHARED FOLDER USING THE CONNECT TO SERVER DIALOG BOX

If the computer sharing the folder doesn't appear in the Sidebar, use the Connect To Server dialog box:

1. Activate the **Finder**.

2. Open the **Go** menu and click **Connect To Server**. Mac OS X will display the Connect To Server dialog box.

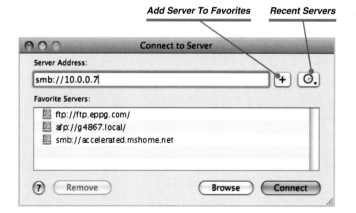

UICKSTEPS

CONNECTING AUTOMATICALLY TO A SHARED FOLDER AT LOGIN

(Continued)

5. Click the **Login Items** tab.

6. Drag each shared folder from the desktop to the These Items Will Open Automatically When You Log In list box.

7. Select the **Hide** check box for each shared folder you add if you want to prevent Mac OS X from displaying a Finder window showing the folder's contents when it connects.

8. Open the **System Preferences** menu and click **Quit System Preferences** to close System Preferences.

If you find that the preceding method doesn't make Mac OS X connect automatically to the shared folders, try creating a URL file to connect to the shared folder:

1. Activate the **Finder**, open the **Go** menu and click **Applications**, and double-click **TextEdit** to open TextEdit.

2. Type the URL for the shared folder using this format: *protocol://username:password@server/ volume*, where *protocol* is afp (for a Mac server) or smb (for a Windows server), *username* is your user name, *password* is your password for the server, *server* is the server, and *volume* is the shared folder. For example, you would use smb:// csmith:secur1ty@accelerated.mshome.net/resource to connect to the shared folder "resource" on the SMB server named "accelerated.mshome.net," using the user name "csmith" and the password "secur1ty."

Continued . . .

3. Specify the server you want to connect to:

- The Server Address text box contains the address of the last server you used (if any). You can type another server's address over this address.

- To select a server you've designated as a favorite, click it in the Favorite Servers list. (You can add the server in the Server Address text box to the Favorite Servers list by clicking the **Add Server To Favorites** button.)

- Click **Recent Servers** and choose a recent server from the drop-down list.

- If you don't know the exact name of the server, click **Browse** to display a Finder window listing the servers on the network. Double-click the server you want, and supply your user name and password as described in the next two steps.

4. Click **Connect**. Mac OS X will display the untitled dialog box shown in Figure 10-1. This dialog box offers you the choice between connecting as a guest and connecting as a registered user.

5. If you have a user account with this computer, select the **Registered User** option button and enter your name and password. Otherwise, select the **Guest** option button.

6. If you want to add the password for this share to your Keychain so that you don't have to enter it when you connect to the share in the future, select the **Remember This Password In My Keychain** check box.

7. Click **Connect**. Mac OS X displays a dialog box listing the volumes you can mount.

Figure 10-1: You can connect to a server as a guest or as a registered user. A guest may be restricted to accessing fewer shared folders than a registered user can access.

3. Select the whole URL in TextEdit and drag it to your desktop. The Finder will create a URL file from it.

4. Open the menu and click **System Preferences**, choose **Accounts**, click your account, and then click the **Startup Items** tab.

5. Drag the URL file from your desktop to the These Items Will Open Automatically When You Log In list box. Select the **Hide** check box if you don't want Mac OS X to open a window showing the folder.

6. Open the **System Preferences** menu and click **Quit System Preferences** to close System Preferences.

7. Drag the URL file from your desktop to the Trash.

8. Click the **TextEdit** window to activate TextEdit, and then open the **TextEdit** menu and click **Quit TextEdit**. When prompted to save the changes to the document, click **Don't Save**.

If you're unable to connect automatically using either of these techniques, you can speed up the process of connecting manually. Create an alias to each shared folder on your desktop (or in another folder of your choice). You can then quickly establish the connection to a shared folder by double-clicking the alias.

8. Choose the volumes you want to mount:

- To select a volume, click it.
- To select a contiguous range of volumes, click the first volume and then **SHIFT**+click the last.
- To select noncontiguous volumes, click the first volume and then ⌘+click each of the other volumes.

9. Click **OK**. Mac OS X will close the dialog boxes and mount the specified volume or volumes on your desktop.

10. Double-click a volume to open a Finder window showing its contents.

Disconnect Your Mac from a Shared Folder

To disconnect your Mac from a shared folder:

- Drag the shared folder's icon on your desktop to the Trash.

  –Or–

- In a Finder window, click the **Eject** icon next to the sharing computer in the Sidebar. This disconnects your Mac from all the shared folders on that computer.

  –Or–

- Click the shared folder's icon on your desktop, open the **File** menu, and click **Eject**. (The Eject command shows the shared folder's name—for example, Eject Public for a shared folder named Public.)

Mac OS X disconnects your Mac from the folder and removes the folder's icon from the desktop (if you have chosen to display connected servers on the desktop).

Copy Network Files and Information

After connecting to a network share, you can access its files and folders in the same ways you access the files and folders on your Mac's hard disk:

- To open a Finder window showing the folders and files on the network share, double-click the icon for the network share on your desktop.

- Drag a file or folder from the network share to your hard disk to copy it there. For example, drag a file to an entry in the Sidebar, and then use the Spring-Loaded Folders feature (see the note under "Customize Finder Preferences" in Chapter 3) to navigate to where you want to store the copy of the file.

- Drag a file or folder from your Mac's hard disk to the network share to copy it there. Again, you can use the Spring-Loaded Folders feature to open the folder in which you want to store the copy.

- Double-click a file on the network share to open it using your Mac's default application for that file type. For example, double-click a document file with a .doc extension to open the file for editing in Microsoft Word (assuming Microsoft Word is installed on your Mac).

Print on Network Printers

After connecting to a network printer, as discussed in "Install a Network Printer" in Chapter 6, you can print using the same techniques as for a local printer (see the "Printing" QuickSteps, also in Chapter 6).

Access a Network Internet Connection

If the network your Mac is connected to has an Internet connection, your Mac is automatically connected to it and can use it directly unless it requires a user name and password. In most cases, you can access the Internet by simply opening your browser (click the **Safari** icon on the Dock) or your e-mail application (click the **Mail** icon on the Dock). See Chapter 4 for more information.

Let Others Access Your Resources

The other side of the networking equation is sharing the resources on your Mac so that others can use them. This includes sharing your files, folders, and disks; your Mac's screen; your printers; and other resources, such as an Internet connection.

Share Your Folders

Mac OS X makes sharing your folders with other users as straightforward as possible.

NOTE

Mac OS X provides folders specifically for sharing files with other users securely. In each user account that you set up, Mac OS X creates a Public folder that's accessible to other users but that can't be changed by them. By putting files in this folder, which you'll find in your Home folder (~/Public, where ~ is UNIX shorthand for your Home folder), and turning on Personal File Sharing (see the following section), you can provide the files to other network users. Each Public folder also contains a Drop Box folder (~/Public/Drop Box) that other users can drop files in, even though they're not allowed to see the contents of the folder (let alone access them).

QUICKSTEPS

CONNECTING TO A WINDOWS COMPUTER

Before you can connect to a shared folder on a Windows computer, you must set up sharing on that computer. To make sharing easier, you should also tell Mac OS X which workgroup your Mac belongs to. This QuickSteps show you how to perform both these tasks.

SHARE A FOLDER ON WINDOWS VISTA

The easiest way to share a folder on Windows Vista is to use the Public folder that Windows automatically creates. This folder contains subfolders including Public Documents, Public Music, Public Pictures, and Public Videos to help you keep different types of files together.

Windows Vista automatically shares the Public folder with all users of the computer. You can also share the Public folder on the network:

1. Click **Start**, right-click **Network**, and then click **Properties**. A Network And Sharing Center window will open.

2. In the Sharing And Discovery list, click the button at the right end of the Public Folder Sharing bar to expand its contents.

3. Click the option button for the sharing you want:

   ● To let network users change or create files, click **Turn On Sharing So Anyone With Network Access Can Open, Change, And Create Files**.

   ● To let network users open files but not change or create them, click **Turn On Sharing So Anyone With Network Access Can Open Files**.

4. Click **Apply**. A User Account Control dialog box for Network And Sharing Center will be displayed.

Continued . . .

1. Open the menu and click **System Preferences** to open the System Preferences window.

2. Click **Sharing** to display the Sharing pane (see Figure 10-2).

3. Check the name displayed in the Computer Name text box and the readout underneath it that gives the name under which your Mac appears on the network. If you want to change the name, click **Edit**, type the new name, and click **OK**.

4. In the left list, select the **File Sharing** check box. Mac OS X turns File Sharing on and displays the list of shared folders.

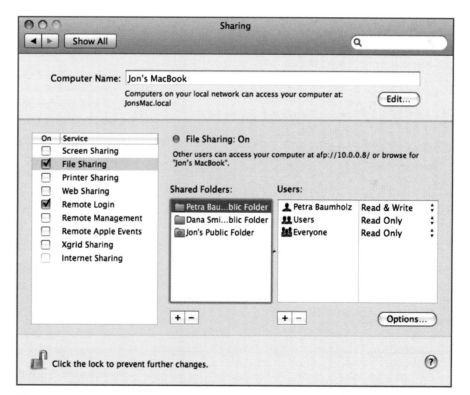

Figure 10-2: To share your files and folders with other computers on your network, turn on File Sharing on the Sharing pane in System Preferences.

QUICKSTEPS

CONNECTING TO A WINDOWS COMPUTER (Continued)

5. Click **Continue**. If you are not an Administrator user for the computer, you will need to supply an Administrator's password.

6. Click the **Close** button (the X button) to close the Network And Sharing Center window.

You can also share other folders. Open a Windows Explorer window, right-click the folder you want to share, and then click **Share** on the shortcut menu. Follow through the steps in the File Sharing Wizard to control which users can access the folder.

SHARE A FOLDER ON WINDOWS XP

The easiest way to share a folder on Windows XP is to use the Shared Documents folder that Windows automatically creates. This folder contains subfolders including Public Documents, Public Music, Public Pictures, and Public Videos to help you keep different types of files together.

To access the Shared Documents folder, open the **Start** menu and click **My Documents**. In the Windows Explorer window showing My Documents, click **Documents** in the Other Places task pane.

Windows XP automatically shares the Shared Documents folder with all users of the computer. You can also share the Shared Documents folder on the network:

1. On the Windows computer, open the **Start** menu and click **My Documents**. A Windows Explorer window will be displayed showing the My Documents view.

Continued . . .

5. Verify that the shared folders are those you want to share. If necessary, change the list:
   - To add a folder, click the + button under the Shared Folders list. On the sheet that appears, select the folder, and then click **Add**.
   - To remove a folder, click it in the Shared Folders list, click the – button, and then click **OK** in the confirmation message box.

6. Verify that the users and permissions shown for each folder are correct:
   - Select a folder in the Shared Folders list. The Users list displays the list of users and their permissions.
   - To add a user, click the + button under the Users list. In the sheet that appears, select the user from this Mac's list of users, and then click **Select**. To add a user (for example, someone who doesn't have an account on this Mac), click **New Person**, type the name in the New Person dialog box, and then click **Create Account**.

   - To set the permissions for a user you've added (or for another user), click the user in the Users list, and then choose **Read & Write**, **Read Only**, or **Write Only (Drop Box)** as appropriate.
   - To remove a user from the list, click the user in the Users list, click the – button, and then click **OK** in the confirmation message box.

7. To set the type of file sharing, click **Options**. The Options sheet will be displayed (see Figure 10-3).
   - Select the **Share Files And Folders Using AFP** check box if you want to share with Macs on the network.
   - Select the **Share Files And Folders Using FTP** check box if you want to share files and folders with any computers via File Transfer Protocol. FTP logins are not encrypted, which means that an eavesdropper can learn them, so it's best to avoid FTP if possible.
   - Select the **Share Files And Folders Using SMB** check box if you want to share files and folders with Windows computers. Select the check box for the user account you want to let access the folders, type the user's password in the Authenticate dialog box, and then click **OK**.
   - Click **Done** to close the Options sheet.

QUICKSTEPS

CONNECTING TO A WINDOWS COMPUTER *(Continued)*

2. In the Other Places task pane, right-click **Documents** and click **Sharing And Security** on the shortcut menu. The Properties dialog box for the folder will be displayed, with the Sharing tab foremost.

3. Select the **Share This Folder On The Network** check box.

4. If necessary, change the default name in the **Share Name** text box to describe the shared folder more clearly. You must keep the name to 12 characters or fewer; otherwise, Mac OS X will not be able to access it.

5. Select the **Allow Network Users To Change My Files** check box if you want network users to be able to change the files rather than just read them.

6. Click **OK**. Windows will close the Properties dialog box and apply the changes.

7. Open the **File** menu and click **Close** to close the Windows Explorer window.

LEARN YOUR WINDOWS WORKGROUP

If you don't know the name of the Windows workgroup to which your computer connects, learn it as follows:

- **Windows Vista** Press **WINDOWS KEY+BREAK**. In the System window, look at the Workgroup readout. Click the **Close** button (the × button).

- **Windows XP** Press **WINDOWS KEY+BREAK**, and then click the **Computer Name** tab in the System Properties dialog box. Look at the Workgroup readout. Click **OK**.

Continued . . .

Figure 10-3: The Options sheet lets you decide whether to share files via AFP (with Macs) or via SMB (with Windows PCs).

8. Open the **System Preferences** menu and click **Quit System Preferences** to close System Preferences.

Users of other Macs can see your Public folder by doing the following:

1. Activate the **Finder** and open a window.

2. In the Shared list, click the entry for your Mac.

3. Click the name of the Public folder they wish to open. (Mac OS X displays a list of all the Public folders—normally, one for each user account.) Mac OS X displays a Finder window showing the contents of your Public folder, including the Drop Box folder (to which users can drag files to make them available to you).

CAUTION

For security, share as conservatively as possible. For example, if your network consists only of Macs, share only via AFP, not via SMB. Avoid FTP sharing unless you find it vital.

TIP

Remember to turn off sharing (clear the **File Sharing** check box on the Sharing pane) when you want to stop sharing your folders on the network.

CONNECTING TO A WINDOWS COMPUTER *(Continued)*

SPECIFY YOUR WINDOWS WORKGROUP

To tell Mac OS X which workgroup to connect to:

1. Open the menu and click **System Preferences** to open the System Preferences window.

2. Click **Network** to display the Network pane.

3. In the left list box, click your regular network connection—for example, **Ethernet** or **AirPort**.

4. Click **Advanced** to display the Advanced sheet for that network connection.

5. Click the **WINS** tab to display its contents (see Figure 10-4). WINS is the acronym for Windows Internet Name Service.

6. Open the **Workgroup** drop-down list and select the workgroup name. If it doesn't appear, type the name.

7. Click **OK** to close the Advanced sheet.

8. Open the **System Preferences** menu and click **Quit System Preferences** to close System Preferences.

Share Your Mac's Screen

You can share your Mac's screen with other Macs running Leopard or with any computer running a Virtual Network Computing (VNC) program. To share your screen:

1. Open the menu and click **System Preferences** to open the System Preferences window.

2. Click **Sharing**. The Sharing pane will be displayed.

3. In the left list box, select the **Screen Sharing** check box. The readout in the middle of the pane gives the addresses that VNC users can use (for example, "vnc://10.0.0.9") and Leopard users can use (for example, "Jon's MacBook").

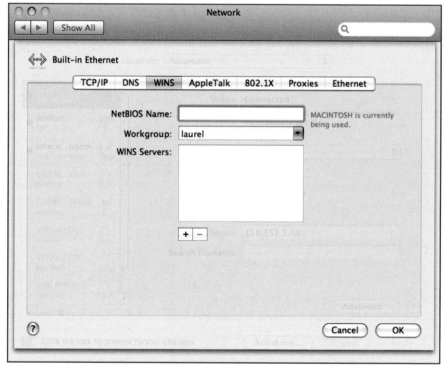

Figure 10-4: Use the WINS tab of the Advanced sheet in System Preferences for a network connection to tell your Mac which Windows workgroup name to use.

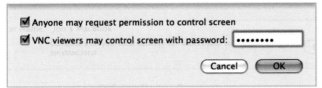

4. Click **Computer Settings** to open the Settings sheet.

5. Select the **Anyone May Request Permission To Control Screen** check box if you want remote users to be able to request permission to control the screen. You can choose whether to allow or deny each request.

6. Select the **VNC Viewers May Control Screen With Password** check box if you want VNC users to be able to take control of the screen. Normally, you will use this capability to control your Mac from another computer via VNC—but anyone who knows the password can also use it. This setting can be very useful, but it makes your Mac much less secure.

7. Click the **OK** button to close the Settings sheet.

8. In the Allow Access For area, choose which users can use screen sharing:

   • If you want all users to be able to use screen sharing, select the **All Users** option button.

   • If you want to restrict the users (as is normally wiser), select the **Only These Users** option button. Click the + button, use the resulting sheet to select the user or users, and then click **Select**.

9. Open the **System Preferences** menu and click **Quit System Preferences** to close System Preferences.

Share Your Printers

You can share the printers attached to your Mac with other users of your network. To share the printers with other Mac users:

1. Open the menu and click **System Preferences** to open the System Preferences window.

2. Click **Sharing**. The Sharing pane will be displayed.

3. In the left list box, select the **Printer Sharing** check box.

4. Open the **System Preferences** menu and click **Quit System Preferences** to close System Preferences.

Share Your Internet Connection

Chapter 4 describes how to set up a dial-up Internet connection. Once you've made such a connection, you can share it with other computers on the network by using Mac OS X's Internet Sharing feature. You can also use Internet Sharing to share a broadband connection that connects directly to your Mac rather than to the switch or router on your network. The Mac that runs the Internet connection is called the "host," and the other computers that use the connection are "clients." Both the host and the clients need to be set up independently.

Sharing your Internet connection is often useful, but it can have three main disadvantages:

- You must keep your Mac running and connected all the time the other computers need the Internet connection available. This may not be convenient, especially if you have a laptop Mac.

- You share the Internet connection's bandwidth (capacity) with the other users. So if other users are using the connection heavily (for example, downloading and uploading large files), the connection may seem slow or unresponsive to you.

- Actions that other users take will appear to come from your IP address, as if you had taken those actions. For example, if a user illegally downloads copyrighted or banned material, it will appear that you have done so.

CONFIGURE THE HOST TO SHARE THE INTERNET CONNECTION

To configure the host for sharing the Internet connection:

1. Open the menu and click **System Preferences** to open the System Preferences window.

2. Click **Sharing** to display the Sharing pane.

3. In the left list box, click the **Internet Sharing** item to display the Internet Sharing controls (see Figure 10-5). Don't select the Internet Sharing check box just yet.

4. In the **Share Your Connection From** drop-down list, select the network connection that you're using to connect to the Internet:

   - Select **Internal Modem** for a dial-up connection.

   - Select **Ethernet** for a broadband connection connected to your Mac via Ethernet.

   - Select **AirPort** if you're using your AirPort to connect to the Internet.

   - Select **FireWire** if your Mac is connected to the Internet connection via FireWire. (This is rare but possible.)

NOTE

You can select multiple connections in the To Computers Using list box. For example, if you have a combination wired and unwired network, you might select both Ethernet and AirPort. You can't use the same connection as you're using to connect to the Internet.

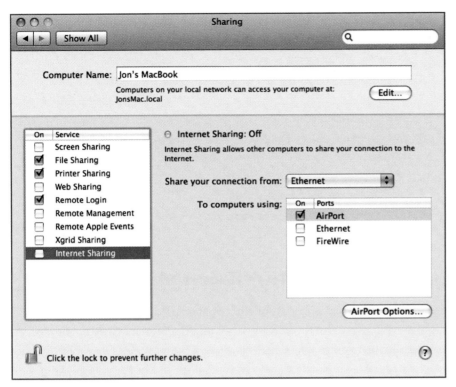

Figure 10-5: Set up Internet sharing on the Sharing pane in System Preferences.

5. In the To Computers Using list box, select the check box for each network interface you'll use for sharing your Internet connection with your other computers. For example, select **AirPort** if you'll use an AirPort connection to share the Internet connection.

6. If you're sharing over an AirPort, click **AirPort Options** and set options on the resulting sheet (see Figure 10-6). You'll recognize these options (for naming the network, choosing the channel, and applying encryption) from the Computer-To-Computer dialog box (discussed in "Set Up a Computer-to-Computer Wireless Network" in Chapter 9). Click **OK** to close this dialog box and return to the previous dialog box.

7. Select the **Internet Sharing** check box in the left list box. Mac OS X will display a message box warning you that sharing your Internet connection may disrupt your network settings.

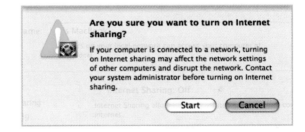

Are you sure you want to turn on Internet sharing?

If your computer is connected to a network, turning on Internet sharing may affect the network settings of other computers and disrupt the network. Contact your system administrator before turning on Internet sharing.

Start   Cancel

8. Click **Start**. Mac OS X starts the sharing.

9. If your Mac is configured to go to sleep, click **Energy Saver** in the System Preferences window and configure it to not go to sleep. (If your Mac goes to sleep, the other computers will not be able to access the Internet through the shared connection.)

10. Open the **System Preferences** menu and click **Quit System Preferences** to close System Preferences.

CONFIGURE THE CLIENTS TO SHARE THE INTERNET CONNECTION

To configure each client Mac to use the shared Internet connection:

1. Open the menu and click **System Preferences** to open the System Preferences window.

NOTE

To stop sharing your Internet connection, clear the **Internet Sharing** check box on the Sharing pane in System Preferences.

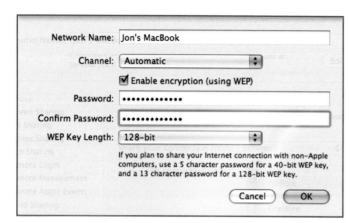

Figure 10-6: Choose wireless network options if you're sharing your Internet connection via AirPort.

2. Click **Network**. The Network pane will be displayed.

3. In the left list box, select the connection you're using to share the Internet connection. This example uses AirPort.

4. Click the Advanced button. The Advanced sheet for the connection will be displayed.

5. Click the **TCP/IP** tab.

6. Click the **Configure IPv4** drop-down list and click **Using DHCP**. This setting will make your Mac request its IP address from the Mac that's sharing the Internet connection.

7. Click **OK** to close the Advanced sheet.

8. Open the **System Preferences** menu and click **Quit System Preferences** to close System Preferences.

TIP

Remote access to your Mac is a wonderful tool for getting you out of a jam when you discover, on the road, that you don't have the files you need with you. But remote access often requires you to use slow dial-up connections, the command line, or VPN. If your computing setup that requires remote access consists of a desktop Mac and a laptop Mac, consider storing your documents on the laptop Mac rather than on the desktop Mac. Network the laptop Mac to the desktop Mac using Gigabit Ethernet or FireWire, and you will be able to access the documents at high speeds using the desktop Mac while you're at home. When you take your laptop Mac on the road, you will have all your documents with you and won't need remote access to your desktop Mac.

Access Your Mac Remotely

If your Mac is a laptop, chances are that you'll take it with you wherever you might need to use it. But if you have a desktop Mac, you may need to be able to access it when you're somewhere else. Mac OS X provides five ways for you to access your Mac remotely: Screen Sharing, Back To My Mac, File Sharing, Remote Login and Secure Shell (SSH), and virtual private networking (VPN).

Connect via Screen Sharing

If you've already set up your home Mac to share its screen (as described in "Share Your Mac's Screen," earlier in this chapter), you can connect to it across your home network. If your network is connected to the Internet, you can even connect to your home Mac across the Internet.

From a Mac running Leopard, you can connect using the Screen Sharing feature. From a Mac running an earlier version of Mac OS X, or from a computer running another operating system, you can connect using a VNC client. Here are some VNC clients:

- **Mac OS X**   Chicken of the VNC (free; various sites, including www.apple.com/downloads/macosx/networking_security/chickenofthevnc.html)

QUICKSTEPS

CONNECTING VIA VPN

Virtual private networking (VPN) uses an insecure public network to handle secure private networking. Most commonly, VPN means using the Internet to connect to a LAN. You can think of VPN as a secure pipe through the Internet connecting computers on either end. VPN replaces both leased lines between facilities and the need for long-distance direct dial-up connections, thus saving considerable amounts of money.

Mac OS X includes the capability to connect to another network by using VPN, but it does not have the capability to host a VPN itself. Your use of VPN is likely to be restricted to calling in to a network that hosts a VPN—for example, a corporate network running Windows. Accordingly, this example uses a Windows computer as the VPN host.

To set up your Mac to connect to a VPN:

1. Open the **** menu and click **System Preferences** to open the System Preferences window.

2. Click **Network** to display the Network pane.

3. Click + below the left list box. Mac OS X will open a sheet (shown here with VPN choices made).

Select the interface and enter a name for the new service.

Interface: `VPN` ▲▼

VPN Type: `L2TP over IPSec` ▲▼

Service Name: `Company VPN`

Cancel   Create

Continued . . .

- **Windows**   VNC Free Edition (free; www.realvnc.com)
- **Linux**   Most distributions include a VNC client, usually named VNC and based on VNC Free Edition

CONNECT VIA SCREEN SHARING ON LEOPARD

To connect via Screen Sharing:

1. Activate the **Finder**.

2. Open the **Go** menu and click **Computer** to open a Finder window.

3. In the Shared section of the Source list, click the Mac that is sharing its screen.

4. Click the **Share Screen** button.

5. Choose how to connect:

   - If you don't have an account on the Mac or you do but you're not allowed to connect remotely, select the **By Asking For Permission** option button. Click the **Connect** button. If the Mac's current user accepts your request, a Screen Sharing window opens.

   - If you have an account on the Mac and are allowed to connect remotely, select the **As A Registered User** option button. Type your name and password. Select the **Remember This Password In My Keychain** check box if you want to store the password for future use. Click the Connect button.

Once you've connected, you can work on the remote Mac much as if you were seated at it—except that the screen will usually redraw much more slowly, so activities such as watching video are out.

- Open the **Edit** menu and click **Send Clipboard** to send the contents of your Mac's Clipboard to the remote Mac so that you can then paste them. Open the **Edit** menu and click **Get Clipboard** to retrieve the contents of the remote Mac's Clipboard so that you can paste them on your Mac.

- Open the **View** menu and click **Turn Scaling On** if you want to scale the remote Mac's screen to your screen. This capability is useful when the remote Mac has a larger screen than your Mac. If you don't turn on scaling, you'll need to scroll the Screen Sharing window to see all of the remote Mac's screen.

- Open the **View** menu and click **Adaptive Quality** if you want Screen Sharing to vary the quality of the picture to best suit network conditions. Open the **View** menu and click **Full Quality** if you want to see the remote screen at full quality, even if it means the picture will be updated slowly.

CONNECTING VIA VPN *(Continued)*

4. In the **Interface** drop-down list, choose **VPN**.

5. In the **VPN Type** drop-down list, choose **L2TP Over IPSec** or **PPTP**, depending on the instructions of the remote network's administrator. (L2TP is more secure than PPTP, so choose this option if you're offered the choice.)

6. In the Service Name text box, type the name you want to give the connection—for example, Company VPN.

7. Click **Create** to create the connection and close the sheet. The VPN connection appears in the Network pane.

8. Type the IP address of the VPN server in the Server Address text box.

9. Type your account name for the VPN server in the Account Name text box.

10. Click **Apply**. Mac OS X finalizes the VPN configuration and saves it.

11. Select the **Show VPN Status In Menu Bar** check box if you want to be able to monitor the VPN's status from a menu-bar icon.

12. Click **Connect**. Your Mac connects to the VPN server.

13. You should now be able to work on the VPN as if you were connected to its network locally, except that your Internet connection will probably act as a bottleneck, making the use of network resources much slower.

Continued . . .

When you've finished, open the **Screen Sharing** menu and choose **Quit Screen Sharing** to close the Screen Sharing window and the session.

CONNECT VIA SCREEN SHARING WITH VNC

To connect via Screen Sharing with VNC:

1. Open your VNC client as usual.

2. Set up a connection to the address your Mac is showing on the Sharing page (click the Screen Sharing item in the Service list, and then look at the readout next to it).

3. If prompted for a password, enter the password.

4. When you have finished the VNC session, close it.

Connect via Back To My Mac

If you have a membership with Apple's .Mac online service, you can use the Back To My Mac feature to connect to your Mac from another Mac.

TURN ON THE BACK TO MY MAC FEATURE

First, turn on the Back To My Mac feature on each Mac that you will use—both the Mac that you will use and the remote Mac to which you will go back:

1. Open the menu and click **System Preferences** to open the System Preferences window.

2. Click **.Mac** to display the .Mac pane.

3. On the **Account** tab, sign in if you haven't already done so.

4. Click the **Back To My Mac** tab.

5. Click **Start** to start Back To My Mac. (If there's a Stop button rather than a Start button, Back To My Mac is already on.)

6. Open the **System Preferences** menu and click **Quit System Preferences** to close System Preferences.

GO BACK TO A MAC

1. Activate the **Finder**.

2. Open the **Go** menu and click **Computer** to open a Finder window showing your Mac's contents.

3. Expand the **Shared** category in the Sidebar if it is collapsed.

CAUTION

Connecting to your home Mac may not work if you use a router or similar device to share a broadband Internet connection. In lay terms, the problem is that when you try to connect to your home Mac across the Internet, the Mac you're using can "see" no farther than the router—it cannot see the Mac behind the router. The Back To My Mac feature gets around this problem by having both Macs sign into the .Mac service, which allows them to communicate across the router.

NOTE

If your home Mac uses a dial-up connection, connecting remotely via File Sharing will probably require a helper at the home Mac to ensure that it is connected to the Internet at the required time and to tell you the dynamic IP address that your ISP has assigned to it. For such situations, the Back To My Mac feature is a better bet— even if you have to pay for a .Mac account.

4. Click the Mac to which you want to connect.

5. Click the **Share Screen** button if you want to share the Mac's screen. Click the **Connect As** button if you want to connect for file sharing. Supply your password when prompted.

Connect via File Sharing

If you've already set up your home Mac to use File Sharing (as described in "Share Your Folders," earlier in this chapter), and your home Mac is connected to the Internet, you may be able to access your home Mac remotely by using this feature without using Back To My Mac. File Sharing lets you copy files to and from your home Mac, but you can't run applications or control your home Mac directly.

You'll need to know the IP address assigned to your home Mac's Internet interface, so check this before you leave home. This assumes that your home Mac is connected to the Internet via a broadband connection that remains connected and that provides a static IP address (one that doesn't change from one session to another).

1. On the remote Mac you're using, activate the **Finder**, open the **Go** menu, and click **Connect To Server**. Mac OS X displays the Connect To Server dialog box.

2. Type your home Mac's IP address in the Server Address text box.

3. Click **Connect**, and then enter your user name and password. Bear in mind that the connection across the Internet will be much slower than a connection over a LAN.

Connect via Remote Login and Secure Shell

If you need to take actions on your home Mac when you're somewhere else, you can do so—but there's a learning curve, as you must use the command-line interface of the Terminal. To connect, you turn on Remote Login on your home Mac, and then use Secure Shell (SSH) from a computer at your remote location.

TURN ON REMOTE LOGIN

1. Open the menu and click **System Preferences** to open the System Preferences window.

2. Click **Sharing**. The Sharing pane will be displayed.

TIP

You can connect via SSH using computers that run operating systems other than Mac OS X. For example, you can connect from a Windows, Linux, or UNIX computer.

TIP

Connecting via Remote Login and SSH is fast, effective, and powerful, but unless you're used to performing actions from the command line, you'll probably find Terminal hard work. If you need to access your Mac remotely with a graphical interface, and neither Screen Sharing nor VNC is a viable choice, consider a remote-control solution such as Timbuktu Pro from Netopia (www.netopia.com).

NOTE

VPN typically uses either the Point-to-Point Tunneling Protocol (PPTP) or Layer 2 Tunneling Protocol (L2TP). Network administrators prefer L2TP because it's considerably more secure than PPTP. Mac OS X can make VPN connections using either PPTP or L2TP. Ask the administrator of the network you're connecting to which VPN protocol you should use.

3. In the left list box, select the **Remote Login** check box.

4. Open the **System Preferences** menu and click **Quit System Preferences** to close System Preferences.

CONNECT VIA SECURE SHELL

To connect via SSH:

1. Activate the **Finder**, open the **Go** menu and click **Utilities**, and then double-click **Terminal**. A Terminal window will open.

2. Type *ssh username@hostname*, where *username* is your user name and *hostname* is your home Mac's IP address or network address ("powerbook.mshome.net"), and press **RETURN**. For example, type ssh chris@192.168.0.44 and press **RETURN**.

3. Terminal will prompt you for your password.

4. Type your password and press **RETURN**. Terminal will display a login message and a prompt for the remote Mac.

5. Type commands for the Terminal (such as the following), pressing **RETURN** after each command:

   - Use the ls command to list the contents of the current directories.
   - Use the cd command to change directories.
   - Use the scp (Secure Copy) command to copy files from one computer to the other.

6. When you've finished, type exit to end your SSH session.

7. Open the **Terminal** menu and click **Quit Terminal** to close Terminal.

Index

R

radio, 148, 150
radio buttons, 12
RealPlayer Music Store, 152
Recent Items submenu, 8, *9*, 24
recovering files, 117–118
    See also Time Machine
regional settings, changing, 42
registering Mac OS X, 3
remote access
    connecting via Secure Shell, 221–222
    connecting via VPN, 219–221
    Remote Login, 221–222
    via Back To My Mac, 220–221
    via File Sharing, 221
    via Screen Sharing, 218–220
renaming icons, 29
resolution, changing, 24–25
Restart button, 3
restarting, 15, 94
RETURN key, 13
rewritable CDs, erasing, 119–120
routers, 190

S

Safari, 70, 71
    blocking pop-up windows, 77–78
    bookmarks, 71–75
    browsing history, 76
    controlling web content, 77
    home page, 75
    Internet browsing, 72–74
    opening a tab in the background, 75
    SnapBack, 77
    starting, 72
    windows and tabs, 74
satellite connections. *See* Internet connections
scanners
    installing, 124
    scanning pictures using Image Capture, 124–126

screen, 6–7
screen savers, 21
    picking a new screen saver, 21–23
Screen Sharing, 214–215
    connecting remotely via, 218–220
scroll arrows, 9
scroll bars, 9
scroll button, 9
searching
    from the desktop, 56–57
    from the Finder, 57–59
    using existing searches, 57
Secure Empty Trash feature, 55
Secure Shell (SSH), 221–222
security
    encrypting your Home folder, 176–179
    firewalls, 182–184
    firmware passwords, 181–182
    Internet, 70, 76–78
    locking files, 176
    Security pane, 179–180
    and wireless networks, 191
    See also passwords; user accounts
selecting objects, 6
servers, 187
setup, user account, 3–4
sharing
    files and folders, 206–209, 210–213
    Internet connections, 215–218
    printers, 215
    your Mac's screen, 214–215
sharing files and folders, 176–177
Sharing Only accounts, 166
sheets, 12–13
short name, 3
shutting down, 15, 94
Sidebar, 10, 45–47
    connecting to a shared folder, 206–207
    See also Finder window
Simple Finder, 170, 171
site navigation, 72–73
sizing handles, 9

sleeping, 14, 94
sliders, 13
Smart Folders, creating to repeat searches, 59–60
SnapBack, 77
software
    installing, 111–113
    removing, 113
Software Update, 8, 104–106
    configuring, 106–107
sound effects, 41–42
Spaces, 31–32
    icon, 32
    keyboard and mouse shortcuts, 34
    rearranging, 35
    setup, 32–34
    switching among, 34–35
spinners, 13
spring-loaded folders and windows, 52
Standard accounts, 165
starting applications, 6, 8
starting Mac OS X, 2
    automatically, 94
status bar, 9
Stickies, 103
stopping Mac OS X automatically, 94
switching users, 14–15
    See also Fast User Switching
system information, 107
System Preferences, 8
    changing the desktop background, 18–20
    navigating, 19
    opening, 17–18
    organizing, 19
    Security pane, 179–180
System Profiler, 107, *108*

T

Tab button, 12
TCP/IP, 197–199
Terminal, starting applications, 101–102
text boxes, 12